VIOLENT MINDS

Just as cultural attitudes toward criminality were undergoing profound shifts in the late nineteenth and early twentieth centuries, modernist authors became fascinated by crime and its perpetrators, as well as the burgeoning genre of crime fiction. Throughout the period, a diverse range of British and American novelists took the criminal as a case study for experimenting with forms of psychological representation, while also drawing on the conventions of crime fiction in order to imagine new ways of conceptualizing the criminal mind. Matthew Levay traces the history of that attention to criminal psychology in modernist fiction, placing understudied authors such as Wyndham Lewis, Dorothy Sayers, Graham Greene, and Patricia Highsmith in dialogue with more canonical contemporaries such as Joseph Conrad, Henry James, Dashiell Hammett, and Gertrude Stein. Levay demonstrates criminality's pivotal role in establishing quintessentially modernist forms of psychological representation and brings to light modernism's deep but understudied connections to popular literature, especially crime fiction.

MATTHEW LEVAY is Assistant Professor of English at Idaho State University. His research focuses on twentieth-century literature, with emphases on modernism, the history and theory of the novel, literary genres, and popular print culture. His essays and reviews have appeared in *Modernism/modernity*, the *Journal of Modern Literature*, *Modernist Cultures*, *MLQ*, and the *Journal of Modern Periodical Studies*.

VIOLENT MINDS

Modernism and the Criminal

MATTHEW LEVAY

Idaho State University

CAMBRIDGE
UNIVERSITY PRESS

University Printing House, Cambridge CB2 8BS, United Kingdom

One Liberty Plaza, 20th Floor, New York, NY 10006, USA

477 Williamstown Road, Port Melbourne, VIC 3207, Australia

314–321, 3rd Floor, Plot 3, Splendor Forum, Jasola District Centre, New Delhi – 110025, India

79 Anson Road, #06-04/06, Singapore 079906

Cambridge University Press is part of the University of Cambridge.

It furthers the University's mission by disseminating knowledge in the pursuit of education, learning, and research at the highest international levels of excellence.

www.cambridge.org
Information on this title: www.cambridge.org/9781108428866
DOI: 10.1017/9781108553698

First published 2019

Printed and bound in Great Britain by Clays Ltd, Elcograf S.p.A.

A catalogue record for this publication is available from the British Library.

ISBN 978-1-108-42886-6 Hardback

Contents

Acknowledgments

Like any monograph, this book has been long in the works. The fact that it's here and finished I owe to the encouragement, advice, and support of several people, all of whom have enriched not only this ominous-sounding project, but also so many other aspects of my life.

My first thanks go to those mentors at the University of Washington who shaped my identity as a scholar, and who exhibited at every turn an inspiring blend of rigor, curiosity, and humor. From our first interaction, Jessica Burstein has been a model of incisiveness and wit, and it is no exaggeration to say that I learn something from her every time we talk. She continues to be the greatest influence on my thinking about modernism (and about a great many other things, too), and I have benefitted enormously from her intellectual, professional, and personal generosity. Brian Reed showed me what true inquisitiveness looks like, and he has no equal as the kindest person in academia. I am sorry that Herb Blau isn't here to read this book: first, because I think he might have liked it; and second, because I know he would have found time to give it a spirited critique. A beautiful writer and a formidable thinker, he challenged me to do better in every way.

I have benefitted from the institutional support of several universities, and from the wisdom of the colleagues and friends I found there. I am tremendously thankful for the Walter Chapin Simpson Center for the Humanities, and for Kathy Woodward, who makes the Simpson Center the extraordinary intellectual space that it is. A Society of Scholars fellowship at the Simpson Center gave me the opportunity to develop my earliest ideas on modernism and criminality and a vibrant audience on which to test them, while the Modernist Studies Group gave me a lively interdisciplinary community that remains, for me, the gold standard of reading and writing groups. I was fortunate to work with some of the best colleagues in the business at the Harvard College Writing Program, and a series of Fuerbringer Summer Faculty Grants from that institution not only allowed me to visit the Beinecke Library at Yale University in order to work with the Gertrude Stein and Alice B. Toklas Papers, but also provided books, journal subscriptions, and other supplies that I simply couldn't have done without. More recently, the Department of English and Philosophy at Idaho State University has cheered me on as I finished the project; I owe special thanks to Brian Attebery, Jennifer Attebery, Dave Lawrimore, and Jessica Winston for all their support, in every sense of that word. Just as importantly, I am also grateful to my students at Washington, Harvard, and Idaho State for reminding me why a day spent thinking, talking, and writing about books is one of the most rewarding days one can have.

I am especially indebted to those who read portions of the manuscript in draft form, and whose comments helped me realize what I actually wanted to say and how I needed to say it. Sarah Cole, Jonathan Eburne, Paul Jaussen, Paul Peppis, and Lisa Siraganian have each made this book infinitely better, and I couldn't have asked for a finer or more generous group of readers. I owe Sarah Cole and Paul Peppis a further debt of gratitude for their guidance through some of the more daunting and opaque elements of the profession; they answered with humor, grace, and astonishing speed every question I threw at them, and never once seemed ruffled by my asking. Marshall Brown gave me early advice on Chesterton and thereby improved everything I've written since, while Chuck Rzepka helped bring my thoughts on Sayers into sharper focus. For inspiring conversations about violent minds and other, lighter matters, I thank Amy Clukey, David Earle, Katherine Fusco, Donal Harris, Aaron Jaffe, Sean Latham, Doug Mao, Michael Valdez Moses, Justus Nieland, Gayle Rogers, Paul Saint-Amour, and Rebecca Walkowitz, all of whom offered advice, gave encouragement, and steered me in new, productive directions, always at exactly the right times.

At Cambridge University Press, Ray Ryan patiently and expertly guided the manuscript to publication, and I am grateful not only for his long-standing commitment to the field of modernist studies, but also for his championing of first-time authors and the work they produce. I also want to acknowledge Cambridge University Press's anonymous readers, whose advice has made this an immensely better book, and me a better writer. Portions of Chapters 2 and 3 appeared, in different form, in *Modernist Cultures* and the *Journal of Modern Literature*, and I am happy to acknowledge Edinburgh University Press and Indiana University Press for granting permission to include them here.

As a teenager I borrowed nearly all the crime novels my father checked out from our local library, while at the very same time I was inspired by my mother's return to teaching. I am grateful, then, to Allan and Beverly Levay for fostering in me a love of books and of the classroom, and for making these things real priorities in their house. I am also fortunate to have shared that house with Elizabeth Levay, whose generosity and dedication are readily apparent and always appreciated. Finally, my greatest debts are to Rachael Levay, whose support for me and for this book has never wavered, and who always inspires me to better thinking, better writing, and better living. From Seattle to Boston and now to Idaho, we have made our way together, and I count myself lucky to have spent these years with the most patient, encouraging, and brilliant partner I could imagine. Our daughter, Mina, provides love and laughter at every moment, and I am continually amazed that I get to spend so much time with as joyous and thoughtful a person as her. This book, like everything else I do, is for them.

Pocatello, Idaho

mother's return to teaching, I am grateful, then, to Allan and Beverly Levey for fostering in me a love of books and of the classroom, and for making these things real priorities in their house. I am also fortunate to have shared that home with Elizabeth Levey, whose generosity and dedication are readily apparent and always appreciated. Finally, my greatest debts are to Rachel Levey, whose support for me and for this book has never wavered, and who always inspires me to be a better thinking, better writing, and better living. From Seattle to Boston and now to Idaho, we have made our way together, and I count myself lucky to have spent these years with the most patient, encouraging, and brilliant partner I could imagine. Our daughter, Mina, provides love and laughter at every moment, and I am continually amazed that I get to spend so much time with as joyous and thoughtful a person as her. This book, like everything else I do, is for them.

Pocatello, Idaho

Introduction
Modernism's Violent Minds

> There is no essential incongruity between crime and culture.
> We cannot re-write the whole of history for the purpose of gratifying
> our moral sense of what should be.
> – Oscar Wilde, "Pen, Pencil, and Poison" (1889)[1]

Just two months after London police discovered the eviscerated body of
Mary Kelly, the last identified victim of Jack the Ripper, in a squalid East
End lodging house, Oscar Wilde made an audacious claim. Flouting the
widespread anxiety surrounding criminal violence that the Ripper murders
engendered, Wilde's essay "Pen, Pencil, and Poison," published in the
Fortnightly Review, offered an ironic yet largely sympathetic portrait of
Thomas Griffiths Wainewright, the notorious artist, critic, forger, and
suspected poisoner, whose criminal talents Wilde deemed "almost without
rival in this or any age."[2] Rather than apologizing for or glossing over his
subject's murderous reputation, Wilde defended it as a vital component of
Wainewright's aesthetic practice, explaining that "[t]he fact of a man being
a poisoner is nothing against his prose," especially since Wainewright's
crimes "seem to have had an important effect upon his art."[3] Though
Wilde undoubtedly crafted his position with the goal of inflaming his
audience, the contention that Wainewright's murders enhanced rather
than hindered his work is not simply a satirical jab at a conservative
Victorian culture, nor does it mimic the incitements of earlier writers
such as Thomas De Quincey, whose infamous essay "On Murder
Considered as One of the Fine Arts" (1827) argued that such a crime should
never "be laid hold of by its moral handle," but should instead be "treated
aesthetically . . . in relation to good taste."[4] For all its debts to provocateurs
such as De Quincey, "Pen, Pencil, and Poison" is the product of a unique
historical moment, as Wilde asks readers to take seriously the idea that
crime can serve as a catalyst for art at the same time that the threat of
criminal violence seemed uncomfortably close at hand. Thus, when Wilde

rejects the notion that criminality precludes aesthetic achievement, chiding those who "still think it necessary to apply moral judgements to history," he advocates for an appreciation of the criminal in stark contrast to the popular condemnations of that figure that circulated in the wake of the Ripper murders.[5]

Wilde was not the only public figure of the time to see Wainewright's criminality as an opportunity to challenge longstanding perceptions of the criminal. In his idiosyncratic study *The Criminal* (1890), the first major English-language account of the burgeoning field of criminal anthropology, psychologist Havelock Ellis proposes Wainewright as an example of the "instinctive criminal" whose abnormal exterior reflects an equally deviant mind.[6] Proceeding from the testimony of one of the poisoner's acquaintances, who took his notably large head, long hair, and "snake-like expression ... at once repulsive and fascinating" as indications of latent criminality, Ellis designates Wainewright "a perfect picture of the instinctive criminal in his most highly developed shape."[7] Potentially "on the verge of insanity, if not, as is more likely, insane," Wainewright represents a kind of "moral monster" whose pathology becomes evident through the empirical methods of modern criminology, which classify criminals according to their deviation from accepted standards of physical normality.[8] By asserting that Wainewright's body betrays his criminal compulsions, Ellis's study confirms how, in Michel Foucault's formulation, criminal anthropology works to "provide the mechanisms of legal punishment with a justifiable hold not only on offences, but on individuals," defining through the imprimatur of scientific reason what certain individuals "are, will be, may be."[9] For Ellis, these positivist developments in the social and biological sciences are what distinguish modern criminology from earlier efforts, as the systematic scrutiny of the criminal body offers a richer, more objective understanding of the motivations that drive it.

In suggesting that the criminal is too often defined by stereotype, and that society can only confront the issue of criminality by using new methods of interpretation, Wilde and Ellis also signal a budding modernist fascination with criminality. Indeed, just as these two late Victorians sought to reposition the criminal within public discourse, so too did a diverse range of British and American novelists, who had become increasingly attentive to an idea of the criminal as a psychological rather than a purely social phenomenon – a social problem, to be sure, but also a problem for fictional representation. This book charts the history of that attention to criminal psychology in modernist fiction from the late nineteenth century to the mid-twentieth, and explains why a surprising number of modernist novels are intensely preoccupied with the representation of criminality as a unique form of subjectivity that both affirms and eludes conventional understandings of interiority and identity. By placing in dialogue a wide swath of fictions, *Violent Minds* presents a more complicated and heretofore unrecognized narrative of literary modernism's formal engagement with crime and criminality, and one that draws upon such nineteenth-century precursors as Wilde and Ellis in order to demonstrate how modernist authors responded to the variety of criminological theories that had so influenced public perceptions of the criminal. For instance, by suggesting that crime could be both the subject of and inspiration for a work of art rather than dismissing it as a moral abomination – a suggestion that foreshadows Ellis's claim that the criminal can fascinate as well as repulse, and that fascination is an essential part of crime's cultural power – Wilde exhibits a pronounced modernist investment in representing criminality without subjecting it to the cultural assumptions and anxieties that had plagued it in previous eras. Likewise, Ellis's interest in the symmetry between criminal bodies and minds was also a key modernist preoccupation, as authors experimented with new forms of psychological representation that might advance more compelling, and ultimately more accurate, depictions of criminal motivation. In both cases, Wilde and Ellis help explain how and why modernists attempted to apprehend the subjectivity of the criminal by registering in their fiction the processes that characterize that figure's mental life. As a result, one can see how modernists began to regard the criminal as less of a moral conundrum than an aesthetic enterprise, a fearsome psychology ripe for examination.

In its contention that criminality served a crucial purpose for modernist literature, *Violent Minds* advances a simultaneously formal and historical argument. It defines the modernist fascination with the criminal as just as much an aesthetic experiment as a social critique, and argues that this fascination originated in authors' desires to utilize the criminal as a figure for assessing the available means of representing fictional characters' inner lives, coupled with their belief that previous theories of criminality had failed to account for individual nuances of motivation and behavior. Since one of the hallmarks of modernism is its attentiveness to psychological advances, it is unsurprising that authors of the period understood the criminal in these terms. After all, if modernism borrowed from Freud what Michael Levenson identifies as a recognition of "the *dislocation* of the rational ego, its loss of mastery in its own house" – a process wherein "[r]ationality endures limits while arational instincts take on new depth and significance" – then the criminal provided modernist authors with a concrete example of how such instincts could shape individual behavior.[10] Levenson hints at this connection when he asserts that, while Freudian therapy aspired to strict laws of treatment, for modernist authors "the great example of [Freud's] work was the image of life beyond the law."[11] Robert Pippin makes a similar point when he observes that modernists strove for artistic autonomy "achieved at the price of a very costly social 'refusal,'" exemplified in an "obsession with gamblers, outlaws, con men . . . those who try to act out or confirm their independence from the mediation of others."[12] For the modernists discussed in this book, the idea of a life ungoverned was not only realized through the insights of a therapeutic method responsive to the fluidity of the unconscious, but also through the criminal, dually defined by a willful rejection of the social contract and a psychology that resists conventional standards of interpretation, representation, and judgment.

Just as modernism developed alongside psychoanalysis, it also appeared at a time when acts of violence in Europe and America had renewed some of the late nineteenth century's most contentious debates regarding the nature of crime and its punishment. Those debates elicited a range of contributions – from scientists, journalists, legal scholars, and social theorists – but they offered no consensus on how crime could be combatted. What they did was prove two things, both of which had profound consequences for the modernist representation of criminality: first, that the criminal had become increasingly fundamental to, if also destructive of, the fabric of modern society; and second, that popular and professional opinions regarding criminality hinged upon the criminal rather than the crime. Consequently, several modernist representations of criminality echoed Gabriel Tarde's 1890 assertion that "[f]rom the social point of view crime may be a monstrosity, but not from the individual or organic point of view, because it is the absolute triumph of egoism and of the organism over the brakes of society."[13] Laudatory yet foreboding, Tarde's characterization of the criminal as an egoistic "organism" unfettered by social limitation demonstrates what Mark Seltzer describes as the nineteenth century's "positing of the category of the dangerous individual," or the codification of criminality as a violent form of individualism that is, paradoxically, posited as a general category of identity.[14] According to Seltzer, during the nineteenth century the criminal's identity became inseparable from the actions he or she committed, and so a "kind of act was now a species of person."[15] For authors of the late nineteenth and early twentieth centuries, this criminal species posed a unique challenge: to represent the interiority of those marginalized figures who embody the violence of modernity, while at the same time acknowledging that those figures are often motivated by desires and internal conflicts that remain ambiguous or unknowable.

In order to illuminate the breadth and depth of modernism's criminal imagination, this book constructs a genealogy of criminality within a variety of late nineteenth- and early twentieth-century British and American fictions. Attending equally to canonical modernists – Henry James, Joseph Conrad, Wyndham Lewis, and Gertrude Stein – and to authors typically neglected by modernist criticism – G. K. Chesterton, Graham Greene, and Patricia Highsmith – *Violent Minds* reveals criminality's pivotal role in establishing quintessentially modernist forms of psychological representation. It also considers the formal devices, often borrowed from popular crime fiction, that modernists deployed in order to render the criminal mind in their work. Rather than hewing to a familiar slate of modernist authors, I argue that the relationship between modernism and the criminal comes more sharply into focus when we situate modernist texts alongside popular genre fictions whose treatment of criminality and its detection pose some of the very same questions of agency, psychology, and narrative possibility that animate modernism. Throughout, I show how modernist fiction was invigorated by the aesthetics and epistemologies of crime fiction, and how certain works of crime fiction might be productively understood as examples of popular modernism, conforming to the conventions of a popular genre while also pressuring those conventions in ways that speak directly to the modernist imperative toward experimentation and novelty. By examining the impact of criminality upon a range of fictions by canonical and neglected modernists, this book uncovers multiple connections among modernism's aesthetics, interrogation of subjectivity, and investment in popular culture, and in so doing expands our understanding of modernism as a pluralistic set of formal innovations that unsettle conventional paradigms of fictional representation.

Criminal Histories

In many respects, modernism's attraction to the criminal as a unique individual consciousness was an unexpected result of a nineteenth-century positivist school of criminology that based its models of criminality on ancestry and physiognomy, those "natural and reasonable methods" for

diagnosing crime that Ellis applauds in *The Criminal*.[16] There is clearly an
irony in this relationship, a rift between Virginia Woolf's famous identification of December 1910 as the point at which "human character changed" – a proclamation that brands modernism as the cultural consequence
of a seismic shift between past and present forms of sociality – and early
criminologists' position that criminality did not reflect a sea change in
human character so much as an individual irruption of past forces that
defied humanity's evolutionary development.[17] While Woolf's modernism
depends upon a conception of the past as surrendering to social and
historical change, criminologists held that past forms of humanity were
precisely what came back to haunt and halt the progress of the present. Sir
Arthur Conan Doyle's "The Adventure of the Empty House" (1903)
models the tension between the two when Sherlock Holmes voices the
latter position to his partner, John Watson:

> "There are some trees, Watson, which grow to a certain height, and then
> suddenly develop some unsightly eccentricity. You will see it often in
> humans. I have a theory that the individual represents in his development
> the whole procession of his ancestors, and that such a sudden turn to good
> or evil stands for some strong influence which came into the line of his
> pedigree. The person becomes, as it were, the epitome of the history of his
> own family."
> "It is surely rather fanciful."
> "Well, I don't insist upon it."[18]

Though it may appear "fanciful" to Watson, Holmes's theory of individual
development draws upon a set of scientific discourses insisting that,
according to historian Martin Wiener, "the will and personality of the
criminal offender had faded into the impersonal conditions from which he
was manufactured," with the criminal becoming "less a moral actor and
more a point of conjunction of forces larger than individuals, a sign of weak
spots in the human (and, to a lesser degree, social) constitution."[19] From
psychiatrists who wondered if patients inherited their symptoms to phre-
nologists who classified the ridges of the human skull according to their
perceived influence on behavior, numerous physicians, anthropologists,
and statisticians in Europe and America posited a connection between
ancestry and criminal action. Their efforts crystallized in the emerging
discipline of criminology, whose practitioners, in hopes of identifying the
causes of criminal behavior, considered family history an attractive culprit.
Consequently, Holmes's conception of the individual as a contemporary
iteration of ancestral patterns reflects a form of scientific inquiry that made
a lasting impression on public consciousness throughout the late

nineteenth century, and led many to suspect that criminal behavior had more to do with familial influence than free will.[20]

For all his apparent certainty, however, Holmes immediately distances himself from this line of thought after Watson expresses reservations, and it is Holmes's dissociation from his theory, rather than the theory itself, that epitomizes the modernist response to criminality. In many ways, the study of crime during the modernist period is also a study of ambivalence, as the issue of criminal motivation was subject to a diverse and often contradictory array of interpretations. While positivist approaches undoubtedly influenced cultural conceptions of criminal behavior, so too did competing arguments that favored environmental and socioeconomic factors as catalysts for crime. Particularly as the Ripper murders fanned the flames of paranoia in London and beyond, social reformers decried the squalid conditions of urban slums, arguing that the weight of poverty could easily turn law-abiding Londoners into violent criminals. Rather than characterizing the Ripper as an atavistic emblem of brutality – a common perception at the time – these arguments took aim at a dysfunctional civic apparatus that had failed to protect the city's most vulnerable residents. As Judith Walkowitz observes, by the time of the Ripper murders the infamous Whitechapel district of the East End "had come to epitomize the social ills of 'Outcast London,'" as high rates of poverty and scarce resources for combating them forced many citizens to turn to crime in order to survive.[21] Criminality, by this logic, was a problem of environment, and not the result of a diseased family tree.

These two schools of thought were not easily distinguished, however, and modernist writing on criminality bears distinct traces of both. Several authors followed the example of reformers such as Henry Mayhew, whose exposé of the city's forgotten corners was serialized in London's *Morning Chronicle* and collected in book form as the three-part *London Labour and the London Poor* (1851). When he added a fourth volume on crime and unemployment in 1861, Mayhew explained criminality in ancestral and economic terms, identifying typical criminal characteristics while noting that the unemployed often perceive crime as an opportunity, albeit meager, for earning a living. Mayhew's collaborator John Binny exemplifies this dual perspective when discussing thieves, whom he proposes are "trained from their infancy in the bosom of crime" by parents "of bad character."[22] Rather than suggesting heredity as the sole factor in adopting a criminal trade, Binny argues that those who become thieves "are often carried to the beershop or gin palace on the breast of worthless drunken mothers," and learn their professions within their "wretched abodes."[23] According to

Binny, crime is both inherited and environmental, with biology and socio-economics fostering a life of lawbreaking.

Like Binny and Mayhew, many nineteenth-century criminologists, social reformers, and journalists found it exceptionally difficult to define criminality with any certainty, and some capitulated to an idea of crime as an unsolvable enigma. As Nicole Rafter explains, several leading criminologists "conceived of dangerousness as irrationality – immoderate, illogical, and inexplicable behavior. To them, these extreme departures from standard ways of reasoning and behaving seemed a departure from human nature itself."[24] In this perception of the criminal as irrational, to commit a crime is to reveal one's essential inhumanity by contradicting the Enlightenment ideal of the human as motivated by logic and reason. By contrast, some legal professionals took the opposite view, and maintained that irrational violence was all too human. According to historian David Taylor, nineteenth-century British courts often reduced murder charges when the accused's faculties appeared diminished at the time of the killing, and so "many domestic killings were treated as manslaughter because the crime was committed (or was presented as having been committed) on the spur of the moment or when the accused was not in full control of his or her reason."[25] In this system, even the most violent crimes could be understood as pitiable failures of will.

As these accounts indicate, no single theory of criminality found universal acceptance during the period, which led modernists to perceive the impasse as an opportunity to explore new methods for representing criminal motivation. And yet, just as those authors attempted to establish their own, distinctive positions on the criminal, the theory of inherited criminality retained a substantial grip on the general public, and so many felt bound to address it in their work. This school of thought originated with French psychiatrist Bénédict Morel, who in 1857 published his theory of degeneration, which held that certain individuals inherited from their ancestors an array of congenital defects that separated them from a healthy populace. The concept was a hazy one, as Morel explained that the "clearest notion we can form of degeneracy is to regard it as a *morbid deviation from an original type*."[26] In his controversial book *Degeneration* (1892), which claimed that degeneracy could also be observed in modern art and culture, Max Nordau explains Morel's theory in even more alarmist terms, arguing that the slightest "deviation" can prove disastrous because, if

under any kind of noxious influences an organism becomes debilitated, its
successors will not resemble the healthy, normal type of the species, with
capacities for development, but will form a new sub-species, which ...
possesses the capacity of transmitting to its offspring, in a continuously
increasing degree, its peculiarities, these being morbid deviations from the
normal form – gaps in development, malformations and infirmities.[27]

Such "malformations" appear in multiple guises, but primarily in "the
unequal development of the two halves of the face and cranium," "imper-
fection in the development of the external ear," and other, smaller features
such as "squint-eyes, harelips," and "webbed or supernumerary fingers."[28]

While such accounts of degeneracy emphasize the signifying powers of
the body, their implications go well beyond physical eccentricity.[29] Rather,
they form a significant component of what Sander Gilman refers to as "the
Western European stereotype of the Other, whether the Other is the lower
class or the exotic," and contribute to a pronounced cultural anxiety
regarding the other's potential for criminality.[30] Daniel Pick makes
a similar point when he references the "tension between the image of the
degenerate and the unseen essence of degeneration," manifest in xenopho-
bic paranoia over "the dangerous classes" of the metropolis – an "anomalous and racially 'alien'" group possessed of an "apparent invisibility in the
flux of the great city."[31] Paradoxically, the degenerate is physically marked
by his pathology yet assimilates into the urban crowd, a criminal outsider
intent on infiltrating an unsuspecting populace.

No one exemplified this approach to the criminal more than Cesare
Lombroso, the Italian physician who founded the discipline of criminal
anthropology by applying the physiognomic indicators of degeneracy to
the identification of potential criminals (and who I discuss in greater detail
in Chapter 2). Through his examination of their bodies and skeletal
remains, Lombroso sought to classify criminals by their physical abnormalities, creating taxonomies of criminality to predict potential threats to
a community. In his seminal *L'uomo delinquente* (*Criminal Man*), which
appeared in five separate editions from 1876 to 1897, Lombroso advocated
for his concept of the "born criminal," defined as an individual predisposed
to crime due to a stunted family history.[32] Since his ancestors had not
evolved along normal lines, and instead retained a consistently low level of
mental and physical development, the born criminal was essentially atavistic in appearance. In the first edition of *Criminal Man*, Lombroso claims
that "there is nearly always something strange" about a criminal's visage, as
"each type of crime is committed by men with particular physiognomic
characteristics, such as lack of a beard or an abundance of hair," attributes

that explain why criminals, on the whole, appear "neither delicate nor pleasant."[33] Characterized as a modern primitive, the born criminal's physical abnormalities marked him as irrational and uncivilized, lacking the restraining influence of reason to deter him from acts of violence.

Through the influence of Lombroso and others, several late nineteenth-century efforts to reduce crime focused on the bodies of suspected offenders. These initiatives relied upon what Simon Cole terms "technologies of skin and bone," which included fingerprinting, a procedure first utilized in the years immediately following the Ripper murders, as well as French biometrician Alphonse Bertillon's invention of anthropometry, which identified criminals according to their physical measurements, personality traits, and other distinguishing characteristics.[34] In his influential history of criminal photography, Allan Sekula notes that such technologies worked to quash the criminal's subjectivity by reducing him or her to pure physicality, "unmask[ing] the disguises, the alibis, the excuses and multiple biographies of those who find or place themselves on the wrong side of the law."[35] By scouring the body for evidence of criminality, proponents of these methods sought to reassure the public that crime could be understood empirically, and that the study of crime, far from being a morbid fascination, actually served the greater good.

At the same time, these approaches also emphasized crime's probable, violent encroachment on everyday life, and complemented the lurid narratives of criminality that filled the daily newspapers. Such narratives escalated dramatically in 1888, when London journalists labeled the rise of Jack the Ripper as either a consequence of the poverty that pervaded the city's slums or an extreme extension of the vice those areas cultivated. Some would have it both ways. Recounting the heated debates over the Ripper featured in the London *Times*, Simon Joyce observes that the editors of that paper saw the killer as "produced by a degenerate environment in which he finds support, but which he also exploits and corrupts still further."[36] In *The Times* and elsewhere, the Ripper murders initiated a broader conversation about the incursion of violence on public life, drawing upon prominent scientific and sociological theories of criminality while reminding readers that a multidimensional problem like crime might never be solved. They also fed into the literary representation of criminality by stimulating a host of fictions that grappled with criminal psychology in ways previously unimaginable. According to L. Perry Curtis, Jr., the lack of resolution in the unsolved Ripper murders "left gaps into which all kinds of theories, daydreams, and nightmares rushed pell-mell," and one of the most significant efforts to fill those gaps came from the crime and detective fictions that flooded the literary marketplace, as well as the work of modernist authors who adapted the popular model of the criminal to new and rapidly evolving ends.[37] While England and America had been inundated with new technologies for understanding criminality by the time the nineteenth century gave way to the twentieth, it was fiction that brought the most probing investigations into the criminal mind.

Criminal Eras

One useful distinction between criminological and fictional approaches to criminality at the turn of the century – and one that underscores the argument of this book – is that fiction allowed authors to imagine multiple iterations of what the criminal mind might look like, whereas criminologists attempted more definitive arguments regarding what that mind necessarily was. While criminology aimed to settle the question of how criminality manifests, modernist fiction suggested that the question was, by definition, open-ended, and therefore subject to a range of potentially valid responses. This is not to say that criminology insisted upon a universal model of criminality, deliberately discounting more nuanced perceptions of criminal motivation, but rather that modernist authors, in their fascination with the lability of character – what Omri Moses describes as the rejection of subjective consistency in favor of characters who "think and act on the basis of attitudes that are not shaped in advance," and "make decisions that transform *themselves* as well as the objects of their actions" – viewed the criminal as perpetually in flux, simultaneously molded and obscured by the idiosyncrasies of individual psychology.[38] For modernists, the idea of the criminal as potentially unknowable was not simply a threat to public safety, but rather an opportunity to test the capacity of literary form to represent such an enigma.

Recent critics have made substantial inroads in documenting fiction's criminal representations, most notably Lisa Rodensky, whose work on third-person narration as a barometer of criminal responsibility in Victorian fiction bears significant weight on my own claims regarding modernism and crime. Proceeding from the fact that the law depends upon inference in determining culpability for a criminal action, since judges and juries can only establish guilt based on physical evidence that implies a connection between the action and the individual accused of committing it, or on witnesses' impressions of the accused's moral fiber, Rodensky shows how nineteenth-century novels' third-person narrators make interior states immediately accessible, offering unfiltered accounts of the logic behind an action so readers can determine the degree of responsibility that an actor might bear for it. "The Victorian novel's power to represent the interior life of its characters," she argues, "both challenges the law's definitions of criminal liability and reaffirms them," as Dickens, Eliot, and others use their narrators to test the legal standards of intention, agency, and justice.[39] Though grounded in the nineteenth century, Rodensky's argument has notable implications for modernism. When she contends that the threads connecting legal and fictional approaches to criminality begin to fray at the close of the Victorian era thanks to "a much more heightened and overt literary modern self-consciousness of and skepticism about the relations between intentions and actions in the context of crime" – a strain due in part to new forms of modernist narration, in which the third-person narrator "either disappears entirely . . . or is only ambiguously present . . . or displays more overtly and consistently his inability to know and to make whole the fragments of the story" – she identifies precisely the shift that defines the modernist representation of criminality.[40] Suspicious of any formula that weds a criminal action to the ideas that motivate it, modernists, Rodensky suggests, were much more likely than Victorians to regard their accounts of the criminal as fundamentally incomplete, an inevitable consequence of both a narrator's failure to grasp another mind in its entirety and the potential obscurity of a criminal's own motivations, to himself and others.

Despite these links between modernism and criminality, critics have been slow to chart their importance for the field. Such hesitation is curious given the absorption of modernist authors in narratives of crime: the lurid exposés of criminality that populated their newspapers, the pseudoscientific rhetoric surrounding inherited criminality, and the popular detective fictions that became a ubiquitous presence at newsstands and bookstores, as well as their own fictional accounts of crime and violence. Yet the most provocative recent work on literature and crime appears largely within the purview of Victorian studies. In addition to Rodensky's account of Victorian narrative's criminal imagination, Elizabeth Carolyn Miller has made a persuasive case for the female criminal as an index of modernity's upheavals in *fin-de-siècle* literature. Characterizing what she terms the "New Woman Criminal" as a "herald of changing political and social conditions, changing gender roles, and changing definitions of 'public' and 'private,'" Miller demonstrates how readers' initial shock at witnessing female criminality inured them to the disruptive sensations of the new, "naturaliz[ing] change" at a moment when change appeared to be the order of the day.[41] Similarly, Simon Joyce troubles the deceptive gap between the literary representation of crime and its social reality in his illuminating study of crime and class in Victorian London. While authors of popular detective fiction appeared to ignore any equation of criminality with urban poverty, setting their works in rarified metropolitan enclaves or rural estates and offering aristocratic villains rather than the hard-edged, desperate residents of the East End, Joyce argues that these contradictions belie a more nuanced relationship between fiction and the geographies it represents; rather than distracting readers from the crime plaguing London's slums, "the principle of escapism embodied in detective fiction developed alongside, and even benefited from, a countervailing desire to learn more about the lives of the urban poor."[42] In these and other studies, critics have methodically and impressively mapped the contours of criminality within the literature and culture of the Victorian era, exploring fictional crime as a distinctive response to the period's most significant social concerns.

Recently, however, modernist critics have begun to challenge the nineteenth century's hold on the subject of criminality. Emphasizing the singularity of the modernist representation of violence, they identify the early twentieth century as the moment at which the horrors of mass violence converged with the experimental aesthetics of the avant-garde to produce a body of literature uniquely attuned to the atrocities of modernity. As Sarah Cole puts it, "[i]t is astonishing ... how thoroughly the problematic of violence as an organizing cultural and aesthetic fact underwrote the literature of the years between 1890 and 1940."[43] Other critics have made similar gestures toward modernism's longstanding infatuation with violence, both metaphorical and actualized, and to the cultivated bellicosity of its most celebrated figures, with Paul Sheehan describing the latter quality as an "association with detachment, emotional reserve and intransigent artistic practices [that] indicates ... that the modernist aesthetic has a strand of compulsive belligerence woven into its DNA."[44] Though more concerned with violence writ large than with specifically criminal violence, Cole and Sheehan's observations suggest a modernism for which the violent criminal act becomes a defining cultural occurrence. From Jonathan Eburne's contention that "the immediate and vulgar realm of everyday crime" serves as one of the chief intellectual foundations of Surrealism, to Rex Ferguson's investigation of the symmetry between the criminal trial and modernist fiction, critics have lately begun to assert that modernism's attraction to violence corresponds with an intense interest in the formal and epistemological dimensions of criminality.[45] Thus, when Ferguson maintains that in both the modernist novel and the twentieth-

century trial, "judgement becomes an issue of prejudicial belief or subser-
vience to an expert authority, identity becomes fragmented into traces and
abstract images, and repetition, as a reliable site of experimental method
and judicial review, becomes an unstable compulsion to repeat a trauma
that never took place," he speaks not only to the relationship between
modernism and the law, but also to a broader set of affinities among
modernism, criminality, and narrative.[46] In this way, he and others powerfully advocate for a modernism enmeshed in the cultural, political, and
legal dimensions of criminality in the early twentieth century.

It is within this critical context that *Violent Minds* makes its most
substantive contributions. Whereas many of the aforementioned works
approach criminality as an essential link between modernist form and the
social phenomena to which it responds, I claim that the criminal functions
as a literary device that helps modernist authors pursue a broader range of
goals: to develop novel forms of psychological representation, to contend
with the social problem of criminal violence in largely formal terms, and to
utilize popular generic conventions, whether to expand the formal boundaries and possible audiences of more obviously experimental fiction or to
make genre fiction more responsive to the aesthetic and thematic preoccupations of modernism. In attending to each of these goals, I aim to show
how criminality reveals profound yet critically underexplored connections
among a range of British and American authors, and so provides new ways
of understanding modernism as a multifaceted attempt to address an
insistent narrative dilemma: how to represent the individual who defies
conventional strategies of representation.

Criminal Forms

Violent Minds thus advances two distinct yet ultimately related arguments:
first, that the criminal is, for modernism, an experiment in representation;
and second, that several modernists turned to the example of crime fiction
in order to conduct that experiment. In those dual claims, this book
combines the expansive cultural turn characteristic of the New
Modernist Studies with an attention to some of the most recognizable
attributes of modernist fiction. In other words, at the same time that
I argue for a version of modernism that reflects the inclusivity of recent
criticism, I also want to emphasize those aspects of modernism that have
traditionally defined the period in order to demonstrate how the issue of
criminality allows us to see figures typically excluded from the modernist
canon as contributing to modernism all along. For instance, while the texts

I consider are quite varied in style and substance – some fit easily into a high modernist avant-garde, while others remain committed to realism or popular genres – all contribute something significant to our understanding of interiority and modernism's perception of it. As I noted earlier, the investment in psychology is one of modernism's hallmarks, but that investment took many forms. As Mark Micale explains, at the turn of the century "artists, philosophers, and scientists probed beneath the surface reality of reason in order to uncover deeper irrational and nonrational levels of human experience and cognition," uniting modernism and psychiatry as "both pioneered new techniques of narration to capture the inner workings of the human mind and the moment-by-moment experience of individual consciousness."[47] At the same time, some authors looked to shed the constraints of rationality by rebelling against the concept of the mind itself, a rejection that Jessica Burstein terms "cold modernism," or a strain of modernism that "engages a world without selves or psychology" and whose narratives present a "story of the individual ... in which the individual has no place."[48] Cold modernism offers an alternative view of modernism's fictional characters as stonily detached, evacuated of the traditional indicators of personhood and represented instead as purely physical entities. Many of the texts I examine demonstrate curious traces of both the dynamic interiority of psychological realism and the calculated blankness of cold modernism, sometimes shuttling between the two. By concentrating on both, I want to stress that modernist fiction does not uniformly represent the minds of its characters, and that the criminal's exemplification of that fact can illuminate overlooked similarities between seemingly disparate novels, thereby expanding the modernist canon while remaining true to its thematic foundations.

These nuances of criminal representation also lead to questions of what precisely counts as a crime, as that concept arises through the intersection of conflicting moral and legal distinctions. As Foucault argues, crime's definition fluctuates with evolving cultural norms: "many crimes have ceased to be so because they were bound up with a certain exercise of religious authority or a particular type of economic activity; blasphemy has lost its status as a crime; smuggling and domestic larceny some of their seriousness."[49] Yet modern crimes do share distinctive traits, albeit ones that accentuate rather than minimize their heterogeneity. According to Jonathan Eburne, the spectacle of crime "presents a disorienting array of cultural extremes: private suffering and public sensation, destruction and production, reason and unreason ... Each crime scene ... becomes a site of contested meanings; each corpse sets in motion waves of public sentiment, popular imagery, and civic action that oscillate between fascination and outrage, between sensationalism and the social process of restoring order."[50] Following Eburne's definition of crime as the locus of cultural extremes, an act whose meaning is produced by the public estimation of its gravity, *Violent Minds* shows how modernist authors conceived of crime as a predominantly violent phenomenon that resists easy classification, and whose occurrence proves the inherent vulnerability of both the social order and individual subjectivity. Of course, modernist fiction engages a wide range of criminal activity, from the white-collar crime of bootlegging in F. Scott Fitzgerald's *The Great Gatsby* to the domestic crime of incest in William Faulkner's *The Sound and the Fury*. To narrow the scope of this book without sacrificing the breadth of criminality that modernists explored, I deal primarily with violent crimes that play outsized roles in public consciousness – murder and terrorism – as well as those, like forgery and identity theft, which blur conventional perceptions of what constitutes a criminal act (and an identity, too). Throughout, I argue that modernist authors did not devote their attention to any single crime to the exclusion of others, but rather examined an assortment of crimes in order to specify how the identity of the criminal is constructed through multiple forms of violence. Many of their texts feature characters whose crimes are not easily distinguished from one another, and serve instead as markers of a holistic criminal identity. Patricia Highsmith's Tom Ripley, for example, is a murderer and identity thief, but in locating the origins of both crimes within Ripley's persistent desire for self-creation, Highsmith offers a protagonist whose individual crimes matter far less than their cumulative effect upon his character. Challenging readers to confront such definitional problems, the novels of Highsmith and others perform what Mark Seltzer describes as "a twin shift in understanding from act to life form – from the character of acts to the character and identity of the actor."[51]

As an instructive example of how modernists conceived of criminality in these terms, consider Faulkner's *Sanctuary* (1931), a pulpy novel once disparaged by its author as a "cheap idea . . . deliberately conceived to make money."[52] While the novel's primary criminal figure, Popeye, commits numerous crimes throughout the narrative – from bootlegging and kidnapping to rape and murder – Faulkner emphasizes his general status as a criminal over any specific offenses that might lead to that designation, highlighting the process by which Popeye becomes legible as a criminal type. Physically diminutive and perpetually dressed in black, Popeye is immediately cast as suspicious in his actions and intentions. He is also impotent, which marks him further as a deviation from the norm.

As Miss Reba, proprietress of the Memphis brothel where Popeye keeps Temple Drake, the woman he has kidnapped and forced into sexual servitude, remarks, "[a] young man spending his money like water on girls and not never going to bed with one. It's against nature" (*S*, 255). Only at the end of the novel does Faulkner explain how the taint of criminality has colored Popeye's life since birth, and there the effect is not so much to offer a motive for his crimes as to account for an innate criminality from which Popeye can never escape: "At first they thought he was blind. Then they found that he was not blind, though he did not learn to walk and talk until he was about four years old" (*S*, 304). Popeye's physical delay corresponds to a developing criminality, as his body's refusal to grow occurs alongside chilling acts of violence. He is sent to "a home for incorrigible children" after murdering a kitten and dismembering two birds, and in these events his criminality appears fully formed, waiting only for his body to catch up (*S*, 309). Popeye is notably indifferent to these and other crimes, but such indifference mirrors his own rejection by his father, who abandoned the family, and the inability of his mother and grandmother to care for him. Here we see the reification of Lombroso's born criminal at the same time that Faulkner implicitly questions the validity of that model, staging the debate between inherited and environmental criminality. Just as importantly, Popeye's apathy regarding the violence he commits also speaks to the challenge of reading the criminal as a coherent subject. Faulkner's novel is remarkably silent on Popeye's perception of his actions – which suggests either that Popeye's motivations for crime are unknown even to him, or that they matter far less to our understanding of Popeye than our more holistic perception of him as an ambiguous figure marked by a general air of criminality – and thus personifies the ambivalence regarding the criminal that permeates modernist fiction.

If Popeye's criminality fulfills the first objective of *Violent Minds* – that is, to show how modernism utilizes the criminal in an attempt to represent a violent, multifaceted subjectivity – then Faulkner's dismissal of *Sanctuary*'s commercial origins fulfills the second, equally important objective of examining the forms of exchange between modernism and genre fiction in the late nineteenth and early twentieth centuries. Indeed, much of my argument centers on how modernism turned to crime fiction for alternative methods for representing criminality, and on how certain crime fiction authors imbued their work with the formal and thematic concerns of high modernism. Consequently, I not only examine authors who are readily identified as modernists, but also nineteenth-century protomodernists such as Edgar Allan Poe and Arthur Conan Doyle, both of whom provide a foundation for understanding the modernist absorption in psychology, as well as late modernists such as Highsmith and Greene, who respond to and repurpose earlier modernist articulations of criminality through the tropes of popular fiction. This broad conception of what counts as modernism might initially seem to strip the term of its descriptive power, since if authors as formally and historically divergent as Poe and Highsmith can both contribute to a study of modernism, then the category of modernism itself could easily be deemed too inclusive. However, calls for inclusivity now dominate modernist studies, buttressed by numerous critics who maintain that expanding the canon provides a more accurate impression of the diversity of modernist cultural production. As Nicholas Daly explains, by establishing "a longer historical *durée* for modernism" and emphasizing the commerce between modernism and popular fiction, critics can offer "a useful corrective to accounts of modernism, or indeed of popular fiction, that treat them as completely *sui generis*," and instead begin "tracing family resemblances across a range of literary expression."[53] This is precisely the kind of critical shift that Douglas Mao and Rebecca Walkowitz identify in their history of the New Modernist Studies, where they note that "canons have been critiqued and reconfigured" through a fundamental reassessment of the "once quite sharp boundaries between high art and popular forms of culture," a significant component of a larger push against the established view of modernism as an exclusive cadre of Anglo-American male authors immune to the demands of the literary market.[54]

Violent Minds makes a related intervention by demonstrating how we can more productively understand modernism by situating traditional examples of it alongside fictions traditionally pitted against it – whether because they are too popular, appear too early or too late, or adopt forms dismissed as marginal to canonical, high modernism. Criminality serves as a fitting vehicle for such an endeavor, as it runs through both the high modernism of Joseph Conrad, Wyndham Lewis, and Gertrude Stein and the genre fiction of Poe, Doyle, Dorothy L. Sayers, and Dashiell Hammett. Of course, any affinity between modernism and crime fiction might appear anomalous, since critics often presuppose vast ideological and aesthetic chasms separating high modernists from their popular contemporaries, succumbing to the stereotype of genre fiction as mere commercial entertainment. Even as vocal a proponent of crime fiction as W. H. Auden, who compared his appetite for the genre to "an addiction like tobacco or alcohol," claimed that "detective stories have nothing to do with works of art."[55] Such stereotypes have experienced a marked critical backlash in recent decades, however, and have not held up especially well. Andreas Huyssen's contention that modernists "insisted on the inherent hostility between high and low" seems dubious given recent work on modernism's engagement with popular culture, and Michael North's claim that the traditional division between an exclusive, elitist modernism and an open, democratic mass culture "has always seemed more a matter of theoretical necessity than of empirical fact" suggests that the idea of modernism's absolute aversion to popular forms is increasingly untenable.[56]

Allowing for the possibility of a modernism that includes popular literature also exposes a remarkable degree of overlap between the modernist imperative to reinvigorate past literary forms and crime novelists' affirmation of their work as a sophisticated manipulation of generic convention. As Paul Peppis argues, even a Golden Age mystery like Gladys Mitchell's *Speedy Death* (1929) can reflect a popular modernism that "interrupt[s] the 'naturalness' of things as they are, especially the established literary, social, and political forms and systems that popular culture is generally held to perpetuate," and thereby repurpose some of modernism's most celebrated innovations within an overtly generic context.[57] Similarly, Sean McCann asserts that some of the most prominent hard-boiled detective novelists – including Hammett, Raymond Chandler, and James M. Cain – "became, in effect, pulp avant-gardists," all of whom saw their work as something more than "pop entertainment."[58] In each of these claims, we see how modernism and popular fiction could pursue similar goals, and draw upon one another in order to explore specific strategies of representation. High modernists such as Lewis and Stein developed some of their most recognizable aesthetic experiments in their engagement with genre fiction, while the formal ingenuity and sustained interest in the social transformations of modern culture displayed in Hammett's and Sayers's detective novels challenge common assumptions that the genre writer and the modernist were mutually exclusive categories. Despite its absence in critical accounts of the period, then, crime fiction played an important, if unheralded, role in modernist writing.

In order to navigate the many strains of modernist criminal representation, *Violent Minds* proceeds in thematic and roughly chronological fashion, with each chapter highlighting a unique focal point along a trajectory of fictional developments. The book's first half focuses largely on the representation of detectives and criminals in the late nineteenth and early twentieth centuries, while the second centers on the overlap between modernism and crime fiction in exploiting literary form to theorize new and innovative models of criminal identity. I do not wish to imply, however, a division between these halves, as each of my chapters unearths powerful and subtle connections among modernism, crime fiction, and criminal representation. Chapter 1, for instance, demonstrates the influence of nineteenth-century approaches to crime and the dictates of the burgeoning detective genre on the modernist representation of criminality; it aligns early detective fictions by Edgar Allan Poe and Arthur Conan Doyle with the Lord Peter Wimsey mystery novels of Dorothy L. Sayers in order to explain how protomodernist conceptions of criminal detection as a form of empirical rationality gave way to twentieth-century notions of the detective as prone to chance, mistake, and error. Examining Sayers's satire of the cold, statistical Victorian sleuth – epitomized by the seeming infallibility of Poe's Auguste Dupin and Doyle's Sherlock Holmes – this chapter illustrates how the conflict between rationality and mindlessness in nineteenth- and twentieth-century detective fiction plays a decisive role in later modernist experiments with psychological representation, using Sayers as a critical example of a popular genre author who, in pursuing the vagaries of psychology in this way, deserves a much more prominent role in modernist literary history than has so far been acknowledged.

Chapter 2 moves from detection to violence by proposing the figure of the anarchist terrorist as a haunting criminal presence on the literary landscape of modernist London. Pairing a historical account of anarchist bombing campaigns with the fictional representation of terror in Henry James's *The Princess Casamassima* (1886), Joseph Conrad's *The Secret Agent* (1907) and *Under Western Eyes* (1911), and G. K. Chesterton's *The Man Who Was Thursday* (1908), this chapter reveals the extent to which political radicalism and metropolitan dynamite attacks became ubiquitous international phenomena at the turn of the century, and dramatically imposed themselves upon the literary imagination. It also argues for the primacy of the terrorist in modernist critiques of criminal anthropology. In examining the psychology of the terrorist and that figure's motives for violence, James, Conrad, and Chesterton dispute the notion of a distinct criminal typology, perceiving significant gaps in any theory of the political criminal as a discrete, coherent subject readily identified by physiognomy. At the same time, one would be mistaken in assuming that, because James, Conrad, and Chesterton all took Lombrosian models of criminality to task, their own conceptions of political crime were entirely sound. Though they aimed to disrupt conventional wisdom regarding terrorism and its adherents, James, Conrad, and Chesterton all fall into critiques of anarchism that are at best historically questionable, and at worst eerily similar to the processes of generalization and abstraction that motivated biological notions of criminality. Consequently, this chapter also reveals how modernist authors often failed to recognize the flaws in their own representations of criminality, their renderings of the anarchist oddly divorced from their understandings of anarchism as a system of political thought.

Combining the themes of Chapters 1 and 2 – that is, the symmetry between modernism and popular literature and the representation of the criminal as a unique instantiation of modern subjectivity – Chapter 3 examines two modernist experiments with crime fiction that blend avant-garde innovation with popular generic convention. Considering Wyndham Lewis's *Mrs. Dukes' Million* (1908–1909; published posthumously in 1977) and Gertrude Stein's *Blood on the Dining-Room Floor* (1933; published posthumously in 1948), I argue that both authors saw in the crime genre the potential for a new mode of writing that might respond to modernism's experimental imperative while also appealing to a mass audience. By confounding crime fiction's traditional emphasis on linear narratives and fixed criminal identities, Lewis and Stein invent an unprecedented kind of fiction that fuses the conventions of a popular genre with the emphases on chance, uncertainty, and play characteristic of modernism, exploring the concept of criminality in order to establish connections between seemingly disparate fictional modes. In so doing, both authors challenge assumed distinctions between modernist fiction and popular culture, and reveal the extent to which modernism took seriously questions of commercial viability and the demands of the literary marketplace. Far from removing their work from the corrupting influence of genre fiction, both Lewis and Stein arrive at their representations of criminality through the fusion of experiment and convention, their texts displaying the curious yet fruitful marriage of modernist aesthetics and popular form.

Chapter 4 extends this line of inquiry to the period of late modernism. I argue that, as authors of the 1930s and after began to conceive of identity, and especially criminal identity, as fluid and ultimately self-determined, they returned to those questions of psychological representation that spurred the early modernist treatment of criminality. Beginning with Dashiell Hammett's *Red Harvest* (1929) and Continental Op stories as exemplary works of popular crime writing that evince a psychological complexity and self-conscious manipulation of literary form characteristic of modernism, this chapter illustrates how late modernist novels such as Graham Greene's *A Gun for Sale* (1936) and *Brighton Rock* (1938), as well as Patricia Highsmith's *The Talented Mr. Ripley* (1955), similarly employ the conventions of crime fiction in order to re-examine early modernist anxieties concerning criminal psychology. In focusing on the representation of murder as a mode of identity formation, I contend that, in the work of these late modernists, crime offers the potential for upward social mobility and the promise of an entirely self-fashioned identity. As characters turn to crime as a viable profession, they approach the act of murder as an opportunity for self-creation, calling into question any notion of a stable, coherent subject, and offering in its place the construction of the career criminal. In presenting identity as a generative process of performance and improvisation, late modernism revisits those questions of criminal subjectivity so prominent in earlier fiction, but responds with more deliberately ambiguous models of the criminal that either evade categorization or use categorization as a paradoxical means of achieving individual ends.

Finally, I conclude with a brief account of how modernism's engagement with criminality inflects the twenty-first-century British novel. Centering on Tom McCarthy's *Remainder* (2005), this conclusion traces the link between the anonymous narrator of that novel, who re-enacts (and eventually initiates) violent crimes in an idiosyncratic effort to manufacture an authentic experience, and modernism's treatment of the criminal as a site for thinking through the psychology of an individual whose identity is defined by the violence he enacts. In so doing, I emphasize how deeply indebted our current perception of identity is to the modernist criminal subject. Far from lying on the periphery of modernism, I argue, the problem of criminality is central to our understanding of both the period itself and our contemporary moment – not simply because modernist authors were intrigued by both factual and fictional accounts of crime, but because their perception of the criminal as an exemplary modern individual continues to resonate with, and to unsettle, the subjects of our own century. If, as McCarthy's novel suggests, modernist conceptions of criminality have never entirely dissipated, then neither has the cultural fascination with crime and violence. Through modernism, we can trace the development of the criminal as an emblem for the vicissitudes of the modern mind, and better comprehend the role of fiction in advancing the criminal to such a position of cultural and literary prominence. In other words, the history of modernism is also a history of violent minds, and the ways in which modernist authors grappled with them form the basis of our current understanding of what crime and criminality signify in a world in which they still persist.

Notes

1. Oscar Wilde, "Pen, Pencil, and Poison," *The Complete Works of Oscar Wilde*, vol. 4, ed. Josephine M. Guy (Oxford: Oxford University Press, 2007), 121.
2. Ibid., 105.
3. Ibid., 120, 121.
4. Thomas De Quincey, "On Murder Considered as One of the Fine Arts," *On Murder*, ed. Robert Morrison (New York: Oxford University Press, 2006), 10–11.
5. Wilde, "Pen, Pencil, and Poison," 121.
6. Havelock Ellis, *The Criminal* (London: Walter Scott, 1892), 17.
7. Ibid., 16, 17.
8. Ibid., 17.
9. Michel Foucault, *Discipline and Punish: The Birth of the Prison*, trans. Alan Sheridan (New York: Vintage, 1995), 18.
10. Michael Levenson, *Modernism* (New Haven: Yale University Press, 2011), 84.
11. Ibid., 84.
12. Robert B. Pippin, *Modernism as a Philosophical Problem: On the Dissatisfactions of European High Culture*, second edition (Malden: Blackwell, 1999), 39.
13. Gabriel Tarde, *Penal Philosophy*, trans. Rapelje Howell (Boston: Little, Brown, and Co., 1912), 221.
14. Mark Seltzer, *Serial Killers: Death and Life in America's Wound Culture* (New York: Routledge, 1998), 4.
15. Ibid., 4.
16. Ellis, *The Criminal*, 283.
17. Virginia Woolf, "Mr. Bennett and Mrs. Brown," *Collected Essays*, vol. 1 (London: Hogarth Press, 1966), 320.
18. Sir Arthur Conan Doyle, "The Adventure of the Empty House," *The New Annotated Sherlock Holmes: Volume II*, ed. Leslie S. Klinger (New York: W. W. Norton, 2005), 812–813. For an insightful reading of this passage in relation to degeneration theory, see Daniel Pick, *Faces of Degeneration: A European Disorder, c.1848–c.1918* (Cambridge: Cambridge University Press, 1989), 155.
19. Martin J. Wiener, *Reconstructing the Criminal: Culture, Law, and Policy in England, 1830–1914* (Cambridge: Cambridge University Press, 1990), 236.
20. On Doyle and family lineage, see Barry McCrea, *In the Company of Strangers: Family and Narrative in Dickens, Conan Doyle, Joyce, and Proust* (New York: Columbia University Press, 2011), 67–93.
21. Judith R. Walkowitz, *City of Dreadful Delight: Narratives of Sexual Danger in Late-Victorian London* (Chicago: University of Chicago Press, 1992), 193.
22. John Binny, "Thieves and Swindlers," in Henry Mayhew, *London Labour and the London Poor*, vol. IV (New York: Dover, 1968), 273.
23. Ibid., 273.

24. Nicole Rafter, *The Criminal Brain: Understanding Biological Theories of Crime* (New York: New York University Press, 2008), 36.
25. David Taylor, *Crime, Policing and Punishment in England, 1750–1914* (New York: St. Martin's, 1998), 29.
26. Bénédict Morel, quoted in Max Nordau, *Degeneration* (Lincoln: University of Nebraska Press, 1993), 16.
27. Ibid., 16.
28. Ibid., 17.
29. For a literary history of degeneration in Britain, see William P. Greenslade, *Degeneration, Culture, and the Novel, 1880–1940* (Cambridge: Cambridge University Press, 1994). See also Dana Seitler, *Atavistic Tendencies: The Culture of Science in American Modernity* (Minneapolis: University of Minnesota Press, 2008), on degeneration's modern political valences.
30. Sander L. Gilman, *Difference and Pathology: Stereotypes of Sexuality, Race, and Madness* (Ithaca: Cornell University Press, 1985), 203.
31. Pick, *Faces of Degeneration*, 52.
32. Although *Criminal Man* was not translated into English until 1911, and then only in abridged form, Lombroso's work circulated widely through the efforts of adherents such as Ellis, who summarized and disseminated its findings. On criminal anthropology's reception in English-speaking countries, see Pick, *Faces of Degeneration*, 176–221; Christopher Pittard, *Purity and Contamination in Late Victorian Detective Fiction* (Burlington: Ashgate, 2011), 105–144; Nicole Hahn Rafter, *Creating Born Criminals* (Urbana: University of Illinois Press, 1997), 110–132; and Rafter, *The Criminal Brain*.
33. Cesare Lombroso, *Criminal Man*, ed. and trans. Mary Gibson and Nicole Hahn Rafter (Durham: Duke University Press, 2006), 51.
34. Simon A. Cole, *Suspect Identities: A History of Fingerprinting and Criminal Identification* (Cambridge, MA: Harvard University Press, 2002), 2.
35. Allan Sekula, "The Body and the Archive," *October* 39 (Winter 1986): 6.
36. Simon Joyce, *Capital Offenses: Geographies of Class and Crime in Victorian London* (Charlottesville: University of Virginia Press, 2003), 175.
37. L. Perry Curtis, Jr., *Jack the Ripper and the London Press* (New Haven: Yale University Press, 2001), 10.
38. Omri Moses, *Out of Character: Modernism, Vitalism, Psychic Life* (Stanford: Stanford University Press, 2014), 2.
39. Lisa Rodensky, *The Crime in Mind: Criminal Responsibility and the Victorian Novel* (Oxford: Oxford University Press, 2003), 7.
40. Ibid., 214, 217.
41. Elizabeth Carolyn Miller, *Framed: The New Woman Criminal in British Culture at the Fin de Siècle* (Ann Arbor: University of Michigan Press, 2008), 2–3.
42. Joyce, *Capital Offenses*, 9.
43. Sarah Cole, *At the Violet Hour: Modernism and Violence in England and Ireland* (Oxford: Oxford University Press, 2012), 4.

44. Paul Sheehan, *Modernism and the Aesthetics of Violence* (Cambridge: Cambridge University Press, 2013), 2–3.
45. Jonathan P. Eburne, *Surrealism and the Art of Crime* (Ithaca: Cornell University Press, 2008), 1.
46. Rex Ferguson, *Criminal Law and the Modernist Novel: Experience on Trial* (Cambridge: Cambridge University Press, 2013), 3.
47. Mark S. Micale, "The Modernist Mind: A Map," *The Mind of Modernism: Medicine, Psychology, and the Cultural Arts in Europe and America, 1880–1940*, ed. Mark S. Micale (Stanford: Stanford University Press, 2003), 2.
48. Jessica Burstein, *Cold Modernism: Literature, Fashion, Art* (University Park: Pennsylvania State University Press, 2012), 2–3.
49. Foucault, *Discipline and Punish*, 17.
50. Eburne, *Surrealism and the Art of Crime*, 7–8.
51. Seltzer, *Serial Killers*, 4.
52. William Faulkner, *Sanctuary: The Corrected Text* (New York: Vintage, 1993), 321–322. Hereafter cited parenthetically, as *S*.
53. Nicholas Daly, *Modernism, Romance and the Fin de Siècle: Popular Fiction and British Culture, 1880–1914* (Cambridge: Cambridge University Press, 1999), 11.
54. Douglas Mao and Rebecca L. Walkowitz, "The New Modernist Studies," *PMLA* 123.3 (May 2008): 737–738.
55. W. H. Auden, "The Guilty Vicarage," *The Complete Works of W. H. Auden: Prose, Volume II, 1939–1948*, ed. Edward Mendelson (Princeton: Princeton University Press, 2002), 261, 262.
56. Andreas Huyssen, *After the Great Divide: Modernism, Mass Culture, Postmodernism* (Bloomington: Indiana University Press, 1986), viii; Michael North, *Reading 1922: A Return to the Scene of the Modern* (Oxford: Oxford University Press, 1999), 10.
57. Paul Peppis, "Querying and Queering Golden Age Detection: Gladys Mitchell's *Speedy Death* and Popular Modernism," *Journal of Modern Literature* 40.3 (Spring 2017): 122.
58. Sean McCann, *Gumshoe America: Hard-Boiled Crime Fiction and the Rise and Fall of New Deal Liberalism* (Durham: Duke University Press, 2000), 4, 3.

CHAPTER I

Modernist Detection
Minds, Mindlessness, and the Logic of Criminal Pursuit

By undue profundity we perplex and enfeeble thought; and it is possible to make even Venus herself vanish from the firmament by a scrutiny too sustained, too concentrated, or too direct.
– Edgar Allan Poe, "The Murders in the Rue Morgue" (1841)[1]

[T]here are certain moments in life which are accessible only at the price of a certain lack of intellectual focus: like objects at the edge of my field of vision which disappear when I turn to stare at them head on.
– Fredric Jameson, "On Raymond Chandler" (1970)[2]

To understand the various forms of criminal representation that emerged during the modernist period – why novelists wavered in their depictions of criminals as irrational offenders prone to inexplicable violence, canny opportunists intent on making their way in an unaccommodating society, or eccentric combinations of pathological unreason and acute self-awareness – we might begin with the Victorian detective. Traditionally perceived as an emblem of stability and social order, the protagonist of nineteenth-century detective fiction is in fact a far more fluid creature, articulating what would become one of modernism's central paradoxes: a simultaneous commitment to representing the nuances of mental life and a recognition that the sheer volume of those nuances makes it impossible for any narrative to deliver a comprehensive, unambiguous portrayal of a character's psychology. Just as high modernists such as Woolf, Joyce, and Lawrence imagined subjectivity as a struggle between competing psychic impulses – some conscious, some unconscious – and fiction as a necessary if imperfect medium for rendering those contradictions, the Auguste Dupin tales of Edgar Allan Poe and the Sherlock Holmes novels and short stories of Sir Arthur Conan Doyle feature detectives beset by similar conflicts, torn between the efficiencies of logic, the entanglements of affect, and the unruliness of a body that alternately

26

expresses and obscures the mind it contains. In presenting the detective as a conglomeration of these and other tensions, these narratives foreshadow later modernist accounts of subjectivity, which attempt, through more explicitly experimental forms, to convey the vicissitudes of modern identity in a process that Christopher Butler describes as an effort "to adapt experimentalist modes of expression to the more precise tracking of actual (elliptical, disjointed, juxtapository) mental processes."[3] The Victorian detective, then, serves as an instructive example of how the mind's functioning became such a vexed issue for twentieth-century literature, and helps us to see how criminality came to play such a substantial role in modernism's fascination with interiority and its representation.

Despite various attempts to shield modernism from the incursion of popular culture, the detective has long been considered one of the period's most notable avatars. According to Brian McHale, the detective genre's epistemological orientation mirrors the modernist effort to apprehend the boundaries of human knowledge. The narrative logic of Faulkner's *Absalom, Absalom!*, McHale argues, "is that of a detective story," as the novel "foregrounds such epistemological themes as the accessibility and circulation of knowledge, the different structuring imposed on the 'same' knowledge by different minds, and the problem of 'unknowability' or the limits of knowledge."[4] Such affinities between modernism and detective fiction not only offer a productive framework for considering modernism in relation to the popular, but also locate the detective at the heart of modernism's formal and thematic concerns. One finds traces of this approach in critical accounts of both modernist and detective fiction, from Slavoj Žižek's claim that "the modern novel and the detective novel are centered around the same formal problem – the *impossibility of telling a story in a linear, consistent way*," to Astradur Eysteinsson's observation that "the modernist hero is frequently in the role of the detective who never solves the crime, for he is of course also the guilt-ridden criminal."[5] Rather than ascribing the resemblance between the two forms to mere historical contemporaneity, these critical perspectives underline a related set of epistemological commitments that link modernism and detective fiction through their shared absorption in questions of knowledge, its transmission, and its occlusions.

Those points of contact do not begin in the twentieth century, but rather arise in the earliest appearances of the Victorian detective. That figure, as a reflection of the increasing modernization of the nineteenth-century police force, is a curiously protean form, adopting a systematic, professional approach to criminal investigation yet deviating dramatically from accepted standards of professional identity and behavior. As Charles Rzepka has argued, though the detective is often characterized as an upholder of hegemonic cultural norms, sleuths in the vein of Sherlock Holmes possess a decidedly individualistic streak, and are just as likely to follow the dictates of their own desires as they are the demands of any legal or social institution. "The evolution in the detective's social status," Rzepka maintains, reflects larger changes in readers' "projected fantasies of what true personal freedom in an increasingly impersonal, bureaucratic, and commercial society might ideally look like, short of outright criminality itself."[6] As a result of this friction between the fictional detective's social and individual obligations – duties to the community and to oneself – critics are split in their assessments of that figure's cultural legacy, juggling views of the detective as an archetype of imperial authority, an affirmation of criminology's scientific aspirations, or an emergent breed of professional committed to ominous intellectual labors. Often these interpretations are mutually reinforcing. Where D. A. Miller makes a persuasive case for the detective's epitomizing of domestic and global surveillance, arguing that the genre "always implicitly pun[s] on the detective's brilliant *super-vision* and the police *supervision* that it embodies," Ronald Thomas applies Miller's Foucauldian perspective to the technologies that translate the physical markings of crime into a logical narrative of culpability.[7] As Thomas explains, "[a]t stake [in detective fiction] is not just the identification of a dead victim or an unknown suspect, but the demonstration of the power invested in certain forensic devices embodied in the figure of the literary detective."[8] What Miller and Thomas share is their conception of the detective as the embodiment of an idea; for Miller the detective is an instrument of the state while for Thomas he is an instrument of science, but for both the character is always a mechanism within a larger system of power, a tool rather than an individual.

As these approaches suggest, most critics characterize the detective as embodying the exactitude of rationality, functioning like a machine whose results are as impressive as its implications are disquieting. Indeed, the Victorian detective's methods reflect an objectivity that removes morality and individual character from the study of crime, making him, in effect, a form of technology uncorrupted by the biases of feeling. According to Martin Wiener, a detective such as Holmes reveals how "the crime-fighting professional changed . . . from a model of character to a model of intelligence, from a knower of the human heart to a master interpreter of circumstances."[9] Here the detective serves as a kind of abstracted intelligence, attuned to physical evidence and environments but stonily unconcerned with people. One could argue that such empiricism improves upon earlier investigative practices that adopted a narrower, more essentialist view of human behavior, yet the detective's apparent disregard for the individual as anything more than a unit within a larger problem also signals the ascendance of a popular fantasy regarding the efficacy of professional detection – namely, the idea that the detective's critical detachment might eliminate any potential for error. By presenting his conclusions as infallible, the detective commands respect in his unfailing accuracy but also exceeds human ability, accentuating what Wiener refers to as "the lack of competence of ordinary human beings," and what Daniel Cottom similarly characterizes as "society's total lack of confidence in itself."[10] In this way, the incredible accuracy of Holmes's brainwork suggests that traditional approaches to criminality are insufficient, and that the act of deduction is, or should be, the exclusive purview of an intellectual elite.

While the Victorian detective's steely devotion to logic and improbable success rate in solving crimes run counter to modernism's attraction to the more opaque elements of human experience, this chapter argues that that character's unique form of thinking is precisely what aligns detective fiction of the period with more overtly modernist narratives. Simultaneously regimented and idiosyncratic, scientific yet immersed in questions of agency that resist empirical scrutiny, the nineteenth-century detective demonstrates how authors experimented with alternative psychological models that depart from traditional perceptions of human reason in order to probe more fully the deep divisions that underscore mental life. This is the same tack that modernists took in presenting consciousness as fragmented and shifting, as their use of stream-of-consciousness narration, interior monologue, and free indirect discourse emphasizes a conception of the mind as a kaleidoscopic assemblage rather than a unified whole. To establish the parallel between modernism and detective fiction as related exercises in psychological representation, I explain how the intellectual gamesmanship of Poe's Dupin and the calculated machinations of Holmes function as instances of protomodernism that initiate some of the early twentieth century's most significant fictional experiments with subjectivity, as both assert and question the value of rationality for navigating an increasingly chaotic modernity. In Poe and Doyle, the dispassionate, scientific approach to crime belies a more radical challenge to the capacity of one mind to understand another, and to the idea of a consistent, stable subject: Dupin relies upon strategies of psychological guesswork so calculated that they eliminate any possibility of being wrong, while Holmes exemplifies a form of cold, systematic reasoning so mechanical that it effectively nullifies his humanity.

While these fraught interrogations of deductive rationality represent a uniquely modernist endeavor in their own right, they come under intense critique in the detective novels of Dorothy L. Sayers, whose underappreciated modernism is the subject of the chapter's second half. Arguing that her protagonist, Lord Peter Wimsey, represents a new, modernist detective who counters the certainties of Dupin and Holmes, I show how Sayers's fiction refashions the protomodernism of its forerunners by embracing their interest in deduction's peculiar mindset while alleging that the process of criminal investigation is, at its heart, illogical, swayed by habits of thought that Victorian detective fiction consistently attempted to negate. Molded by the traumas of World War I yet strangely lacking in psychological depth, immensely capable as a detective yet solving his cases through epiphany, Wimsey is plagued by the contradictions of his era, his profession, and his mind. Far removed from the mechanical rationality of the Victorian sleuth, Sayers's detective is defined by his fluctuation between mindfulness and mindlessness, and so advances pressing questions about the ability of any fictional narrative – generic or modernist – to articulate the individual's inner life.

While her work offers a significant counterpoint to that of Poe and Doyle, Sayers, too, is typically excluded from conversations about modernism. She also sustained withering criticism from influential genre writers, most notably Raymond Chandler, who famously dismissed her in his 1944 essay "The Simple Art of Murder." There Chandler condemned Sayers's dictum that the detective story, as a form of escapism, can never reach "the loftiest level of literary achievement,"[11] and argued that her adherence to convention imposed severe limits on her abilities in characterization:

> [Sayers's] kind of detective story was an arid formula which could not even satisfy its own implications . . . If it started out to be about real people (and she could write about them – her minor characters show that), they must very soon do unreal things in order to form the artificial pattern required by the plot. When they did unreal things, they ceased to be real themselves. They became puppets and cardboard lovers and papier mâché villains and detectives of exquisite and impossible gentility.[12]

At issue here is the problem of artificiality within generic constraints, as Chandler claims that Sayers's reliance on narrative formula leads to a corresponding disregard for psychological realism. Sayers's fiction lacks a level of authenticity that, Chandler contends, one finds only in those works that resist the "artificial pattern" of plot. The clue puzzles of British mystery novelists such as Sayers – a subgenre best known for its strict adherence to notions of "fair play," or the idea that readers must have at their disposal every clue necessary for solving the mystery at hand along with the detective protagonist – would thus appear unconcerned with interiority, favoring instead those stock characters whose shallowness allows them to serve as formal devices that further an engaging yet ultimately sterile plot.[13]

Despite its pointedness, Chandler's appraisal of Sayers as either unable or unwilling to explore the inner lives of her characters instead of reducing them to purely functional roles within the narrative fails to appreciate how a figure such as Wimsey adheres to the conventions of detective fiction only to underscore their inherent hostility to the idea of a transparent and fully realized mind, and in so doing reflects a decidedly modernist commitment to narrative forms that lay bare their own status as convention. Like Poe and Doyle, Sayers invents a detective whose methods are undeniably successful, but also parodies her Victorian predecessors by suggesting that the very notion of an infallible sleuth governed by pure logic is a patently artificial construction, a critique personified in Wimsey's unabashed artifice and intuitive approach to detective work. Her fiction inherits the focus on deductive process popularized by Poe and Doyle at the same time that it skewers that tradition to bring the genre more firmly in line with modernist perceptions of the individual as defined by illogic, self-consciousness, and fragmentation, and of representation as an attempt to utilize formal conventions to expose the complexities of mental life as well as the relative ability of narrative to represent them. This chapter, then, parses the ways in which all three authors, far from being irrelevant to modernism's history of subjective engagement, are essential to understanding that history. Whereas Poe and Doyle represent a gradual transition into the aesthetic paradigms of modernist fiction, Sayers's novels offer a more aggressively modernist account of the detective's distinctive blend of preternatural acumen and comic inadequacy. By approaching their work as underexplored moments in an expanded history of modernism, I aim to counter the prevailing critical narrative that separates modernism from genre fiction, and instead propose that we conceive of modernism and early detective fiction as formally and thematically intertwined.

Poe's Games

In many ways, Poe is an ideal starting point for a study of the nineteenth-century detective story's developing protomodernism, since much of his output has long been regarded as modernist *avant la lettre*. Indeed, Poe's influence on figures such as Walter Benjamin and Charles Baudelaire, the latter of whom deemed Poe "the most powerful pen of our age," has been well documented.[14] At the same time, his status as an innovator of popular genre fiction has complicated that position. As Jonathan Elmer explains, "Poe stands simultaneously as the germinal figure of a central modernist trajectory ... and as the much-acknowledged pioneer of several durable mass-cultural genres: detective fiction and science fiction, as well as certain modes of sensational or gothic horror."[15] Perhaps unsurprisingly given the longstanding critical effort to segregate modernism from popular culture, Poe has been "much acknowledged" for his detective fiction, equally so for his modernism, but almost never for both. To redress that imbalance, I take his eccentric, misanthropic amateur sleuth, the Chevalier C. Auguste Dupin, as a model of detection that anticipates later modernist efforts at understanding the vagaries of mental life. Using the detective as a figurehead for emerging forms of psychological perception and statistical rationality, Poe's Dupin stories bear a profound yet largely overlooked importance for the history of modernism, and for informing modernism's criminal imagination.

Poe's enigmatic synthesis of modernism and detective fiction is perhaps best understood through his elaborate account of games and their relationship to the psychological maneuverings of detection. While it may seem flippant to refer to criminal investigation as a game – implying as that term does that the stakes of winning or losing are not terribly high – the metaphor is nonetheless appropriate for the Dupin stories, which compare the practice of ratiocination to an intellectual exercise not unlike that derived from a tense round of card playing or a heated checkers match. In each of the stories – "The Murders in the Rue Morgue" (1841), "The Mystery of Marie Rogêt" (1842–43), and "The Purloined Letter" (1844) – the protagonist and his unnamed companion (who also serves as the narrator) regard the process of deduction as a form of play, characterizing detective work as a serious endeavor with serious consequences, but also as an amusing way to spend one's time. In portraying detection in this fashion, Poe not only inaugurated the deductive method that Roger Caillois equated with psychological gamesmanship – "Tell me how you play," Caillois claimed, "and I'll tell you if you've murdered anyone"[16] – but also inspired numerous fictional sleuths who identify their work as a private intellectual occupation rather than a civic-minded pursuit of justice. Thus, when Sherlock Holmes cribs from Shakespeare in "The Adventure of the Abbey Grange" (1904) and exclaims that "[t]he game is afoot," he adopts Dupin's assessment of detection as a rousing expenditure of intellectual energy.[17]

In the opening paragraph of "The Murders in the Rue Morgue," Poe's narrator compares the pleasurable effects of brainwork with those of physical exercise, emphasizing the playfulness of deductive thought:

> As the strong man exults in his physical ability, delighting in such exercises as call his muscles into action, so glories the analyst in that moral activity which *disentangles*. He derives pleasure from even the most trivial occupations bringing his talent into play. He is fond of enigmas, of conundrums, of hieroglyphics; exhibiting in his solutions of each a degree of *acumen* which appears to the ordinary apprehension præternatural. ("MRM," 92)

For a character such as Dupin – an "analyst" in his methodical, systematic "disentangling" of the complexities of human behavior – deductive reasoning offers both challenge and pleasure, as the act of problem solving becomes an intellectual sport wherein the thinker can enjoy a test of his abilities. To stave off charges of frivolity, however, the narrator is quick to distinguish between the substantial import of Dupin's "trivial occupation" and the self-aggrandizement of the hobbyist. Using the simple game of draughts – or checkers, to use the game's more common name – as a model of deductive analysis, he explains how the system of calculation employed in a complex game like chess serves as little more than a distraction to the untrained eye. Admiring draughts as an "unostentatious" game in which "the higher powers of the reflective intellect are more decidedly and more usefully tasked ... than by all the elaborate frivolity of chess," the narrator claims that, in the latter game, "where the pieces have different and *bizarre* motions, with various and variable values, what is only complex is mistaken ... for what is profound" ("MRM," 92). By contrast, moves in draughts "are *unique* and have but little variation," and because "the probabilities of inadvertence are diminished ... what advantages are obtained by either party are obtained by superior *acumen*" ("MRM," 93). In other words, a game of chess will feature innumerable moves, strategies, and tactics, and can conclude with a seemingly endless number of outcomes. Yet such possibilities are complex without being profound, requiring an ostentatious style of play rather than a thoughtful one; "in nine cases out of ten," the narrator declares, "it is the more concentrative rather than the more acute player who conquers" ("MRM," 92–93).

Unlike the "elaborate frivolity" of chess, draughts favors the player who does not simply master a set of rules, but instead learns to predict the behavior of the competition. As the narrator explains, "the analyst throws himself into the spirit of his opponent, identifies himself therewith, and not unfrequently sees thus, at a glance, the sole methods (sometimes indeed absurdly simple ones) by which he may seduce into error or hurry into miscalculation" ("MRM," 93). While the chess master perfects a style of play by memorizing a dizzying array of potential moves and countermoves, an adept player of draughts looks beyond the rules of the game and into the face across the board, searching for and then exploiting those expressions and mannerisms that expose an opponent's intentions. A card sharp does exactly the same thing, as a game of whist becomes a test of psychological perspicacity, with more skillful competitors observing "every variation of [an opponent's] face as the play progresses, gathering a fund of thought from the differences in the expression of certainty, of surprise, of triumph, or of chagrin" ("MRM," 94). Here Poe advances a deliberately unsettling proposition by arguing that other minds, for the analyst, are completely transparent, their expressions catalogued and filed into a readily accessible inventory of human emotion. The qualities of psychological observation that one hones in order to win a game thus prove useful for other, more serious purposes – for instance, to detect truth, falsity, or criminality. Consequently, Dupin, in Mark Seltzer's formulation, becomes a detective when he "observes observers observing," a seemingly superficial process that actually reveals a profound psychological engagement.[18]

Significantly, however, the game of detection is never as tidy an affair in the Dupin stories as these anecdotes suggest. In perceiving the faces of his opponents as reliable indicators of their intentions, the analyst expresses two related convictions: first, a faith in the interpretive value of physiognomy, which Lucy Hartley describes as providing to its earliest adherents "a spiritual guarantee that anyone could read the appearances of things in the world and then form a judgement on the basis of their essential though hidden value"; and second, a belief in the predictability of human behavior.[19] By this logic, faces, as objects of interpretation, inadvertently reveal those thoughts and emotions that betray the individual's objectives, and offer up such revelations to anyone willing to look for them. At the same time, though, Dupin's own visage is remarkably impassive. Whereas "most men," according to Dupin, "wore windows in their bosoms," his own manner is "frigid and abstract; his eyes ... vacant in expression" ("MRM," 96). Unlike the easy legibility of those he encounters, Dupin appears impervious to the kind of analysis he performs, remaining inscrutable and therefore unavailable for interpretation. Moreover, Dupin also voices a profound skepticism regarding the consistency of other people. In "The Mystery of Marie Rogêt" he maintains that "[n]othing is more vague than impressions of individual identity," and in "The Murders in the Rue Morgue" he bases his deductions on the empirical evidence of a crime scene rather than on the testimony of potentially unreliable witnesses.[20] Just as the narrator of the latter story insists upon the face as a readable surface and upon the analytical thinker's ability to predict an individual's behavior based on a voluminous "fund of thought" collected through past experience, Dupin himself alternates between views of human beings as entirely knowable and insistently obscure.

What accounts for this contradiction in Dupin's attitude regarding the symmetry between bodies and minds, or the capacity for reading the physical body as evidence of a mind's working? One solution lies in the "fund of thought" concept, which compares an individual to others in order to ascertain that individual's future behavior. Through this motif, Poe implies that people become transparent when one understands them as part of a larger set of data; take, for example, the successful whist player, who spends his first few games studying his competitors in order to collect such a wide sampling of their preferred styles of play that he invariably wins every subsequent hand. In many ways, this tactic of perceiving the individual in relation to a group anticipates Sherlock Holmes's systematic approach to collective behavior. In *The Sign of Four* (1890), Holmes offers an uncharacteristically emotive response to the crowd before reverting to a more statistical method of predicting its actions. Watching a mass of London's workers leaving their jobs for the day, Holmes delivers the following judgment:

> "Dirty-looking rascals, but I suppose every one has some little immortal spark concealed about him. You would not think it, to look at them. There is no *a priori* probability about it. A strange enigma is man!"
> "Someone calls him a soul concealed in an animal," [Watson] suggested.
> "Winwood Reade is good upon the subject," said Holmes. "He remarks that, while the individual man is an insoluble puzzle, in the aggregate he becomes a mathematical certainty. You can, for example, never foretell what any one man will do, but you can say with precision what an average number will be up to. Individuals vary, but percentages remain constant. So says the statistician."[21]

In this pronouncement the statistician and the detective become one and the same, and Holmes continues to follow his mathematical approach to humanity – analyzing individuals as data, groups as percentages, actions as probabilities – throughout his literary career. Similarly, Poe's "fund of thought" motif indicates that the analytical mind gains its power not from initial impressions of human character, but from the memories of an individual's past actions accumulated over long stretches of time, which it then uses in order to arrive at a perfect understanding of that individual's present thoughts and future behaviors. Deduction, in both cases, is therefore an act of prediction, utilizing a law of large numbers in order to limit any individual unit's ability to surprise.

This line of thought owes much to contemporaneous developments in the social and physical sciences, particularly the advent of modern statistics, which focused on the relationship between past action and future probability. In their shared skepticism toward individual behavior and their firm belief in the essential predictability of human action, Dupin and Holmes reflect the attitudes of early statisticians, who sought to clarify the opacity of modern experience. According to Louis Menand, "[s]tatistics conquered uncertainty by embracing it," as practitioners took error as a given within any particular system, reassuring a potentially doubtful public with the idea that mistakes might be admitted and thereby accounted for without invalidating an experiment.[22] This practice becomes even more significant when one recalls that early statisticians functioned much like contemporary social scientists. As Theodore Porter explains, they "sought to bring a measure of expertise to social questions, to replace the contradictory preconceptions of the interested parties by the certainty of careful empirical observation. They believed that the confusion of politics could be replaced by an orderly reign of facts."[23] For many, the idea of statistics' social function tempered the unsettling forces of chance and accident, and Menand notes that statistical approaches to crime exerted a calming effect on an occasionally alarmist society. "The broader appeal of statistics," he argues, "lay in the idea of an order beneath apparent randomness. Individuals – molecules or humans – might act unpredictably, but statistics seemed to show that in the aggregate their behavior conformed to stable laws."[24] In this light, one can perceive Holmes and Dupin as the literary embodiments of statistical thinking, employing mathematical formulae in order to master the range of human action in a process that enables them not only to detect criminals at a far greater speed than their official police counterparts, but also to assert the fundamental order of a seemingly chaotic world.

At the same time, however, Dupin expresses a profound antipathy toward statistics as a reliable indicator of human behavior, and claims in "The Purloined Letter" that mathematics' appeal to universality falters when confronted with the quirks of individual motivation. "Mathematical axioms are *not* axioms of general truths," he maintains:

> What is true of *relation* – of form and quantity – is often grossly false in regard to morals, for example. In this latter science it is very usually *un*true that the aggregated parts are equal to the whole ... In the consideration of motive [mathematical axiom] fails; for two motives, each of a given value, have not, necessarily, a value when united, equal to the sum of their values apart.[25]

For Dupin, the problem is not that statistical thinking is entirely fallacious, but rather that some subjects remain immune to its logic, and are better understood through different instruments. His complaint that human behavior defies categorization due to its inherent unpredictability resembles Holmes's observation regarding the "strange enigma" of man, but goes a step further by questioning the idea that one can predict future behavior by relying on one's knowledge of past motivations. While Holmes views the concept of criminal motivation as a subjective factor for which statistical thinking can account, Dupin emphasizes the importance of individual perception in identifying criminality, and distrusts statistical models for quantifying mental states.

This is not to suggest, however, that Dupin never avails himself of statistics, or that his investigative approach is purely impressionistic. Rather, Dupin fuses statistical reasoning with psychological perception while openly proclaiming the limits of both, perversely refusing to adopt a consistent methodology. To illustrate how these patterns of thought coexist, Dupin references another game. The goal of this particular contest, just as in draughts and whist, is to identify with an opponent's thinking and thereby predict the moves that individual is likely to attempt:

> I knew [a schoolboy] about eight years of age, whose success at guessing in the game of "even and odd" attracted universal admiration. This game is simple, and is played with marbles. One player holds in his hand a number of these toys, and demands of another whether that number is even or odd. If the guess is right, the guesser wins one: if wrong, he loses one. The boy to whom I allude won all the marbles of the school. Of course he had some principle of guessing; and this lay in mere observation and admeasurement of the astuteness of his opponents. For example, an arrant simpleton is his opponent, and, holding up his closed hand, asks, "are they even or odd?" Our schoolboy replies, "odd," and loses; but upon the second trial he wins, for he then says to himself, "the simpleton had them even upon the first trial, and his amount of cunning is just sufficient to make him have them odd upon the second; I will therefore guess odd;" – he guesses odd, and wins.

Now, with a simpleton a degree above the first, he would have reasoned thus: "This fellow finds that in the first instance I guessed odd, and, in the second, he will propose to himself, upon the first impulse, a simple variation from even to odd, as did the first simpleton; but then a second thought will suggest that this is too simple a variation, and finally he will decide upon putting it even as before. I will therefore guess even;" – he guesses even, and wins. ("PL," 257)[26]

Though the method here appears to be one of statistical probability, since the boy's attempt to guess his opponent's maneuver depends upon his understanding of potential options within a field of possibilities, his strategy is also reflexive, and resembles an equally psychological and mathematical contest. In order to win any game beyond the second, the boy must adapt his understanding of an opponent's mental capacity to account for elements of probability – in other words, he must consider both what his opponent is intellectually capable of doing and how that individual might alter his style of play based on the number of games that have transpired. This strategy bears fruit in the arena of detection as well, and figures prominently in "The Murders in the Rue Morgue" when Dupin, in the midst of a silent stroll, casually reads his companion's mind. In explaining how he arrived at the conclusion that the narrator was privately ruminating on the suitability of a particular actor for the title role of Prosper Jolyot de Crébillon's 1714 drama *Xerxes*, Dupin "miraculously" retraces the steps of his friend's logic, describing each turn of the narrator's attentions that brought him from thoughts of a fruit vendor to the inability of a novice performer to handle tragic roles. The narrator, understandably amazed, demands that Dupin explain "the method – if method there is – by which you have been enabled to fathom my soul in this matter," plainly intimating that Dupin's method appears decidedly unmethodical ("MRM," 97). As in the anecdote of evens and odds, however, Dupin's manner of thinking is primarily a way of demystifying human behavior, wherein detection serves as a balancing act between statistics (what the narrator could have thought in a given instant, based on Dupin's familiarity with his past actions) and psychology (what Dupin knows of his interests and preferred topics of conversation). Whereas in Holmes's formulation statistics serve as a reliably impersonal substitute for psychology, Dupin maintains that the rigidity of statistics requires the tempering force of psychology in order to prove useful.

In comparing these games to the processes by which one apprehends a criminal or solves a crime, Poe offers an account of detective work that can seem to elevate psychological impressions to mathematical certainties, advocating for a deductive method that, as Jean-Michel Rabaté points out, is distressingly pseudoscientific.[27] Despite their professed misgivings regarding individual character, the Dupin stories assume a correspondence between exterior and interior, with the protagonist utilizing a method so successful in its conclusions as to suggest that, even as certain individuals can frustrate in the eccentricity of their actions, they nonetheless conform to universal categories of behavior. If man is, as Holmes puts it, "a strange enigma," then Dupin makes him entirely ordinary through statistical and psychological acuity. However, Dupin relies neither on simple guesswork nor on prejudiced notions of human behavior in order to accomplish the task. Rather, his deductive games are better understood as experiments in conditioning the mind to accident as a defining feature of experience. In both his games and his detective work, Dupin's success rides on his ability to balance the probability of a given move with the inevitable chance inherent in any fair contest. Dupin, therefore, is neither entirely statistical nor entirely subjective in his deductions, and instead engages in a form of intellectual gambling that attempts to account for and thereby negate the potential for accident. Dupin explains this form of deduction in "The Mystery of Marie Rogêt" by referencing the centrality of chance in human history:

> [E]xperience has shown, and a true philosophy will always show, that a vast, perhaps the larger portion of truth, arises from the seemingly irrelevant. It is through the spirit of this principle, if not precisely through its letter, that modern science has resolved to *calculate upon the unforeseen* ... It is no longer philosophical to base, upon what has been, a vision of what is to be. *Accident* is admitted as a portion of the substructure. We make chance a matter of absolute calculation. We subject the unlooked for and unimagined, to the mathematical *formulae* of the schools. ("MMR," 174)

By accounting for accident, or the implausible move that could disrupt the entire game in its unpredictability, Dupin marries the mindset of the statistician to that of the gambler, in that the traditional aim of the latter is to minimize the degree of risk involved in placing a wager by calculating the probability of a certain outcome in any given contest. Ironically, the gambler's wager is often characterized as an attempt to thwart statistical probability, or to bury it under the excitement generated by a moment of uncertainty. As Thomas Kavanagh explains, "[t]he risk-taking we call gambling, and the subjective scenarios it generates, initiate for those who play a suspension of the certainties of probability theory and the law of large numbers."[28] To gamble "is to proclaim that there exists, beyond the calm dictates of law, a subjective wildness cosubstantial with who I am and

with the bets I place."[29] Walter Benjamin addressed that very wildness
when he claimed that gambling "is a means of conferring shock value on
events, of loosing them from the contexts of experience."[30]

Compared with these accounts of gambling as a form of self-assertion, or
of the subject's capacity to recognize its own power and frailty in the face of
chance, Dupin's game of detection seems coldly detached from the whims
of the illogical risk taker, and resembles a mechanical form of thinking that,
as I will argue in the next section of this chapter, suffuses the protomodernist impersonality of Holmes. Indeed, one of Dupin's most remarkable
talents is his neutrality in the face of seemingly inexplicable evidence, even
if such evidence leads him, as it does in "The Murders in the Rue Morgue,"
to the ostensibly preposterous conclusion that the mutilated bodies of two
women were the end result of an orangutan's rampage (a conclusion that,
in the end, proves true). Unlike those gamblers who embrace the risky bet
as a means of asserting their existence, Dupin makes familiar and even
logical the "shock value" of coincidence, accepting that accidents "happen
to all of us every hour of our lives, without attracting even momentary
notice" ("MRM," 114). Dupin's deductive games, then, are never pure
instances of uncertainty, but shrewd engagements with the world of rules,
strategy, and psychology – rational if idiosyncratic investigations that attest
to and assuage the inevitability of chance. By eliminating the potential for
error, these fusions of statistics and psychology illustrate the detective's
mastery of apparently uncontrollable circumstances, and reveal how the act
of thinking, in Poe's detective fiction, becomes a means of gaining certainty in a perilously uncertain world.

Doyle's Calculating Machine

If Poe's Dupin tales display a fascination with how private thoughts
become public knowledge, apprehended through the detective's combination of perception and prediction, then the Sherlock Holmes novels and
short stories of Arthur Conan Doyle turn that fascination inward, establishing the process of deduction as the foundation of the detective's
professional and personal identity. Just as it exposes what Stephen Arata
dubs "the pathology of bourgeois life," Doyle's work also highlights the
detective's social and subjective indeterminacy, an ambiguity manifested in
those forms of logic, detachment, and automatism that divorce Holmes
from traditional notions of personhood while at the same time making him
especially qualified to probe the criminal underbelly of late Victorian
England.[31] On the one hand, Holmes's unflinchingly analytical mind

exemplifies the nineteenth century's veneration of professional objectivity, and Amanda Anderson could easily be referring to him when she explains how the ideal of critical distance animated Victorian intellectual life, with "the doctor, the writer, and the professional [representing] the distinct promises of modernity: progressive knowledge, full comprehension of the social totality, and the possibilities of transformative self-understanding."[32] On the other hand, her claim that this ideal was not wholeheartedly embraced, and that in fact "many Victorians were wary of certain distancing effects of modernity, including the overvaluing and misapplication of scientific method as well as the forms of alienation and rootlessness that accompanied modern disenchantment, industrialization, and the globalization of commerce," equally describes Holmes's forbidding stoicism and disregard for traditional social bonds.[33] Appearing at the intersection of these conflicting attitudes, Holmes represents both the promise of objective reason and the threat of subjective impoverishment that accompanies it; he amplifies the statistical psychologism and investigative objectivity of Dupin by perceiving his clients as mathematical quantities, his life as an unceasing hunt for intellectual engagement, and idleness as a threat to his existence. As Charles Rzepka puts it, Holmes "does not work to live, but lives to work," pursuing his aims so fixedly that he takes no interest in anything outside of them.[34] In granting his detective such an unyielding devotion to a single, professional purpose, Doyle presents the deductive mind as disturbingly mechanical, impervious to any emotion that might make its bearer appear fallible or human.

As a symptom of the "distancing effects of modernity," Holmes's combination of intellectual, social, and emotional detachment also reflects other trends within late Victorian culture. For instance, several critics have recognized in Holmes's isolated intellection a current of *fin-de-siècle* alienation and aestheticism that emphasizes cerebral over physical action and social antagonism over collective unity. This is, after all, the detective who "loathe[s] every form of society with his whole Bohemian soul,"[35] suspends an investigation to attend a series of concerts in "The Red-Headed League" (1891), and, at the outset of *The Sign of Four*, reveals that he has injected himself with a 7 percent solution of cocaine "[t]hree times a day for many months" (*SF*, 5). Such aspects of his character align remarkably with the credos of the Aesthetic Movement, which, Anderson notes, "directly and flagrantly espoused the cultivation of radical detachment."[36] Importantly, however, Holmes does not experience these moments of misanthropy and sensory pleasure in the same way as other people. According to Watson, Holmes's abrupt visit to the concert hall is a necessary catalyst for detection, since, in the midst of such idleness, "the lust of the chase would suddenly come upon him, and . . . his brilliant reasoning power would rise to the level of intuition, until those who were unacquainted with his methods would look askance at him as on a man whose knowledge was not that of other mortals."[37] Likewise, Holmes takes no pleasure in using cocaine, explaining that he only resorts to the drug when he has nothing else to occupy his mind, and "can dispense . . . with artificial stimulants" once a suitable case appears: "My mind . . . rebels at stagnation. Give me problems, give me work, give me the most abstruse cryptogram, or the most intricate analysis, and I am in my own proper atmosphere" (SF, 6). Here and elsewhere, Holmes exhibits the cultivated detachment of the aesthete, but only as an inspiration or substitute for the more stimulating experience of work. His leisure is not a pleasurable diversion from a taxing and dangerous career, but an admission that he cannot exist apart from the mental occupations of his "proper atmosphere."

Understandably, Holmes's flirtation with aesthetic and sensory experience appears to complicate what I have identified as his status as a mechanical, wholly professional thinker. Yet this schism between Holmes as machine and Holmes as aesthete is by no means irreconcilable, as Susan Buck-Morss's notion of anesthetics and their relation to the "autogenetic" man – an individual who is self-created, self-sustaining, and immune to the charms of the senses – makes plain.[38] Tracing the term "aesthetics" back to its origin as a referent for sensory experience (aisthitikos in ancient Greek), Buck-Morss shows how the fantasy of the autogenetic individual becomes a common figuration of modernity descended from Kant's transcendental subject, who "purges himself of the senses which endanger autonomy not only because they unavoidably entangle him in the world, but, specifically, because they make him passive ('languid' [schmelzend] is Kant's word) instead of active ('vigorous' [wacker]), susceptible, like 'Oriental voluptuaries,' to sympathy and tears."[39] Like Holmes with his indifference to society or Dupin with his unreadable face, the autogenetic man earns "potency . . . in [his] lack of corporeal response," gaining cultural capital through "asensual" or anesthetic pretensions.[40] Created through the force of his own will, such a man is purely autonomous, disengaged from his surroundings and acting decisively toward self-determined ends. However, the autogenetic fantasy breaks down when faced with the shock and stimuli of modernity, and Buck-Morss argues that, as a result, the late nineteenth century witnessed a proliferation of self-anesthetization, characterized by a flurry of attempts to make "a narcotic . . . out of reality itself" through the concept of the phantasmagoria, or the controlled aesthetic environment in which every surface provides a different form of stimulation, and so anesthetizes "not through numbing, but through flooding the senses."[41] By equating Holmes's flinty detachment with Buck-Morss's theory of autogenesis, we can see that Holmes pursues pleasures such as cocaine and music not simply in order to overwhelm his senses, but rather to conquer them and thereby affirm the supremacy of analysis and reason. More importantly, we can better understand how the detective's tendency to eradicate any emotion that might compromise his objectivity, which Stephen Knight compares to "the superego mastering the ancient morass of the human id," represents a uniquely autogenetic approach to criminal investigation and to thought itself, a protomodernist ideal of scrupulous, even superhuman critical detachment.[42]

To understand Holmes's autonomy in these terms, we can begin with his eccentric profession, a regular topic of conversation in the early stories. Doyle's detective famously maintains a liminal professional status: never an official member of Scotland Yard, Holmes is an autodidact in criminology who investigates cases that others deem unsolvable or that clients bring to him directly, aiding the police in their efforts without adopting their methods or acquiescing to their institutional demands. While critics have noticed that Holmes regularly employs a scientific approach to crime in an effort to neutralize colonial threats to the Empire, with Laura Otis characterizing the detective as an "imperial immune system," Holmes's refusal to join the London police marks the lengths to which he will go to remove himself from civic and professional obligations.[43] In fact, in *The Sign of Four* Holmes congratulates himself for fashioning an entirely unprecedented career, telling Watson that his work with (but never for) the police allows for extraordinary autonomy:

> "I abhor the dull routine of existence. I crave for mental exaltation. That is why I have chosen my own particular profession, or rather created it, for I am the only one in the world."
> "The only unofficial detective?" I said, raising my eyebrows.
> "The only unofficial consulting detective," he answered. "I am the last and highest court of appeal in detection. When Gregson, or Lestrade, or Athelney Jones are out of their depths – which, by the way, is their normal state – the matter is laid before me. I examine the data, as an expert, and pronounce a specialist's opinion. I claim no credit in such cases. My name figures in no newspaper. The work itself, the pleasure of finding a field for my peculiar powers, is my highest reward." (*SF*, 6–7)

By labeling himself an "unofficial consulting detective," Holmes can practice the art of detection under a self-designed rubric, "finding a field" for "peculiar powers" that do not conform to any recognized discipline or methodology. As Vicki Mahaffey argues, Holmes is "bound to no authority other than the accumulated knowledge on the subject," and as a result "is responsible ultimately to himself."[44] In this manner, the autogenetic Holmes evades the omnipresent state power that many critics contend he enforces, as he insists upon a professional independence that troubles any attempt to classify him as a synecdoche for imperial strength.

Throughout the Holmes canon, Doyle stresses the character's professional autonomy by pointing out that even his study of criminal science is a haphazard, personal endeavor, an independent education whose utility arises from its rejection of traditional disciplinary categories. Far from a regimented scholar, Holmes is a dilettante who masters several branches of the physical and natural sciences in an impressively unsystematic fashion. In the first Holmes novel, *A Study in Scarlet* (1887), a man named Stamford elusively describes Holmes as "an enthusiast in some branches of science," and remarks that "[h]is studies are very desultory and eccentric, but he has amassed a lot of out-of-the-way knowledge which would astonish his professors."[45] Such an unorthodox course of study may seem surprising given the prodigious knowledge of criminology that Holmes gains as a result of it, but, as Barry McCrae observes, Holmes's career is founded upon "the breaking of expected routine," and so his education naturally follows a wayward course in order to arrive at forms of knowledge unavailable through the traditional academic programs of the nineteenth-century university.[46] Holmes's enthusiastic approach thus remains firmly beyond the bounds of conventional, systematic research, and connects him to a course of study that his teachers regard with suspicion. In some ways this eccentric education reflects a larger professional shift of the late nineteenth century, when, according to Lawrence Rothfield, "clinical medicine, once queen of the human sciences, [became] subordinated as a form of knowledge to the more exact sciences of bacteriology, chemistry, and microscopic anatomy," but while this situation might help to account for Watson's shortcomings in criminal detection – the general practitioner being unable to read the evidence of a case in a manner equal to a specialist such as Holmes – it does not alleviate a nineteenth-century audience's suspicion of Holmes as a man who lacks a proper discipline, a kind of mad scientist whose chosen field exists at the margins of respectability.[47] Such is the attitude inherent in Watson's bafflement over the object of Holmes's research – "Surely no man would work so hard or attain such precise information unless he had some definite end in view," he posits – and in Stamford's complaint that Holmes's steady engagement with science's more macabre elements "approaches to cold-bloodedness" (*SS*, 32, 19).

However, we might also interpret Stamford's distress at Holmes's "cold-bloodedness" as voicing a more specific anxiety regarding the detective's autogenetic habits of mind, an anxiety that identifies a key element of Doyle's protomodernism. In this reading, Holmes does not arouse suspicion through the gruesome objects of his scientific inquiries – poisons, wounds, and blood spatters, in the opening chapters of *A Study in Scarlet* – but in his utter lack of emotion toward them. In other words, Stamford does not take issue with Holmes's morbid empiricism, but rather with how it prohibits any affective response toward the evidence of cruelty, suffering, and death that it examines. Such emphatic impersonality – Holmes's inability or unwillingness to display feelings of disgust, sympathy, or sexual attraction – is almost certainly his defining feature; Doyle said as much in an 1892 letter to Joseph Bell, the model for Sherlock Holmes, when he explained that his detective "is as inhuman as a Babbage's Calculating Machine, and just about as likely to fall in love."[48] Admittedly off-putting, this resolute blankness connects Holmes to a burgeoning tradition of cold modernism, which Jessica Burstein distinguishes from other paradigms of modernist representation by its flouting of "[p]sychology, with its investment in motive; the unconscious, with its emphasis on hidden depths"; and "emotion, with its emphasis on affect and binding relations to the world."[49] The cold modernist investment in the mechanical – most readily apparent in the work of Wyndham Lewis, whose potboiler crime novel *Mrs. Dukes' Million* I discuss in Chapter 3 – helps to distinguish a central paradox of Holmes's autogenesis: his uncanny ability to fathom the depths of other people while obscuring any trace of his own. By figuring Holmes as an abstracted symbol of a powerful yet distant intelligence that does not express evidence of an interior life, Doyle anticipates later, cold modernist articulations of character as based in external forces and functions. Far from the psychological nuance of other modernist fictions – for instance, the rich interiority exhibited in the novels of Woolf, Joyce, and Conrad, which privilege stream-of-consciousness narration and its unfiltered access to a character's thoughts – Doyle's early stories focus on the protagonist's impassive exterior, the expressionlessness that shrouds any trace of emotion, or else reveals its absence. Holmes, to apply Burstein's phrase, is "all outside, and surface all the way down."[50]

Perhaps the most potent illustration of Doyle's incipient cold modernism is the claim, repeated by several characters in the early Holmes works,
that the detective's mind functions much like a machine, and as such does
not conform to the usual processes of human reasoning. Watson describes
Holmes in the opening paragraph of "A Scandal in Bohemia" (1891) as "the
most perfect reasoning and observing machine that the world has seen,"
and in *The Sign of Four* he grows exasperated with Holmes's lack of
emotion: "You really are an automaton – a calculating machine ...
There is something positively inhuman in you at times" ("SB," 5; *SF*, 17).
True to form, Holmes responds to Watson's jab with a terse defense of his
opposition to feeling:

> "It is of the first importance," [Holmes] cried, "not to allow your judgment
> to be biased by personal qualities. A client is to me a mere unit, a factor in
> a problem. The emotional qualities are antagonistic to clear reasoning.
> I assure you that the most winning woman I ever knew was hanged for
> poisoning three little children for their insurance-money, and the most
> repellent man of my acquaintance is a philanthropist who has spent nearly
> a quarter of a million on the London poor."
> "In this case, however–"
> "I never make exceptions. An exception disproves the rule." (*SF*, 17)

For Holmes, subjective feeling deters effective judgment, and blinds lesser
investigators to the possibility that anyone, no matter how "winning" her
personality, can commit a crime under the right circumstances. If a client is
always a "mere unit," stripped of subjectivity, then one's investigation can
never be swayed by anything other than empirical facts. Holmes, then,
abides by an intractable conviction in the necessity of coldness, and, even
more strikingly, seems not to struggle with his belief. Indeed, he reveals his
mechanicity not just by perceiving his clients as mathematical units, but
also by emphasizing each unit as "mere," unexceptional and divested of any
distinguishing qualities.

Whereas the concept of individual character is anathema to Holmes's
rigidly statistical outlook on humanity, the detective does express a belief in
the body as a site where one can discern the traces of another's interiority
without sacrificing the objectivity required for deep analysis. Perceiving the
body as a set of physical clues that speak directly to their bearer's past
experiences, personal motivations, and social position, Holmes sees clients
and criminals in terms of what Lawrence Rothfield identifies as "a corpus
of isolated, discrete elements, a congeries or consilience of particulars"
rather than "an organized totality of qualities woven biologically into
a person."[51] By attending to bodies rather than unified subjects, Holmes

purports to an emotional neutrality for which individuals are nothing more than the sum of their parts, channeling his view of individuals, expressed in *The Sign of Four* as broad "mathematical certainties," into a more specific notion that those individuals can be further understood through a symbolic dissection of their bodies. In so doing, he exhibits a mechanical devotion to the logic of appearances that aligns with Ronald Thomas's comparison of nineteenth-century fictional detectives and lie detectors; for Thomas, the former "may be regarded not just as truth producers but as truth machines for their societies – as 'devices' that sort out fact from illusion."[52] Watson echoes this idea of the detective as device in "A Scandal in Bohemia" when he speculates that, for Holmes, "[g]rit in a sensitive instrument, or a crack in one of his own high-power lenses, would not be more disturbing than a strong emotion in a nature such as his" ("SB," 5). In both claims, Holmes is more machine than man, his antagonism to emotion a key safeguard that ensures both the detachment of his scientific approach to criminality and, more importantly, its consistent accuracy. What these metaphors offer for a study of Holmes's cold modernism, however, is not a simple equation of Holmes's methods with scientific instruments, but rather their insistence that Holmes *is* a machine, a "sensitive instrument" capable of grasping the totality of other people yet invulnerable to the messy entanglements of feeling. Malfunctions of the machine, by this logic, are disturbing yet fixable – "a strong emotion" is impossible to comprehend.

Doyle furthers Holmes's resemblance to the machine through the detective's collection of newspaper clippings, which constitutes an eclectic index of disparate yet potentially useful information. The collection not only features accounts of criminal activity, but also those minor scraps of *arcana* that Holmes believes might someday prove beneficial to his work. In "A Scandal in Bohemia," Watson refers to this odd assemblage of information as "a system of docketing all paragraphs concerning men and things, so [thorough] that it was difficult to name a subject or a person on which he could not at once furnish information," and notes with evident amusement how, when searching for something on Irene Adler, the subject of their investigation, he "found her biography sandwiched in between that of a Hebrew Rabbi and that of a staff-commander who had written a monograph upon the deep sea fishes" ("SB," 17). From the index, Holmes fashions what he describes in "The Red-Headed League" as a mental inventory of criminal cases, not unlike Poe's description of the successful game player's "fund of thought": "As a rule, when I have heard some slight indication of the course of events I am able to guide myself by the thousands of other similar cases which occur to my memory" ("RHL," 42). In both instances, Doyle presents the index not only as a physical collection of printed matter, but also as an abstract "system" of filing, organizing, and referencing information that imposes itself upon Holmes's thoughts. Rather than opening itself up to the reader's scrutiny through a detailed display of its deductive processes, Holmes's mind is indexical in function, a closed storehouse of data that consistently proves its utility. It is also autogenetic, as seen in *A Study in Scarlet*, where Holmes equates the human brain with "a little empty attic, [which] you have to stock ... with such furniture as you choose," and argues that the wise individual counts among his furnishings "nothing but the tools which may help him in doing his work, but of these he has a large assortment, and all in the most perfect order" (*SS*, 32, 34). Of course, thanks to his irregular criminological education, Holmes's own supply of mental furniture is vast but eclectic, as Watson acknowledges in the list he prepares of Holmes's areas of knowledge and ignorance. In this deliberately partial inventory, Watson characterizes Holmes's understanding of literature, philosophy, and astronomy as "nil" while noting that his knowledge of sensational literature is "immense," and reports that his grasp of anatomy is "[a]ccurate, but unsystematic" (*SS*, 34–35). Undoubtedly intended to reveal the gaps in Holmes's knowledge, and consequently reduce such an alienated thinker to the condition of the mass of ordinary individuals, Watson's list ironically reinforces the notion that Holmes's mindset is essentially that of the index, discriminating in that it contains only what it needs in order to perform its duties, but comprehensive in that it lacks nothing required for accomplishing those tasks.

By characterizing Holmes's indexical mind as unfailingly accurate in its exertions, Doyle not only extends the tradition of dispassionate analysis that originated in Poe's Dupin stories, but also suggests that such a mode of thinking might reassure a late Victorian readership incapable of possessing Holmes's intellectual ingenuity. According to Srdjan Smajić, Holmes's index "operates as a mechanism for coping with the anxiety about ever-retreating horizons of new information," a palliative for the ever-present fear that there is simply too much to be known.[53] In much the same way, Holmes's autogenetic character is also a form of compensation, in which the detective's infallibility assuages a cultural crisis of faith regarding the ability of any individual to maintain autonomy in an increasingly interconnected, chaotic society. Holmes comforts, then, by demonstrating that both information and the self can be equally mastered. Still, any peace of mind that Holmes might have brought to early readers – a cultural balm that Michael Holquist describes as "the magic of mind in a world that all too often seems impervious to reason" – cannot be separated from the fact that the detective's lack of affect and resemblance to a machine expose an underlying suspicion that such detached objectivity might not be possible without a corresponding evacuation of humanity.[54] In segregating the rational mind from the feeling mind, Doyle proffers a cold modernist account of the deductive process in which truly objective thought is only obtained through the renunciation of selfhood, an austerity popularized in subsequent works of detective fiction. Indeed, Holmes's privileging of the mechanical over the human, the autonomous over the collective, soon became the currency by which readers valued the protagonists of later detective fictions, and is precisely what authors such as Dorothy Sayers would target as they rethought the genre's position in a new century.

Dorothy L. Sayers and the Artificial Sleuth

In stark contrast to the penetrating psychological stratagems of Dupin and the robotic, self-assured analysis of Holmes, Sayers introduced the world to Lord Peter Wimsey, her own amateur sleuth, in the midst of an all-too-human mistake. Delivering a playful yet pointed rebuke to the infallibility of detectives past, the opening scene of *Whose Body?* (1923), the first of Sayers's eleven Wimsey novels, features the aristocratic detective admitting his own failure, albeit over an especially banal occurrence. "Oh, damn!" he exclaims en route to a rare book auction, "I've left the catalogue behind . . . Uncommonly careless of me."[55] Though Wimsey characterizes his lapse as "uncommon," and though the mistake itself is a minor incident rather than a colossal blunder, the consistency of Dupin and Holmes makes any hint of absentmindedness, no matter how ordinary, an immediate cause for suspicion. Whereas those earlier detectives perform acts of deduction so accurate that they become alarming, Wimsey is conspicuously flawed – an important distinction for a character who debuted in the aftermath of the Great War, and whose residual shell shock from that conflict can interrupt his investigations and push him to question his suitability for detective work. As Robert Kuhn McGregor and Ethan Lewis argue, by the early 1920s the professional detachment of a figure such as Holmes "had become an impossibility," while Sayers's detective personified the era's most profound struggles with isolation, trauma, and self-doubt: "Peter Wimsey was more the man of the twenties, brilliant but scarred and unsure . . . His was a brilliant mind but a mind that acknowledged the existence of factors beyond his control. Wimsey would never be the complete master of a situation."[56] Viewed in light of the historical moment in which his detective career takes shape, Wimsey's forgetfulness at the outset of *Whose Body?* becomes a more ominous indication that he, unlike his predecessors, is always at the mercy of his environment and his mind, mired in circumstances rather than rising above them through the force of an autogenetic will. Wimsey is, from his first appearance, no Sherlock Holmes, but that inadequacy is precisely the point, as Sayers stresses the fact that no detective working in the 1920s could conceivably possess the kind of uncanny exactitude or self-assurance that the Victorian sleuth represents.

Instead, Sayers offers a new and openly contradictory model for the twentieth-century detective, which borrows certain elements of Dupin and Holmes while emphatically rejecting others. Wimsey is capable despite his carelessness, haunted by memories of the war yet affable in the face of present violence, conflicted about the friction between his socioeconomic privilege and his work as an amateur investigator, and hesitant to serve a legal system that still administers capital punishment. That combination of confidence and self-doubt underscores Wimsey's liminal position within the novels, and emblematizes the detective genre's modernization. Just as Dupin and Holmes represent one facet of the genre's protomodernism – the mechanical functioning of a cold modernist mind that performs its task to perfection, with its attendant ambivalence regarding antihumanism, logical consistency, and the mind–body divide – Wimsey reflects detective fiction's adaptation to the collective uncertainty that followed the Great War, and, in the process, to the historical and philosophical conditions of modernism. As a shell-shocked aristocrat whose attempt to create a unique professional identity is part of a larger struggle to affirm his value for a country that increasingly rejects its nobility and its veterans, Sayers's detective builds upon the formal precedents of Poe and Doyle while negotiating the existential concerns of a tumultuous twentieth century. If, as Modris Eksteins argues, "the integrity of the 'real' world, the visible and ordered world," fell victim to the War's confusion of national allegiances, the chaos of modern warfare, and the hopelessness of extracting meaning from such carnage, then Wimsey becomes the prototype for a new, modernist detective who goes about his work under a shadow of perpetual doubt.[57] Forced to reckon with a fraught historical era for which he appears strikingly ill equipped, and to speak for and to a generation struggling to reconcile the legacy of its ancestors with the bleak reality of the present, he represents an effort to make the detective novel, as a genre, more responsive to a radically transformed cultural landscape.

Wimsey also signals a shift in the formal parameters of genre fiction, for just as Sayers positions him as the exemplary detective of the postwar era, defined by anxiety, error, and uncertainty, she also figures him as a two-dimensional collection of habits and quirks that simultaneously replicates and critiques the nineteenth-century detective novel's traditional forms of characterization. Ironically, given the gravity of Wimsey's profession, much of the humor of Sayers's novels arises from the fact that her protagonist is preposterously annoying. The seriousness of his business, Gill Plain argues, is "masked by the meaningless babble of his affected, self-conscious idiocy," and several critics have offered a version of Ariela Freedman's quip that the Wimsey of the early novels is "more Bertie Wooster than Sherlock Holmes."[58] Edmund Wilson famously bristled at Wimsey's apparent vacuity in his notorious 1945 *New Yorker* essay "Who Cares Who Killed Roger Ackroyd?," where he blamed his inability to read Sayers's *The Nine Tailors* (1934) on the novel's protagonist, whom he ridiculed as "a dreadful stock of English nobleman of the casual and debonair kind" who insists on speaking in an "awful whimsical patter."[59] Its humorlessness aside, Wilson's assessment of Wimsey as a stock character is well founded. Sayers's hero breaks into song without any prompting, cracks jokes that his interlocutors seem never to find funny, and speaks in hasty monologues rife with linguistic affectations popular among the English upper class (for example, his habit of dropping the "g" at the end of a word). These are not benign moments of comedy, however, nor do they prove that Wimsey is a unique individual with a substantial inner life. Rather, Wimsey's eccentricities echo the cultivated intellectual strangeness of past detectives, as Sayers borrows the tropes popularized by her forerunners only to satirize them in a deliberate reworking of the generic traditions she inherits. Whereas Dupin's obsessions with strategy and gamesmanship and Holmes's index of miscellaneous trivia are meant to communicate the genius of those detectives, Wimsey's oddities and arcane interests – a devotion to rare book collecting; an impressive knowledge of art, literature, music, and wine; and a penchant for quoting classical authors in purposely awkward moments – are so clearly exaggerated that they signal a wariness of the concept of analytical genius more generally. Thus, to complain, as Raymond Chandler did, that Sayers's works suffers from a formalistic stiltedness, and to assume that her subscription to convention demonstrates a lack of authorial ability (as Chandler claimed, she either "could not or would not give her characters their heads") is to misunderstand how the Wimsey novels adapt those protomodernist elements of Poe and Doyle for a new century, and ultimately reveal Sayers's modernism rather than discrediting it.[60]

All this is to suggest that Wimsey functions as a register of formal as well as historical change, and that Sayers's novels knowingly proclaim their affinities with and departures from the models of detection popularized by Poe and Doyle in order to show how the two-dimensionality of those earlier detectives reflects not only an outdated mode of critical detachment, but also a set of formal principles that need to be reshaped before ossifying into dogma. This is another reason why Wimsey appears so cartoonish in the early novels, as Sayers highlights his artificiality by presenting him not as a figure of machinelike rationality or as preoccupied with games of chance, but as an ebullient critique of both generic archetypes. That is, Wimsey is not a fully realized, three-dimensional sleuth with demonstrable psychological depth, and as such is not a mere corrective to the inhuman rationalism of Holmes's logic or the statistical psychologism of Dupin's games, but instead represents a parodic retooling of the detective genre's tenets; embodying a traumatic national past while also calling into question those methods of characterization detailed in previous detective fictions, Wimsey demonstrates the fragility of seemingly stable social and aesthetic forms, a position that Samantha Walton identifies in his "flout-[ing] of the genre's perceived demand for the validation of the objective over the subjective," an essentially modernist move that "alters the traditional authority of the detective in fundamental ways, mounting a critique of the rationalism that, ostensibly, had hitherto defined the form."[61] Through its dual emphasis on generic convention and the precariousness of postwar society, Sayers's work offers a provocative assessment of how popular literature might serve an aesthetic and historical function similar to modernism, using its protagonist as a vehicle for critiquing popular fiction's stereotypical predictability while also pointing out new methods for exploring the inconsistencies of human behavior and logical thought. In the process, her Wimsey novels exhibit some of the central objectives of modernist fiction, making the detective genre more receptive to cultural and historical change ("making it new," in a sense) by subjecting its nineteenth-century conventions to more overtly modernist experiments with form and content.

Because of its unique position in relation to other works of the period, Sayers's fiction has recently made small but significant inroads into modernist criticism. Indeed, Sayers is one of only a few detective novelists admitted into the modernist canon, for reasons of chronological and formal affiliation. For McGregor and Lewis, such critical acceptance stems from the fact that Wimsey serves as a barometer of English national identity during periods of intense transition: "Born in 1890, with one foot in the Victorian era and the other in the postwar world, Peter emerged as a balance of opposites. He became Sayers's literary embodiment of a culture trying hard to accommodate the newly modern."[62] Meanwhile, other critics have recognized Sayers's importance for modernist literary history not because her protagonist personifies the transition into a tumultuous postwar climate, or because she released the bulk of her generic output in the 1920s and '30s alongside some of the best known modernist touchstones, but because the aesthetic and philosophical concerns of her work neatly overlap with those of her more experimental contemporaries. As Sean Latham has argued, although her novels are "far from the modernist experimentalism of Joyce and Woolf," their "attentiveness to questions of form and style becomes increasingly apparent as philosophical considerations of human guilt, gender identity, and psychological instability rise to challenge and even overwhelm the generically predetermined consideration of clues and alibis."[63] By infusing detective fiction with elements largely considered beyond its purview, Sayers provides a generic alternative to modernism that nonetheless engages with the period's most prominent formal and philosophical questions, complicating easy distinctions between modernism and popular literature while challenging traditional notions of detective fiction as an entirely formulaic genre, with inviolable rules for its composition.

This is not to suggest, however, that Sayers abandoned the tenets of detective fiction to become a full-fledged experimentalist. On the contrary, she was a vocal advocate for rules concerning plot, character development, and narrative logic who argued that authors must abide by a flexible yet established set of formal conventions in order to qualify as participants in the genre. As she maintained in her introduction to *The Omnibus of Crime* (1929), the detective story "possesses an Aristotelian perfection of beginning, middle, and end," as "[a] definite and single problem is set, worked out, and solved" with the "rounded (though limited) perfection of a triolet."[64] To her critics, such pronouncements revealed an overly rigid approach to literary production, and many dismissed her novels as entertaining yet perfunctory forms of escapism too dependent upon arbitrary guidelines that foreclosed any possibility of innovation. Sayers did little to help her cause when, in the same introduction, she infamously argued that detective fiction can never be considered a serious art form, since "it rarely touches the heights and depths of human passion."[65] This was the claim that drew Chandler's ire, leading him to blast Sayers's characters as "puppets and cardboard lovers and papier mâché villains and detectives of exquisite and impossible gentility."[66] Frustrated by what he perceived as an artificiality in Sayers's writing that results from an uncritical attachment to generic convention, Chandler panned the Wimsey novels as unduly stuffed with two-dimensional characters who lack realistic motivations or psychological depth, and who exist for the sole purpose of furthering a plot. Moving unreflectively through a series of tropes that cannot deviate from a predetermined course, Sayers simply builds her characters upon the model of Sherlock Holmes, a detective Chandler mocked as "mostly an attitude and a few dozen lines of unforgettable dialogue."[67] Therefore, even if Wimsey is meant to critique Holmesian perfection as a modern impossibility, for Chandler that intention does not do enough to make him resemble an actual person, as any critique Sayers might advance is fatally rooted in Doyle's own conception of the detective as the emotionless embodiment of an abstract idea. Her characters, to borrow her own phrase from the introduction to the *Omnibus*, "live more or less on the *Punch* level of emotion," and so fail to live up to Chandler's standards for literary realism.[68]

Though she undoubtedly contributed to the stereotype of detective fiction as an escapist genre whose characters never waver from a heavily circumscribed course of action, Sayers was keenly aware of the problems with writing according to oppressive formal guidelines. As she explained in a 1925 letter to John Cournos, "[t]he trouble is, that writers tend, after a time, always to work to the same formula, so that, after reading half a dozen stories by one man, one begins to see the formula and solve the thing automatically."[69] For Sayers, detective fiction must adhere to certain criteria in order to qualify as genre writing, but never so much that the act of composition becomes automatic, a process of implementing interchangeable conventions from which an author can never deviate. Because she was equally committed to formula and spontaneity, we can productively understand her work as neither acquiescing to nor rebuking the tropes of nineteenth-century detective fiction, but as parodying that genre's most common and therefore restrictive characteristics. In so doing, we can see how Sayers inhabits a form that is both critical and appreciative, transgressing established boundaries without dismissing them entirely, and how her modernism emerges through her work's implicit claims regarding literary history and innovation. If parody is, as Linda Hutcheon contends, "one of the major modes of formal and thematic construction of texts" during the twentieth century, utilized by modernist authors who "recognized that change entails continuity" and whose work offers "a model for the process of transfer and reorganization of that past," then the Wimsey novels demonstrate Sayers's own attempt to reconfigure the detective novel in order to push it toward new and necessary forms of experimentation.[70] Such an effort obviously entails its own set of challenges, and Allison Pease's warning about the dangers of misunderstood parody identifies one of the key sticking points in the early reception of Sayers's fiction: "If a reader is not complicitous with the parodic attitude, unable to understand the tropes as deconstructed, such technique may work against the agent of parody, for parody equally highlights its own artifices in such a way that the parodic text becomes a site of contestation, despite the mutually constitutive nature of such parody."[71] In failing to recognize the contestation at the heart of the Wimsey novels, Chandler and others also miss an essential element of Sayers's modernism – namely, how the detective genre can provocatively skewer its own customs in a way that both innovates and entertains, deploying a modernist attitude of inter-rogation to upend the conventions of a popular form.

As I have suggested, the most strikingly modernist aspect of Sayers's parody is its insistent questioning as to the role of interiority in detective fiction. By flaunting their differences from and similarities to the examples of Poe and Doyle, the Wimsey novels ask whether generic characters can or should possess the psychological complexity of actual people, and whether established conventions regarding characterization can offer unexpected moments of formal invention. Arguing in *The Omnibus of Crime* that the detective genre scrupulously avoids depicting "human passion" in favor of the analytical problem, Sayers would appear to uphold the cold modernist suspicion of psychology, as demonstrated in her presentation of Wimsey as a vacuous collection of verbal tics. Likewise, her contention that "the whole difficulty about allowing real human beings into a detective-story" occurs when characters become romantically entwined – as she claims, "either their emotions make hay of the detective interest, or the detective interest gets hold of them and makes their emotions look like pasteboard" – suggests a formal unease with the concept of psychological representation rather than a market-based concern that readers will automatically reject genre fiction that favors characterization over plot.[72] At the same time, though, Wimsey's experience with shell shock reasserts the centrality of psychology within Sayers's detective fiction, and distances him from both the cold modernism of Holmes and the inscrutability of Dupin. Indeed, Sayers's vivid renderings of Wimsey's hallucinations point to a character whose interiority is an essential element of the narrative for reasons that go well beyond the demands of plot. When Wimsey correctly deduces the identity of the murderer in *Whose Body?*, for example, the narrative does not speed toward the denouement that most readers would expect, but pauses to describe Wimsey's disorientation upon imagining himself returned to the trenches, a disturbing flashback that immediately follows his moment of insight. Here we find that Wimsey has moved seamlessly from professional triumph to personal trauma, incapacitated by the dangers of an imagined No Man's Land:

> "[I]t's the water," said Lord Peter with chattering teeth; "it's up to their waists down there, poor devils. But listen! can't you hear it? Tap, tap, tap – they're mining us – but I don't know where – I can't hear – I can't. Listen, you! There it is again – we must find it – we must stop it . . . Listen! Oh, my God! I can't hear – I can't hear anything for the noise of the guns." (*WB*, 140)

Wimsey's war neurosis is extraneous to the novel's plot – that is, it makes little difference in solving the mystery at hand – but it powerfully distinguishes him from his expressionless, mechanical predecessors, and reveals how his apparent superficiality masks a profound capacity for emotion. This is a detective for whom the work of deduction cannot be separated from the human being who pursues it, and a mind whose residual trauma, pain, and fear can bubble to the surface without warning, adding psychological nuance to an otherwise flat character.

Sayers pushed the question of Wimsey's affective life even further when she introduced a love interest for him later in the series, a decision that not only rebukes the tradition of Holmesian autonomy, but also endows her protagonist with an emotional attachment that blatantly contradicts her previous positions regarding the necessary shallowness of the detective archetype. Reflecting on *Gaudy Night* (1936), in which the mystery novelist Harriet Vane agrees to marry Wimsey, Sayers observed that "Peter had got to become a complete human being, with a past and a future, with a consistent family and social history, with a complicated psychology and even the rudiments of a religious outlook," and she acknowledged that this developing personality "would have to be squared somehow or other with such random attributes as I had bestowed on him over a series of years in accordance with the requirements of various detective plots."[73] Though in one sense a tacit admission that the cold modernism of the nineteenth-century detective is untenable in modern fiction – Sayers would appear to concede that even a static character cannot remain static forever, as human emotion will necessarily creep into a set of connected fictions concerned with a central protagonist – this description of the tension between

Wimsey as a formal device and Wimsey as a "complete human being" also reflects a more crucial concern over whether a character in a genre fiction can ever possess a fully realized psychology, and, if he can, whether such possession will impede the narrative machinery he is meant to fulfill. By this logic, we can read the problem of Wimsey's romance, which led to the abrupt conclusion of the series with *Busman's Honeymoon* (1937), as the inevitable impasse that results from a character who fluctuates between surface and depth. If Wimsey is at once a shell-shocked veteran, a devoted lover, and a set of formal conventions, then he is, above all, a parodic experiment in characterization that adheres to no single philosophy of what characterization should entail.

Sayers addresses this ambivalence toward psychological nuance in one of her most popular novels, *The Unpleasantness at the Bellona Club* (1928), which begins with the discovery of an oddly animated corpse. An expected element of any detective fiction, this particular corpse literalizes the question of how generic characters can shuffle between stock qualities and richer, more developed forms of interiority. On the afternoon of Armistice Day, the elderly General Fentiman is found dead in his chair at the eponymous London veterans' club, one leg swinging freely and independently of the rest of his body, which appears to be in an advanced state of rigor mortis. Due to a bizarre complication involving the simultaneous death of the General's estranged sister and the division of their combined estates, the Fentiman family solicitor enlists Wimsey's help in determining when General Fentiman actually died, and under what circumstances. While Wimsey's investigation exhibits several features of the classic British mystery – a steady proliferation of potential suspects once Wimsey deduces that General Fentiman was murdered, an emphasis on the financial imperatives of inheritance as catalysts for criminal investigation, and a firm resolution in which the guilty party is identified and forced to answer for his crimes – the narrative consistently returns to the corpse as an ambiguous yet profoundly resonant site of evidence. More than a physical marker of past violence through which one pieces together a coherent narrative of the crime's events, Fentiman's corpse provokes acute anxiety in the living, who either distance themselves from this chilling reminder of death's ubiquity by adopting an attitude of ironic detachment, or view it as yet another casualty of an increasingly dehumanizing modernity. It intrigues Wimsey, who claims that he has "rather a turn for corpses" and sees the body as an occasion for putting his grisly hobby to productive use.[74] Other characters, by contrast, experience the corpse as a metonymic figure for the increasing violence and inhumanity of twentieth-century life, or as a fearsome reminder of death's proximity. Learning of his grandfather's passing just after he and Wimsey had ridiculed the Bellona Club as a stultifying enclave for ancient veterans in which a dead man wouldn't be noticed for some time, General Fentiman's shell-shocked grandson, George, is overwhelmed by the absurdity of the situation: "He's been dead two days! So are you! So am I! We're all dead and we never noticed it!" (*UBC*, 5).

One could certainly read George's outburst as a product of his instability, an overpowering expression of grief filtered through the trauma of shell shock, which culminates in a harrowing vision that he and Wimsey have escaped the trenches only to learn that they and their fellow soldiers never actually made it out alive. However, the scene represents far more than a grim acknowledgment of the ravages of world war. In his description of the Bellona Club as filled with the walking dead – a mausoleum of long-retired military men who unthinkingly perform the same routines day after day, and perhaps the future haunt of veterans such as George and Wimsey, both of whom have returned to England with shattered nerves and increasing doubts regarding their place in a transformed society – George voices some of Sayers's most distinctively modernist questions concerning the blurry boundaries between interior and exterior, character and convention. What, George demands, is the difference between the wounded veteran and the dead body for a postwar society that pays little attention to either? And, at the level of form, what distinguishes George, a living character within a genre fiction, from the enigmatically lively corpse of General Fentiman, which sets the rest of the plot in motion? The latter question reflects the plight of the literary character more generally, as George's situation is no different than that of the plot device that his grandfather has become, or of any of the book's other characters. As George indicates, everyone who populates the novel, living or dead, serves a purely narrative purpose, existing as a formal instrument rather than a distinct individual. Thus, the confrontation between Wimsey, George, and General Fentiman's corpse not only parodies the unthinking, unfeeling behavior that makes automatons of the living ("We're all dead!"), with its implicit critique of the emotional stasis of postwar British society, but also stages a modernist interrogation of form. In a work of fiction, the scene suggests, psychological representation can never transcend the formal conventions that constitute it, and so a detective novel like Sayers's becomes experimental when it makes plain the fact that all characters exist as generic devices, animated but ultimately artificial. In positioning her novels between the formal and thematic imperatives of modernism and detective fiction, Sayers disrupts some of the latter's most fundamental conventions by presenting them as a paradoxically vital set of dead ends, necessary to sustain a narrative but never able to escape their status as formulae.

Through the multiple narrative functions of General Fentiman's body, which simultaneously confirms George's affective life and emphasizes his strictly formal existence, Sayers also parodies other mandates governing the figure of the detective and that character's role within a work of genre fiction. In admitting its own conventionality – indeed, in its presentation as a purely narrative device – General Fentiman's corpse casts a long shadow over Wimsey, who vacillates between moving emotional displays and the empty gestures of the stock character.[75] Wimsey's resemblance to the dead expresses itself physically, as the narrator of *Whose Body?* memorably describes him as possessing "a long, amiable face [that] looked as if it had generated spontaneously from his top hat, as white maggots breed from Gorgonzola" (*WB*, 1). More significantly, Wimsey's alternation between shallowness and depth stresses his liminal status within the narrative more generally, as he toggles between the private emotiveness of the shell-shocked veteran and the public superficiality of the antic amateur sleuth who masks his interiority by making a spectacle of himself. Several of the novel's other characters are taken in by Wimsey's erratic amiability, perceiving him as a cartoonish, two-dimensional figure sprung from popular entertainment rather than a perceptive, emotionally nuanced individual. In *The Unpleasantness at the Bellona Club*, Major Robert Fentiman, General Fentiman's other grandson and George's older brother, teases Wimsey for resembling a stock character. "I find you refreshing," he explains. "You're not in the least witty, but you have a kind of obvious facetiousness which reminds me of the less exacting class of music hall" (*UBC*, 3). Sayers's detective is "less exacting" on his fellow characters – and, by extension, his readers – by virtue of his resemblance to an established literary type. Both groups can recognize him according to their experience with popular generic conventions, understanding his flippant personality, to borrow Sean Latham's description, as "cobbled together from popular clichés."[76] In this respect, he bears a striking similarity to the corpses he discovers, in that he too is read largely in terms of surfaces, as a performing body that, like any generic device, behaves exactly according to form.

What is most notable about Wimsey's generic personality, however, is just how readily he admits to it. From the beginning of the Wimsey series, Sayers's detective mocks himself as a pale imitation of Sherlock Holmes, and the parody of the early novels earns much of its force through Wimsey's repeated attempts to cast himself in the guise of Doyle's impassive sleuth. In *Whose Body?*, Wimsey begins his investigation into a case involving an unidentified corpse found in a bathtub with overly dramatic flair: "Exit the amateur of first editions; new motive introduced by solo bassoon; enter Sherlock Holmes, disguised as a walking gentleman" (*WB*, 5). By announcing his investigation with manic pomp and elaborate stage directions, he alludes to what his readers already know: in the early decades of the twentieth century, Doyle's iconic detective seems less relevant to a modern milieu, and any attempt to replicate his mechanical methods can only be seen as an elaborate joke whose comedy never quite conceals the fact that the comfortable certainties of Holmesian logic are ill-suited for a modern narrative. Other references to Doyle's creation make explicit the ways in which twentieth-century detective fiction has abandoned Victorian convention in favor of a messier form of verisimilitude. In *Whose Body?*, Wimsey explains that for a murder to go undetected the killer must "prevent people from associatin' their ideas," since "it's only in Sherlock Holmes and stories like that, that people think things out logically" (*WB*, 123). Similarly, in *Clouds of Witness* (1927), he quotes his mother on the subject of deductive prowess, repeating her conviction that what formerly passed for superior critical acumen is now recognized as female intuition: "you can give it a long name if you like, but I'm an old-fashioned woman and I call it mother-wit, and it's so rare for a man to have it that if he does you write a book about him and call him Sherlock Holmes."[77] In both cases, the references to Holmes deflate both that detective's critical detachment and the essential logic of the world he occupies, while at the same time advancing a broader assertion that those forms of rationality demonstrated in Doyle's fiction obscure more haphazard, intuitive, and subjective modes of thought. Wimsey's allusions expose the logic of a Holmes narrative as little more than mystification, drawing upon convention in order to reveal its limitations.

As these moments indicate, Wimsey exists between the poles of artificiality and realism. He draws attention to his divergences from Holmesian perfection in order to underline his believability for a twentieth-century audience, but those comparisons inevitably highlight the fact that Wimsey is a literary character, his psychological depth in conflict with, if not secondary to, his narrative purpose. It is ironic, then, that interiority is such a central focus of Wimsey's investigations, as Sayers emphasizes both the mental processes by which Wimsey ferrets out the criminals he pursues and the habits of mind that distinguish criminals from other, innocent characters within a genre fiction. Perhaps the most pointed instance of this phenomenon appears in *Whose Body?*, when Wimsey identifies the novel's murderer as Sir Julian Freke, a renowned psychiatrist whose publications include *Criminal Lunacy, The Application of Psycho-Therapy to the Treatment of Shell-Shock,* and *An Answer to Professor Freud, with a Description of Some Experiments Carried Out at the Base Hospital at Amiens* (*WB*, 139). Wimsey confirms his suspicion of Freke's guilt while reading the doctor's latest book, *Physiological Bases of the Conscience,* which takes a Nietzschean view of the individual's freedom to obliterate his or her moral compass. Alarmed by Freke's cold materialism, Wimsey grows increasingly wary of the book's position on conscience as an impediment to pure egoism:

> Mind and matter were one thing, that was the theme of the physiologist. Matter could erupt, as it were, into ideas. You could carve passions in the brain with a knife. You could get rid of imagination with drugs and cure an outworn convention like a disease. "The knowledge of good and evil is an observed phenomenon, attendant upon a certain condition of the brain-cells, which is removable." (*WB*, 136)

Wimsey pronounces this outlook "an ideal doctrine for the criminal," and justifies his rationale for targeting Freke by telling his friend and colleague (and, eventually, brother-in-law), Scotland Yard inspector Charles Parker, that the psychiatrist simply "likes crime" (*WB*, 136, 170). He elaborates by arguing that

> In that criminology book of his he gloats over a hardened murder. I've read it, and I've seen the admiration simply glaring out between the lines whenever he writes about a callous and successful criminal . . . After all, he thinks conscience is a sort of vermiform appendix. Chop it out and you'll feel all the better. Freke isn't troubled by the usual conscientious deterrent. (*WB*, 170)

Freke's murderousness, then, becomes legible within the violence of his ideas, and Wimsey's repeated references to the brutal indifference of Freke's philosophy indicate a murderer whose danger, paradoxically, lies more in thought than in deed. Freke, like Wimsey, has "rather a turn for corpses," and yet he represents a threat where Wimsey does not because his imagination abjures the ethical. Freke has an individual psychology, but one bereft of the kind of social conscience that allows Wimsey, for all his two-dimensionality, to appear more fully human than the stoic, impersonal detectives of past fictions. All this is to say, then, that we can read Wimsey's distaste for Freke's blasé materialism as another indictment of Holmesian cold modernism. More than a straightforward condemnation of psychoanalysis or of the Nietzschean *Übermensch*, Freke's status as the novel's killer exemplifies Sayers's critique of a psychology that evacuates all traces of affect in favor of a ruthlessly mechanical approach to thought.[78]

Whereas Freke displays all the hallmarks of a distant, objective mind, the method by which Wimsey identifies him as the narrative's guilty party delivers an equally potent blow to Holmesian logic. Indeed, the divide between Wimsey and Holmes appears nowhere as sharp as when the former detective flouts traditional systems of deduction, as he solves his cases through sudden bursts of inspiration rather than the systematic analysis of the calculating machine. In *Whose Body?*, for instance, Wimsey solves his case through an immediate flash of insight:

> And then it happened – the thing he had been half-unconsciously expecting. It happened suddenly, surely, as unmistakably, as sunrise. He remembered – not one thing, nor another thing, nor a logical succession of things, but everything – the whole thing, perfect, complete, in all its dimensions as it were and instantaneously; as if he stood outside the world and saw it suspended in infinitely dimensional space. He no longer needed to reason about it, or even to think about it. He knew it. (*WB*, 136–137)

Here, the "logical succession" of reason is of no use, as Wimsey remembers something he already knows in order to arrive at his conclusion, the unconscious "whole thing" made immediately and completely manifest. The answer to this mystery emerges inevitably, with the predictability and naturalness of a sunrise, but also "instantaneously," as a sudden burst of knowledge rather than a methodically considered judgment that takes time and rigor to work out. In effect, Sayers ignores the tradition of detective fiction that demands a series of logical deductions, carefully explained in painstaking detail, that lead to the revelation of the narrative's criminal, and instead focuses on the single moment of brilliance, isolated from rational thought, which simultaneously reveals and obscures a powerful mind. Wimsey's moment of clarity appears as exactly that – a jolt of inspiration that attests to his mental acuity without revealing anything so specific as a thought process ("he no longer needed . . . to think about it") – and so reaffirms his position as a modern departure from nineteenth-century generic convention.

In contrast to Dupin's psychologism and Holmes's mechanical logic, Wimsey solves his case through the immediate insight of epiphany, one of modernism's most recognizable forms of psychological representation. Following Joyce's valorization and subsequent ironizing of the concept, epiphany has been a hallmark of modernists' attempts to depict arational interiority, or those modes of feeling that unite mind and body through a transcendent, unanticipated moment of knowledge. As Pericles Lewis argues, one of the modernist project's most distinctive features was its attempt to "make the structure of the novel more capable of describing transcendent experiences," or those subjective moments, combining physical and psychological self-awareness in an instant of quasi-religious sensation, that "originated in the ordinary world ... but that opened some sort of insight beyond the realm of the ordinary."[79] Charles Taylor characterizes epiphany in a similar fashion, using the term to denote the aesthetic revelation, within a particular object, of "something only indirectly available, something the visible object can't say itself but only nudges us towards."[80] In both cases, epiphany functions as a means of accessing that which appears fundamentally unavailable, leading the individual who experiences it toward forms of complete knowledge paradoxically derived from the partial, the mundane, and the indirect. Thus, when Sayers presents Wimsey's solution to the crime as epiphanic, she deliberately rejects the detective genre's favoring of logic and objectivity by adopting a strategy largely associated with modernist subjectivity.[81] Samantha Walton furthers the point when she claims that, in Sayers's fiction, "detection is treated as a creative act over which the detective has limited control," as "excessive rationalism is associated with domination, while affective forms of knowing and relating to the world are granted a privileged ethical status."[82] By this logic, Wimsey's epiphany at the end of *Whose Body?* not only reiterates the lack of mastery that marks him at the novel's outset, but also, and more importantly, proclaims this "limited control" a virtue rather than a shortcoming. The epiphany is both an example of modernist formal experiment and a kind of professional ethics, an affective response to criminal violence that replaces Holmesian coldness with a more humane, and perhaps honest, approach to detection within a modern, postwar world.

Given the distance she establishes between her protagonist and his Victorian precursors, it is ironic that Sayers also equates Wimsey's epiphanic detective work in *Whose Body?* with a game not unlike those favored by Dupin. As soon as Wimsey identifies Freke as a murderer, the narrator compares his thought process to that involved in solving a word puzzle:

There is a game in which one is presented with a jumble of letters and is required to make a word out of them, as thus:
COSSSSRI
The slow way of solving the problem is to try out all the permutations and combinations in turn, throwing away impossible conjunctions of letters, as:
SSSIRC
or
SCSRSO
Another way is to stare at the inco-ordinate elements until, by no logical process that the conscious mind can detect, or under some adventitious external stimulus, the combination:
SCISSORS
presents itself with calm certainty. After that, one does not even need to arrange the letters in order. The thing is done.(*WB*, 137)

While undoubtedly alluding to Dupin's games of draughts and whist, this game distinguishes itself as a different sort of contest by downplaying the psychological acumen required in Poe's examples. Here the game's outcome depends upon "no logical process that the conscious mind can detect," with the act of statistical reasoning dismissed as an inefficient, "slow" approach to problem solving trumped by the immediate certainties of epiphany.[83] Even more significantly, Wimsey derides the very game he plays, worried that his attitude toward the business of solving crimes is too amateurish, too focused on the game's entertainment value rather than its resolution. When Parker chastises Wimsey for treating murder as a triviality, Wimsey glumly agrees: "That's what I'm ashamed of, really ... It is a game to me, to begin with, and I go on cheerfully, and then I suddenly see that somebody is going to be hurt, and I want to get out of it" (*WB*, 129). While Wimsey may joke that he considers amateur detection a more engaging hobby than the traditional pursuits of his social class, he sheds such posturing during moments in which the game of detection takes a more grisly turn. When in *Unnatural Death* (1927) the novel's killer hangs herself while awaiting trial after Wimsey's sleuthing leads to her arrest, the usually cheerful detective turns somber: "Wimsey said nothing. He felt cold and sick. While Parker and the Governor of the prison made the necessary arrangements and discussed the case, he sat hunched unhappily upon his chair" (*UD*, 264). For Wimsey, the game of detection ceases to provide enjoyment when one faces the consequences of its resolution. The objective distance of Holmes gives way to a more empathetic and ultimately uncertain approach to detective work as a serious game, wherein one can be wrong rather than unfailingly right, intuitive rather than statistical or logically consistent, and unmoored by the ethics of leading a criminal, even one who is unmistakably responsible for a serious crime, to her own death.

In positioning Wimsey between two extremes – a flat, unthinking character who reiterates the detective genre's central conceits and a sharp, satirical original who parodies the traditions from which he descends while also imbuing the game of detection with an ethical imperative – Sayers's novels offer a new way of understanding the pleasures and pitfalls of detective fiction itself, a genre that many of her characters and readers alike describe, quite lovingly, as a way to avoid thinking. In *The Unpleasantness at the Bellona Club*, Wimsey reveals that he became absorbed in detective novels while convalescing in a war hospital, taking them up as a way of isolating himself from otherwise traumatic thoughts; though at first he belittles the genre as the preferred literature of "dull men in offices," he eventually admits that such novels "were about the only thing I could read. All the others had the war in them – or love . . . or some damn thing I didn't want to think about" (*UBC*, 214–15). For Wimsey, detective fiction becomes the vehicle for escapism that Sayers praised in *The Omnibus of Crime*, but to so radical a degree that it distracts its reader from any emotional entanglement or self-awareness. When another character explains her admiration for the genre by labeling it as something that "keeps your brain occupied" in the same manner as chess, Wimsey highlights its virtues as a game that simultaneously engages and lulls:

> Yes – that would keep one's mind off things with a vengeance. Draughts or dominoes or patience would be even better. No connection with anything. I remember . . . one time when something perfectly grinding and hateful had happened to me. I played patience all day. I was in a nursing home – with shell-shock – and other things. I only played one game, the very simplest . . . the demon . . . a silly game with no ideas in it at all. I just went on laying it out and gathering it up . . . hundred times in an evening . . . so as to stop thinking. (*UBC*, 215)

In his assessment of patience as "a silly game with no ideas in it at all," Wimsey plays upon the common critical refrain against detective fiction, a genre he admits to reading in order to circumvent more painful forms of emotional connection, losing himself in an undemanding – some might say "mindless" – form of entertainment. For him, detective fiction serves a dual function, putting a stop to thinking by offering an immersive reading experience while also operating according to instantly recognizable conventions, proceeding by rote and thus presenting no discernible ideas of its own. One can simply continue "laying it out and gathering it up" ad infinitum, with each novel a link in an unbroken chain of affective deadening.

The obvious irony here is that Sayers levels her critique within the pages of a detective novel, and it is precisely this fact that sharpens the bite of her modernist parody rather than blunting its force. While Wimsey's account of detective fiction as anti-intellectual would seem to imply a profound limitation to the genre's experimentalism, the idiosyncrasies of his deductive practice, coupled with his constant negotiation of psychological depth and vacuity, offer the competing perspective that the rational approaches of Dupin and Holmes are entirely out of place in an increasingly chaotic modernity, and that a detective who desires to stop thinking, and who can often appear quite successful at that task, is, paradoxically, a far more radical and ultimately modernist parody of generic convention. Sayers does not simply reject the tenets of detective fiction outright, but rather demonstrates the need for a brand of detective fiction more aware of its own history and conventions, and more willing to take both of these to task in charting new possibilities for representation. If, as Leonard Diepeveen claims, parody functions as a mode of argument, "not only about the value of a work or movement, but . . . about what constitutes its relevant features, and what allows it to attract attention," then Sayers's parody of detective fiction's form and consumption represents a multifarious effort to rejuvenate the genre, albeit one pulled in so many directions that it becomes difficult to see clearly where a reader's sympathies are meant to lie.[84] Do Sayers's novels aim to unsettle readers from their passive consumption of entertainment, jabbing, perhaps, at readers like Wimsey, who view genre writing as a bulwark against more engaged, difficult, or experimental forms of self-understanding? Or do they represent an ironic modernist parody of generic form, illustrating a popular genre's potential for innovation through its suspicion of deductive rationality and traditional methods of characterization? As I have argued throughout this chapter, both possibilities are correct, and this is precisely why the Wimsey novels represent a much more radical, modernist reimagining of the detective genre than critics have so far considered. Sayers's parody is essential to our understanding of why modernism turned to detective fiction as an invaluable resource for theorizing the contradictions of an individual mind, and helps to explain why the criminal, recognized as an even less logical and ultimately more troubling figure, took up such a prominent position in modernist fiction's engagement with the representation of mental life.

Notes

1. Edgar Allan Poe, "The Murders in the Rue Morgue," *Selected Tales,* ed. David Van Leer (Oxford: Oxford University Press, 1998), 106. Hereafter cited parenthetically, as "MRM."

2. Fredric Jameson, "On Raymond Chandler," *The Poetics of Murder: Detective Fiction and Literary Theory,* ed. Glenn W. Most and William W. Stowe (San Diego: Harcourt Brace Jovanovich, 1983), 125.

3. Christopher Butler, *Early Modernism: Literature, Music, and Painting in Europe, 1900–1916* (Oxford: Oxford University Press, 1994), 95–96.

4. Brian McHale, *Postmodernist Fiction* (London: Routledge, 1987), 9.

5. Slavoj Žižek, *Looking Awry: An Introduction to Jacques Lacan through Popular Culture* (Cambridge, MA: MIT Press, 1992), 48–49 (emphasis in original), and Astradur Eysteinsson, *The Concept of Modernism* (Ithaca: Cornell University Press, 1992), 120.

6. Charles J. Rzepka, *Detective Fiction* (Malden: Polity, 2005), 48.

7. D. A. Miller, *The Novel and the Police* (Berkeley: University of California Press, 1988), 35.

8. Ronald R. Thomas, *Detective Fiction and the Rise of Forensic Science* (Cambridge: Cambridge University Press, 1999), 2.

9. Martin J. Wiener, *Reconstructing the Criminal: Culture, Law, and Policy in England, 1830–1914* (Cambridge: Cambridge University Press, 1990), 224.

10. Ibid., 223; and Daniel Cottom, "Sherlock Holmes Meets Dracula," *ELH* 79.3 (Fall 2012): 559.

11. Dorothy L. Sayers, "Introduction," *The Omnibus of Crime,* ed. Dorothy L. Sayers (New York: Harcourt, Brace, 1929), 37.

12. Raymond Chandler, "The Simple Art of Murder," *Later Novels and Other Writings* (New York: Library of America, 1995), 987.

13. On the English clue-puzzle mystery, especially during the interwar years, see Lee Horsley, *Twentieth-Century Crime Fiction* (Oxford: Oxford University Press, 2005), 37–52; Stephen Knight, *Crime Fiction since 1800: Detection, Death, Diversity,* second edition (Basingstoke: Palgrave Macmillan, 2010), 81–109; and Rzepka, *Detective Fiction.*

14. Charles Baudelaire, "The Painter of Modern Life," *The Painter of Modern Life and Other Essays,* trans. and ed. Jonathan Mayne (London: Phaidon, 1995), 7. See also Richard Kopley, *Edgar Allan Poe and the Dupin Mysteries* (New York: Palgrave Macmillan, 2008), for the early-twentieth-century appreciation of Poe's detective fiction, particularly by T. S. Eliot, G. K. Chesterton, and Dorothy Sayers.

15. Jonathan Elmer, *Reading at the Social Limit: Affect, Mass Culture, and Edgar Allan Poe* (Stanford: Stanford University Press, 1995), 2.

16. Roger Caillois, "The Detective Novel as Game," *The Poetics of Murder: Detective Fiction and Literary Theory,* ed. Glenn W. Most and William W. Stowe (San Diego: Harcourt Brace Jovanovich, 1983), 2.

17. Sir Arthur Conan Doyle, "The Adventure of the Abbey Grange," *The New Annotated Sherlock Holmes: Volume II*, ed. Leslie S. Klinger (New York: W. W. Norton, 2005), 1158. Versions of the phrase appear in both *I Henry IV* and *Henry V*.

18. Mark Seltzer, *True Crime: Observations on Violence and Modernity* (New York: Routledge, 2007), 68.

19. Lucy Hartley, *Physiognomy and the Meaning of Expression in Nineteenth-Century Culture* (Cambridge: Cambridge University Press, 2001), 1.

20. Edgar Allan Poe, "The Mystery of Marie Rogêt," *Selected Tales*, ed. David Van Leer (Oxford: Oxford University Press, 1998), 171. Hereafter cited parenthetically, as "MMR."

21. Sir Arthur Conan Doyle, *The Sign of Four* (London: Penguin, 2001), 84. Hereafter cited parenthetically, as *SF*. Holmes refers to William Winwood Reade's *The Martyrdom of Man* (1872), which denounces Christianity in favor of a conception of human history with deep ties to social Darwinism and contemporary advances in the natural sciences. Holmes praises the book earlier in the novel as "one of the most remarkable ever penned," probably for its rationalist approach to its subject (*SF*, 17).

22. Louis Menand, *The Metaphysical Club: A Story of Ideas in America* (New York: Farrar, Straus and Giroux, 2001), 182.

23. Theodore M. Porter, *The Rise of Statistical Thinking, 1820–1900* (Princeton: Princeton University Press, 1986), 27.

24. Menand, *The Metaphysical Club*, 194.

25. Edgar Allan Poe, "The Purloined Letter," *Selected Tales*, ed. David Van Leer (Oxford: Oxford University Press, 1998), 260. Hereafter cited parenthetically, as "PL."

26. For perhaps the most famous reading of this scene, and of the story more generally, see Jacques Lacan, "Seminar on 'The Purloined Letter,'" *The Poetics of Murder: Detective Fiction and Literary Theory*, ed. Glenn W. Most and William W. Stowe (San Diego: Harcourt Brace Jovanovich, 1983), 21–54.

27. Jean-Michel Rabaté, *Given: 1° Art 2° Crime: Modernity, Murder and Mass Culture* (Brighton: Sussex Academic Press, 2007), 84.

28. Thomas M. Kavanagh, *Dice, Cards, Wheels: A Different History of French Culture* (Philadelphia: University of Pennsylvania Press, 2005), 11.

29. Ibid., 11.

30. Walter Benjamin, *The Arcades Project*, trans. Howard Eiland and Kevin McLaughlin (Cambridge, MA: Belknap, 2003), 513.

31. Stephen Arata, *Fictions of Loss in the Victorian Fin de Siècle* (Cambridge: Cambridge University Press, 1996), 143.

32. Amanda Anderson, *The Powers of Distance: Cosmopolitanism and the Cultivation of Detachment* (Princeton: Princeton University Press, 2001), 4.

33. Ibid., 4.

34. Rzepka, *Detective Fiction*, 47.

35. Sir Arthur Conan Doyle, "A Scandal in Bohemia," *The New Annotated Sherlock Holmes: Volume I*, ed. Leslie S. Klinger (New York: W. W. Norton, 2005), 5. Hereafter cited parenthetically, as "SB."
36. Anderson, *The Powers of Distance*, 147.
37. Sir Arthur Conan Doyle, "The Red-Headed League," *The New Annotated Sherlock Holmes: Volume I*, ed. Leslie S. Klinger (New York: W. W. Norton, 2005), 62. Hereafter cited parenthetically, as "RHL."
38. Susan Buck-Morss, "Aesthetics and Anaesthetics: Walter Benjamin's Artwork Essay Reconsidered," *October* 62 (Autumn 1992): 8.
39. Ibid., 6, 9.
40. Ibid., 8.
41. Ibid., 22.
42. Knight, *Crime Fiction since 1800*, 61.
43. Laura Otis, *Membranes: Metaphors of Invasion in Nineteenth-Century Literature, Science, and Politics* (Baltimore: Johns Hopkins University Press, 1999), 90–118.
44. Vicki Mahaffey, *Modernist Literature: Challenging Fictions* (Malden: Blackwell, 2007), 80.
45. Sir Arthur Conan Doyle, *A Study in Scarlet, The New Annotated Sherlock Holmes: Volume III, The Novels*, ed. Leslie S. Klinger (New York: W. W. Norton, 2006), 18. Hereafter cited parenthetically, as *SS*.
46. Barry McCrae, *In the Company of Strangers: Family and Narrative in Dickens, Conan Doyle, Joyce, and Proust* (New York: Columbia University Press, 2011), 88.
47. Lawrence Rothfield, *Vital Signs: Medical Realism in Nineteenth-Century Fiction* (Princeton: Princeton University Press, 1992), 141.
48. Quoted in Ely M. Liebow, *Dr. Joe Bell: Model for Sherlock Holmes* (Madison: Popular Press, 2007), 173.
49. Jessica Burstein, *Cold Modernism: Literature, Fashion, Art* (University Park: Pennsylvania State University Press, 2012), 12.
50. Ibid., 12.
51. Rothfield, *Vital Signs*, 135.
52. Thomas, *Detective Fiction and the Rise of Forensic Science*, 32.
53. Srdjan Smajić, *Ghost-Seers, Detectives, and Spiritualists: Theories of Vision in Victorian Literature and Science* (Cambridge: Cambridge University Press, 2010), 126.
54. Michael Holquist, "Whodunit and Other Questions: Metaphysical Detective Stories in Postwar Fiction," *The Poetics of Murder: Detective Fiction and Literary Theory*, ed. Glenn W. Most and William W. Stowe (San Diego: Harcourt Brace Jovanovich, 1983), 159.
55. Dorothy L. Sayers, *Whose Body?* (New York: HarperCollins, 1995), 1. Hereafter cited parenthetically, as *WB*.

56. Robert Kuhn McGregor and Ethan Lewis, *Conundrums for the Long Week-End: England, Dorothy L. Sayers, and Lord Peter Wimsey* (Kent: Kent State University Press, 2000), 23.
57. Modris Eksteins, *Rites of Spring: The Great War and the Birth of the Modern Age* (Boston: Houghton Mifflin, 2000), 211.
58. Gill Plain, *Women's Fiction of the Second World War: Gender, Power and Resistance* (New York: St. Martin's, 1996), 48; Ariela Freedman, "Dorothy Sayers and the Case of the Shell-Shocked Detective" *Partial Answers* 8.2 (June 2010): 380.
59. Edmund Wilson, "Who Cares Who Killed Roger Ackroyd?," *Classics and Commercials: A Literary Chronicle of the Forties* (New York: Farrar, Straus and Giroux, 1950), 258–259.
60. Chandler, "The Simple Art of Murder," 987.
61. Samantha Walton, *Guilty but Insane: Mind and Law in Golden Age Detective Fiction* (Oxford: Oxford University Press, 2015), 222, 223.
62. McGregor and Lewis, *Conundrums for the Long Week-End*, 2.
63. Sean Latham, *"Am I a Snob?": Modernism and the Novel* (Ithaca: Cornell University Press, 2003), 198.
64. Sayers, "Introduction," 31.
65. Ibid., 37.
66. Chandler, "The Simple Art of Murder," 987.
67. Ibid., 980.
68. Sayers, "Introduction," 33.
69. Dorothy L. Sayers, *The Letters of Dorothy L. Sayers, 1899–1939: The Making of a Detective Novelist*, ed. Barbara Reynolds (New York: St Martin's, 1996), 241.
70. Linda Hutcheon, *A Theory of Parody: The Teachings of Twentieth-Century Art Forms* (Urbana: University of Illinois Press, 2000), 2, 4.
71. Allison Pease, *Modernism, Mass Culture, and the Aesthetics of Obscenity* (Cambridge: Cambridge University Press, 2000), 81–82.
72. Sayers, "Introduction," 40.
73. Quoted in Barbara Reynolds, *Dorothy L. Sayers: Her Life and Soul* (New York: St. Martin's, 1993), 256.
74. Dorothy L. Sayers, *The Unpleasantness at the Bellona Club* (New York: HarperCollins, 2006), 30. Hereafter cited parenthetically, as *UBC*.
75. During the war, Wimsey became an even more literal embodiment of a corpse. A brief biographical sketch that prefaces several Wimsey novels states that "In 1918 he was blown up and buried in a shell-hole near Caudry," after which his sergeant (who becomes his butler back in London) must dig him up to save his life. Dorothy L. Sayers, *Unnatural Death* (New York: HarperCollins, 1995), x. Hereafter cited parenthetically, as *UD*.
76. Latham, *"Am I a Snob?,"* 177.
77. Dorothy L. Sayers, *Clouds of Witness* (New York: HarperCollins, 1995), 117. Hereafter cited parenthetically, as *CW*.
78. By contrast, Stacy Gillis positions the relationship between Wimsey and Freke within the context of postwar shell shock and the increasingly tenuous

relationship between patient and analyst. See her "Consoling Fictions: Mourning, World War One, and Dorothy L. Sayers," *Modernism and Mourning*, ed. Patricia Rae (Lewisburg: Bucknell University Press, 2007), 185–197.

79. Pericles Lewis, *Religious Experience and the Modernist Novel* (Cambridge: Cambridge University Press, 2010), 20.

80. Charles Taylor, *Sources of the Self: The Making of the Modern Identity* (Cambridge, MA: Harvard University Press, 1989), 469.

81. This is not to suggest that other fictional detectives do not employ the kind of epiphanic solutions to a mystery that Wimsey does, but rather to argue that Wimsey's epiphanies bear a distinct and deliberate parallel to those more commonly associated with high modernism.

82. Walton, *Guilty but Insane*, 238–239.

83. Note the distinction between this account of logic as an impediment to successful game playing and Sayers's own devotion to word games. As Barbara Reynolds explains in her biography of Sayers, "there was ... a strong rational bent to [Sayers's] mind which delighted in the intellectual side of detective fiction, as it delighted in puzzles of all kinds – cryptograms, codes, and especially crossword puzzles, a new craze in the 1920s to which she at once became addicted" (*Dorothy L. Sayers: Her Life and Soul*. New York: St. Martin's, 1997: 195).

84. Leonard Diepeveen, "Introduction," *Mock Modernism: An Anthology of Parodies, Travesties, Frauds, 1910–1935*, ed. Leonard Diepeveen (Toronto: University of Toronto Press, 2014), 9.

CHAPTER 2

Criminal Types
Anarchism, Terrorism, and the Violence of Chance

Anyone who relies on abstraction will die in it.
— Mikhail Bakunin, *Statism and Anarchy* (1873)[1]

As representations of the detective shifted during the transition from the nineteenth to the twentieth century, with writers such as Sayers parodying the foolproof rationalism of Doyle and Poe in order to cultivate more nuanced, contradictory, and ultimately modernist forms of characterization, fictional accounts of the criminal also started moving in new directions. Increasingly attuned to an idea of the criminal as a unique, multifaceted subject motivated by individually specific desires, beliefs, and loyalties, but also struggling to overcome earlier prejudices against criminality as indicative of a pathological or morally corrupt character, authors of the late nineteenth and early twentieth centuries engaged vigorously with popular and scientific perceptions of crime in an effort to redefine the concept in more dynamic, less essentialist terms. While, as I have argued in the Introduction, late Victorian notions of the criminal depended in many respects upon positivistic theories of hereditary deviance and cultural degeneration popularized by criminal anthropologists such as Cesare Lombroso, there arose near the century's end a chorus of dissent within literary circles, which sought to undo such rigid taxonomies of biological criminality. Unconvinced that a life of crime was a foregone conclusion for the unlucky inheritors of pathological deviance, and troubled by the abdication of free will that such a notion entailed, these authors challenged the prevailing school of criminology by attacking its core assumptions. Whereas scientists and social reformers pointed to Lombroso's statistical gaffes and methodological inconsistencies, writers' critiques pivoted on the question of how an avowedly analytical approach to crime could be so impressionistic, its findings supported by stereotypes yoked to empirical evidence that, as Daniel Pick argues, aimed to restrict "the problem of crime to certain distinct and immutable creatures."[2] Such

72

findings were doubly suspicious in that they effectively ignored rival explanations for criminal acts. French anthropologist Paul Topinard complained that Lombroso's conclusions seemed "fashioned in advance," and several authors protested what they perceived as criminal anthropology's attempt to evade the complexities of individual subjectivity by standardizing the criminal as a homogenous character type.[3] Though the discipline still retained a fair measure of its cultural influence at the dawn of the twentieth century, in literature the criminal began to appear much more psychologically ambiguous, and much less readily explained by any single, generalized account of the violent mind.

Such was not always the case. In the latter half of the nineteenth century, Lombroso achieved a sizeable reputation as the pioneer of criminal anthropology, and became its most celebrated proponent.[4] Building upon French physician Bénédict Morel's theories of degeneration, which equated individual instances of mental illness and physical deformity with global processes of biological devolution, Lombroso staked his career on a similar belief in criminality as an inherited pathology, permanently etched upon bodies that deviate dramatically from the norm.[5] In the first edition of his landmark *Criminal Man* (1876), he writes that "[n]early all criminals have jug ears, thick hair, thin beards, pronounced sinuses, protruding chins, and broad cheekbones," and infers that those physical markers, like the blunted features of prehistoric man, reveal a latent predisposition to criminality, an atavistic aggression rooted in a distant past and unchecked by modern civilization.[6] In this system, criminals are born, not made, and are incapable of behaving in ways that contradict their birthrights; since criminality is inherited, the crimes that an individual commits are simply functions of that person's being, lacking any motivation other than the unconscious need to act in the manner ascribed by a criminal lineage. Lombroso puts the matter in stark terms, arguing that "most criminals really do lack free will."[7]

The foremost challenge that critics of criminal anthropology faced was not the difficulty of mounting an offensive against Lombroso's theories, but of contending with their ubiquity in the public sphere. Though controversial, criminal anthropology played a key role in nineteenth-century debates regarding criminality, and was widely promoted as a modern, evidence-based method for identifying and punishing potential offenders. Lombroso and his adherents were especially successful in disseminating that message through the popular press, where they underscored their discipline's ability to bring a cool, detached logic to bear on a chaotic and value-laden phenomenon.[8] According to Nicole Rafter, this "scientific separation of the orderly from the disorderly" was the crux of criminal anthropology's appeal, as Lombroso's emphasis on the signifying properties of the criminal body, epitomized in his generous use of photography and medical illustration, established a powerful, seemingly empirical link between the criminal's features and the violence toward which he or she is pathologically inclined.[9] Through a positivist approach that stresses the contrast between the aberrational appearance of the criminal and the normality of the law-abiding majority, "the visual and verbal languages of criminal anthropology ... reduce themselves to thin air, claiming to be media through which perception flies, unobstructed, straight to the essence of the criminal body."[10] By making criminality transparent to the skilled observer, criminal anthropology functions, in Daniel Pick's phrase, as "a pure medium of description," or a methodology whose "scrupulous impartiality" attempts to immunize its findings against the biases of other approaches by positing the criminal as an incontestable example of an empirically diagnosed corporeal otherness.[11] As a result of its claims to objectivity, championed in popular and professional publications, Lombroso's method encouraged a perception of the criminal body as a window into the criminal mind, and validated itself as an antidote to the moralism of the past. Consequently, any refutation of the discipline also had to unsettle the popular faith in it that Lombroso had nurtured, shaking the public's conviction in the essential legibility of the criminal body, which will always announce the actions it must, by nature, commit.

In addition to the difficulty of displacing criminal anthropology from the popular imagination, writers found it hard to avoid other means of criminal representation that, while not directly influenced by Lombrosian scientism, nonetheless reinforced general stereotypes of criminality. They chafed at the models set by social reformers such as Henry Mayhew, who, in a series of articles for London's *Morning Chronicle*, later collected as *London Labour and the London Poor* (1851; a supplementary volume on crime was added in 1861), classified the capital's criminals according to the illicit activities in which they engaged rather than cataloguing any distinguishing anatomical features they possessed. In his expansive analysis of London's criminal classes, Mayhew identified four varieties of criminal – beggars, cheats, thieves, and prostitutes – and refined those categories to include more specialized types of criminal behavior.[12] For these individuals, a life of crime resembles a profession without exactly being one, as Mayhew conceives of crime as a release from destitution and honest labor, a means of shirking legal forms of work for which one is constitutionally incapable. While his system succeeded in circumventing biology in order to address social concerns such as urban poverty, inadequate infrastructure, and the lack of economic opportunity in London's neglected East End, its alternately statistical and anecdotal approach largely affirmed the cultural purchase of criminal "types," shoring up a belief that criminality operates according to class-based hierarchies, and therefore might be confined to particular locations and kinds of persons (primarily the poor). As David Taylor observes, "Mayhew's analysis was comforting [to nineteenth-century readers], insofar as the criminal districts were, first, clearly defined in geographic terms, and, second, contained, and controlled by the police."[13] In providing such reassurance, however, Mayhew's superficially holistic approach to crime ignored the particulars of the individual criminal in order to define that individual's experience within generalized taxonomies of the criminal trades, essentially swapping the criminal body for the criminal profession or address.

How, then, could modernist authors chart a new course for criminal representation, particularly since so many late Victorian writers followed Lombroso and Mayhew in imagining the criminal as an irredeemable character type? According to Martin Wiener, fictions published at the height of criminal anthropology's reputation reflected the discipline's influence, offering a version of criminality "more deeply rooted within the offender's nature than in the moral consciousness or the rational intellect."[14] Likewise, William Greenslade argues that even during criminal anthropology's decline at the turn of the century, Lombroso "was still being called up as a familiar and legitimised source of criminological authority" in fiction and cinema, perpetuating through mass media ideas that the scientific community increasingly regarded with derision.[15] Given the popular durability of Lombrosian positivism as well as Mayhew's account of criminality as a problem of poor communities, authors' efforts to reimagine the criminal took on a special urgency. Dissatisfied with what they viewed as overly restrictive models that failed to register the idiosyncrasies of the criminal's inner experience, modernist writers of the late nineteenth and early twentieth centuries combined their formal interest in subjectivity with an ambivalence toward fixed demarcations of criminal identity that swallowed the individual within broader categories of personhood. This is not to suggest that modernists were wholly immune to depersonalized accounts of criminal nature, but rather that their work offered an alternative position by depicting criminals as malleable, oftentimes contradictory subjects best understood as unique combinations of personality, experience, and affiliation, if they could be understood at all.

The primary vehicle for this effort was psychological representation, through which modernists sought to convey the tangle of motivations that drive one toward the criminal act. In the process, they revealed the circumstances that disrupt the exchange between motive and action, challenging the criminal's autonomy by showing how external forces can lead to incongruous behavior. Whereas Lombroso and Mayhew described criminality as a relatively transparent category of subjectivity applicable to large groups – an inherited pathology or indisposition to a respectable trade – fiction allowed readers to trace the movements of a single criminal negotiating an obscure thicket of motivations: independent experience and belief; environmental, social, and economic pressures; and group affiliation. In this way, it could reveal how a criminal's warring motivations often fail to illuminate that individual's actions, making criminality, like all identity, a potentially unsolvable enigma. We can understand this effort to represent the criminal mind as fulfilling what Kevin Bell describes as "modernism's imagining of subjectivity as an endless interstitiality," or "a liquid constellation of singularities of experimentation and experience," overlapping so thoroughly that one cannot parse the individual strands in order to arrive at a single, concrete explanation of the subject.[16] Significantly, this interstitiality weaves the subject's singular desires with equally pressing external demands, and modernist authors necessarily represented the criminal as pulled between disparate poles, neither wholly autonomous nor the avatar of a general type. The challenge, then, was to explain the varieties of criminal behavior without reducing them to a typology or hewing too closely to any single explanation of criminality, pursuing as many options as possible in order to convey an idea of the criminal as a mutable, potentially inscrutable subject.

This chapter focuses on three novelists who took up that challenge through the figure of the terrorist, specifically the anarchist terrorist, who made a dramatic impact on the world stage after Alfred Nobel's 1867 invention of dynamite. As Sarah Cole has persuasively demonstrated, the anarchist charged the imaginations of numerous authors through the flagrance of his ambiguities and the spectacle of his violence, the unpredictability of which "suggested a future with unknowable and potentially frightful contours."[17] Examining the ambivalent accounts of anarchist terror in novels by Henry James, Joseph Conrad, and G. K. Chesterton, I argue that these three authors address in distinct yet ultimately related ways one of anarchism's fundamental mysteries, which speaks more broadly to the representation of criminality in fiction: "the question of what kind of person would or could become an anarchist and how to amalgamate such people into an understandable frame of reference."[18] By exposing the collisions of political fervor, individual affect, and social allegiance within the mind of the terrorist, while also wrestling with cultural assumptions regarding innate criminality that lingered in the public imagination, these authors testify to the terrorist's signifying power as an emblem of political criminality, and to the importance of fiction as a demystifying frame of reference that affords more diverse and psychologically penetrating models of the criminal subject.

Of course, an aesthetic investment in inner experience is not the same thing as an undivided attention to it, and while all three authors present the terrorist as resisting biological and socioeconomic models of criminality, their inability to reject entirely the notion of the criminal type leads to fictions that are revealingly inconsistent. James, for instance, wavers between portrayals of anarchist revolutionaries as, on the one hand, born criminals with an inherent penchant for violence, and, on the other, idealistic laborers for whom terror is a viable defense against economic exploitation. Similarly, Conrad presents the act of terror as an inherently unpredictable event susceptible to the whims of chance while depicting other violent acts in terms that echo Lombroso's theories on inherited (and hence unavoidable) criminality. Chesterton's impression of anarchism as a vague political philosophy designed to ignite the fervor of a crowd is perhaps the most conflicted of all, in that its studious indifference to anarchism as an ideology belies its interest in the clashes between individual desire and political commitment. Rather than seeing these contradictions as evidence of an unwitting or hypocritical acceptance of criminological theories dependent on typology and generalization, and therefore as concessions to traditional modes of criminal representation, this chapter argues that such ambiguities are an essential component of a larger formal project, in which authors use the criminal as a way of imagining the subject as a constellation of individual and social traits. James, Conrad, and Chesterton do not simply reveal their own prejudices by depicting the terrorist in this fashion, nor do they exemplify a failed attempt at resisting popular attitudes toward criminality. Instead, their alternation between individual and categorical accounts of the criminal reflects what Michael Levenson poses as an animating question for modernist characterization more generally: "whether it is a higher value to be the luminous representative of a general possibility or to be a possibility wholly *sui generis*."[19] Taken together, the novels discussed in this chapter powerfully demonstrate how modernists took the issue of political criminality as a clarion call to rethink the representation of literary character as a vacillation between individuality and collectivity, and to foster an idea of the individual as simultaneously autonomous and embodying larger social and political forces.

By examining these three authors in tandem, one can also understand how the issue of criminal subjectivity inflects more traditionally modernist notions of the fragmentation of identity and the problem of psychological representation. It is no coincidence that modernism's celebrated engagement with interiority arises alongside a broader cultural fascination with terrorism and the mindset of its acolytes, as writers such as James, Conrad, and Chesterton use the political criminal to test the capacity of narrative to express subjectivity as it negotiates the demands of the self and the collective. Consequently, this chapter reveals the extent of the relationship between modernist aesthetic practice and conceptions of insurrectionary violence that combine individual motivations for terror with generalized categories of human possibility (political, anthropological, and socioeconomic), and illustrates how modernist depictions of terrorism evince a profound skepticism regarding narrative's ability to account fully for its perpetrators.

Terror as a Type

In many ways, late nineteenth- and early twentieth-century terrorism represented an entirely new species of criminality. Whether inspired by political ideology, personal experience, or the grisly thrill of wreaking havoc on a grand scale, the terrorist appeared to act on multiple and mutually exclusive impulses, and left both criminologists and the general public uncertain of where to assign blame for his deeds. Even more than the numerous assassinations of public figures – which included two American presidents, a French president, an Austrian empress, a Russian tsar, and an Italian king[20] – the indiscriminate violence of terrorist bombing campaigns provoked outrage and confusion, and stirred up animosity toward any group that might be held responsible. In the United States, bombings in Chicago (the infamous Haymarket Square incident of May 4, 1886), Los Angeles (the destruction of the *Los Angeles Times* building on October 1, 1910), and New York (the attack on the J. P. Morgan bank on Wall Street, on September 16, 1920) made headlines not only for the damage they caused, but also for the blanket denunciations of potential perpetrators they elicited. As Paul Avrich contends, Haymarket "provoked a nationwide convulsion of deep-rooted and violent prejudice" against all stripes of political radicalism, the shudders of which reverberated through editorials in the *Chicago Times*, which deemed anarchists associated with the bombing "arch counselors of riot, pillage, incendiarism and murder," and the *New York Tribune*, which characterized the perpetrators as a "mob ... crazed with a frantic desire for blood."[21] In these and other responses, journalists borrowed the pathologizing discourse they employed for other forms of criminality – demonstrating what Richard Bach Jensen identifies as "print media's relentless tendency to oversimplify and to exploit dominant stereotypes" when dealing with political crime – and described the terrorist in terms that reflected both Lombroso's born criminality and Mayhew's ersatz professional.[22] In this way, a previously unimaginable, idiosyncratic form of violence was quickly incorporated as a general category of criminality, as newspapers dispatched established notions of the criminal to provide "the essential glue that bound together and transformed disparate incidents into a formidable edifice of terrorism."[23]

Similar attitudes surfaced in Britain and Continental Europe, where terror was more frequent and acute. English editorial cartoonists used racialized caricatures to depict the Fenian bombers of Clerkenwell Prison (1867), Scotland Yard (1884), London Bridge (1884), the Tower of London (1885), and the Houses of Parliament (1885) in an effort to defuse public panic and quash sympathy for Irish independence,[24] while French newspapers' sensational portraits of anarchist terror – for instance, their frenzied coverage of the infamous Ravachol, who became a figurehead for the movement after bombing the homes of a judge and lawyer in 1892, and of Émile Henry, whose blithe toss of a bomb into Paris's Café Terminus in 1894 encapsulated the anarchist principle of "propaganda by deed" – stoked public fears over violence whose anticapitalist political objectives were overshadowed by attackers' willingness to harm any member of the bourgeoisie regardless of individual identity, in what Deaglán Ó Donghaile terms a "dialectic of unrestricted class warfare."[25] In each case, the press depicted the terrorist as simultaneously typical and extraordinary. Indeed, the fact that organized groups like the Fenians and independently operating anarchists employed the same technique to achieve far different ends led to a contradictory understanding of the terrorist as a kind of criminal mongrel; both a steadfast political martyr and a volatile sociopath devoted to "an apocalypse of smoke and blood," the terrorist was perceived as a resolute yet erratic figure, psychologically indeterminate and hence far more dangerous than other criminals.[26] Such ambiguity could mitigate the terrorist's fearsome persona by labeling him an outsider, an impassioned but misguided radical who acted on behalf of fringe political crusades, but it could also enhance it by acknowledging that acts of terrorism occur without warning, often without apparent rationale or aim. Paradoxically, then, the terrorist reinforced the idea of criminality as otherness while becoming yet another criminal type, representing at once novel forms of individual violence and more familiar stereotypes of madness and pathological deviance.

As these contradictions suggest, journalists' codification of the terrorist into a general type of offender was never a seamless process, and did little to calm public anxiety over what many feared was a new era of unpredictable mass destruction. Much as Lombroso's theory of born criminality could suggest an irrevocably declining society besieged by violence when it meant to reassure audiences that the spread of crime could actually be kept in check, efforts to neutralize terrorism's threat through caricature and stereotype struggled to overcome the frightful reality that most bombings looked like chance occurrences, unexpected and thus unavoidable for even law-abiding citizens. While turn-of-the-century terrorism was often carefully orchestrated, the fact that one could never predict an outbreak made all such acts seem random, the maleficent results of inscrutable events and perpetrators. As Jeffory Clymer argues, the bomber, often described as a "dynamite fiend" or "dynamitard," "exploited what is most ghastly about modern terrorism, the fateful dance of chance and innocence that indiscriminately turns everyday citizens into public victims."[27] Because they aimed for symbolic, collateral damage rather than the deaths of specific people, bombing campaigns fueled intense cultural apprehension, illustrating just how readily "everyday citizens could . . . become the random targets of terrorists."[28] This notion of terrorism as an unforeseen and indiscriminate attack on people from all backgrounds produced a corresponding fear that the entire world might be vulnerable, and anyone, anywhere, a potential victim. Through such "impersonal randomness," Alex Houen explains, dynamite attacks "revealed to people that they were *already living as potential statistics*, already living as anonymous figures in a crowd."[29] But whereas Sherlock Holmes's perception of the crowd as a statistical aggregate showed late Victorian readers an orderly model of deduction in the midst of a chaotic urban modernity – a reliable way of compartmentalizing human behavior that subsumes chance within the comforting certainties of probability – the terrorist's vision did precisely the opposite. In the act of bombing, the terrorist turns an individual into a statistic at the moment of the latter's death or injury, and does so through a form of violence whose spontaneity flouts the effectiveness of probability as a preventative tool. Shattering the illusion of social order, the terrorist reveals in its place two grim realities: first, that victims are not only discrete subjects, but also, unavoidably, members of an anonymous collective that functions as a blunt political instrument; and second, that a criminal, rather than a detective, is now the one who exerts individual mastery over the masses.

If we understand the phenomenon of terrorism, like other forms of criminality, as a reduction of specific persons to broader groups or categories – victim, fiend, bystander, fanatic – then we can also see why the international anarchist movement so beguiled writers of fiction.[30] For many authors, the anarchist mission to destroy the mechanisms of the state in hopes of liberating the individual carried with it a fearsome yet romantic tinge, and coupled neatly with an emerging modernist egoism, the shock of whose violent aesthetic, Paul Sheehan observes, marked "an explosive intervention in literary culture."[31] More significantly, though, anarchism intrigued through its apparent amorphousness. Since its fundamental principles differed markedly from one anarchist group to the next, several cultural critics flattened anarchism's unique distinctions into a single, homogenous whole.[32] As William Phillips puts it, "[a]narchists could not be contained in tidy labels, and this lack of definition and unified voice created a perceptual vacuum ... which outsiders filled by making anarchism stand for many cultural developments that were perceived as threatening or disorderly."[33] Readers of contemporary newspapers thus saw anarchism as primarily a provocation to violence instead of a political philosophy, never learning, for example, that Mikhail Bakunin's ardent brand of insurrectionism was not the same thing as the anarchist philosophy of Pyotr Kropotkin, which borrowed from evolutionary theory to argue that the cooperation among species seen in the physical world might counter the capitalist emphasis on competition as the most effective method for human advancement. At the same time, the popular press's habit of ignoring distinctions between rival anarchist positions to focus on atrocities committed in the movement's name does not deserve all the blame for this state of affairs, since several anarchist leaders openly resisted the yoke of a definite ideology, believing that an established creed would enact the very oppression it hoped to overthrow. Bakunin, for instance, claimed that he would "cleave to no system," since "[n]o theory, no ready-made system, no book that has ever been written will save the world."[34] Without a consistent definition of anarchist ideology, journalists and critics were left to fill what they perceived as gaps in anarchism's philosophical coherence, and so the figure of the anarchist came to serve as a kind of revolutionary straw man, or generalized exemplar of political violence. In this way, anarchism became synonymous with terrorism, forming an inextricable link between the two in the popular imagination. "The bomb and the anarchist," Sarah Cole argues, "were partners; to understand the cultural significance of one is to penetrate the world of the other."[35]

Given the correlation of anarchism with violent criminality, public perceptions of the anarchist tended toward the pathological. According to historian George Woodcock, "[t]he stereotype of the anarchist is that of the cold-blooded assassin who attacks with dagger or bomb the symbolic pillars of established society. Anarchy, in popular parlance, is malign chaos."[36] This stereotyping of the anarchist proved a fruitful, if frustrating topic for criminal anthropologists such as Lombroso, who struggled to place anarchism within his atavistic framework. For Lombroso, anarchists resembled other types of criminals in that they too displayed physical markers reflective of an innate propensity for violence; as Daniel Pick observes, Lombroso initially characterized the surge of anarchist sentiment in late nineteenth-century Europe as "a form of epidemic disease."[37] Soon, however, Lombroso was forced to answer nagging questions regarding his methods in approaching politically motivated crime, which critics found disturbingly reductionist in dealing with the complexities of such a specific brand of violence. Though he long maintained that terrorist violence is, like other forms of criminality, a byproduct of heredity, Lombroso eventually refined his position to claim that "political crime," as he called it, could not be understood in the same way as other criminal actions. In the fifth and final edition of *Criminal Man* (1896–1897), he contends that political criminals "share the characteristics of criminals of passion and therefore are the opposite of the criminal type."[38] While the astute observer can spot those born to crime by searching for distinctively asymmetrical physiognomies, Lombroso concedes that political criminals act on irrational, fleeting impulses, and, far from appearing atavistic, "have beautiful or ... anticriminal faces with broad foreheads, rich beards, and gentle, serene countenances."[39] Here the anarchist's physical beauty represents the very antithesis of criminality, but also cements his status as a criminal other; the anarchist deviates in dramatic fashion from the norms of criminality (which, in turn, deviate from other physical norms), and thereby becomes even more sinister than his criminal peers.

In spite of this revised approach to the political criminal, Lombroso was skeptical of his assertions, and insisted on separating such criminals from the mass of ordinary individuals. Perhaps to defend his methods from charges of ineffectiveness – or, worse, from the embarrassment of appearing to lose faith in their fundamental principles – Lombroso described other avenues by which one might identify potential terrorists and thereby preserve criminal anthropology's social utility. Moving from physical characteristics to more subjective categories of emotion, psychology, and motivation, Lombroso nonetheless found within political violence a kernel of biological criminality. He notes in *Criminal Man*'s fifth edition that "anarchists are often inspired by an overdeveloped sense of altruism and an exaggerated sensitivity to the pain of others," and argues that the "contradiction between their altruism and the cruelty of their deeds can only be understood in the light of the behavior of hysterics. Hysteria, the sister of epilepsy and a disease linked to the loss of sensitivity, usually combines extreme egotism with excessive altruism. This proves that altruism is often no more than a variant of moral insanity."[40] The staggering ethical repercussions of this final sentence aside, Lombroso's equation of anarchism and disease is significant in that it pulls the discussion of terrorism away from psychology and toward the original, physiological foundations of criminal anthropology, hovering somewhere between the two. Never quite diverging from his earlier, corporeal focus, Lombroso implies that one should understand the political criminal in psychosomatic rather than wholly psychological terms. By explaining the altruism of the anarchist through mental and physical illness – hysterical behavior characterized by a loss of sensitivity – Lombroso ends up exactly where he began, with the criminal body serving as the outward manifestation of the psyche.

That the founder of criminal anthropology could never make up his mind about the origins of political violence – whether terrorists were born to lives of crime, acted upon independent ideological convictions, or lost themselves in fitful passions – mirrors the ambivalence that defined literary responses to the subject in the late nineteenth and early twentieth centuries. For James, Conrad, and Chesterton, anarchist terrorism exposed the rifts between rival approaches to criminality while also demonstrating their pervasiveness within the cultural landscape. Consequently, their depictions of the terrorist shuttle between pathological conceptions of criminality and those that acknowledge the exercise of free will and the inexplicable sways of chance, offering new ways of representing criminal psychology without shirking entirely the concept of the criminal type. In so doing, all three authors attest to the anxieties that anarchism instigated during the period, and, more importantly, to the formative influence of terrorism upon modernist efforts to complicate traditional understandings of criminality, subjectivity, and psychological depth.

Henry James and the Born Criminal

For Henry James, the threat of political violence may have been a disquieting feature of modern life, but it also made for a fascinating spectacle. Describing the increasingly bloody fight over Irish independence in an 1881 letter to Thomas Sergeant Perry, James expresses interest in visiting the beleaguered colony, not to participate in the conflict, but rather because, as he puts it, "I should like to see a country in a state of revolution."[41] Careful to acknowledge that this desire does not reflect his political sympathies, James characterizes the English as pragmatic reformers and the Irish as "a totally impractical people," describing the situation in Ireland as more of a diplomatic impasse than a justification for anti-imperialist violence.[42] Yet this pedestrian view of the Irish question is hardly the most notable element of James's letter. More significant is its remarkably aesthetic approach to politics, which styles the battle for Irish independence as a spectacle to experience rather than a topic of political debate. While he presents the Irish as an immovable group intent on rebuffing a government ready to negotiate, James's interest in a problem he proclaims "insoluble" is never wholly political, but instead an aesthetic appreciation of political struggle.[43] James suggests that politically motivated violence is something to see and be seen, a phenomenon whose politics are less important than, or at least inseparable from, its properties as art.

As for his desire to witness a revolution, James came close to getting his wish, not in Ireland, but in his adopted home of London. During the years he spent writing *The Princess Casamassima*, his fictional study of London's anarchist subculture and the widening chasm between the city's upper and lower classes, which he published serially in the *Atlantic Monthly* beginning in September 1885 and collected in book form in 1886, the capital was rocked by efforts to destabilize its most prominent institutions.[44] Barbara Arnett Melchiori has dubbed 1884–1885 "the year of the dynamitards" on account of the Fenian bombings of Victoria Station (February 25), Scotland Yard (May 30), and London Bridge (December 13) in 1884, as well as the simultaneous explosions at Westminster Hall, the Houses of Parliament, and the Tower of London executed by Fenian rebels on January 24 of the following year.[45] In addition to Fenian attacks, political protests were ubiquitous during these years, and caused just as much panic as the dynamite outrages. An unemployed workers' demonstration at Trafalgar Square on February 8, 1886, led to days of rioting and vandalism, while an 1887 protest against a ban on public assembly at the Square yielded multiple clashes with police and severe damage to local businesses.[46]

Though the city was hardly swept up in the intense revolutionary spirit of Continental Europe, its streets nonetheless experienced their share of political violence, exemplified by the mass of individuals who came together to demonstrate and revolt against the injustices inflicted upon them by what they perceived as a stifling political order.

These uprisings clearly spurred James's imagination, given his long-standing interest in urban crowds.[47] As Lionel Trilling put it in his seminal essay on *The Princess Casamassima*, James, at this stage of his career, conceptualized the social world as a conflagration of "crowds and police," or "a field of justice and injustice, reform and revolution."[48] Stressing James's attention to both the crush of bodies surging through the metropolis and the authorities charged with providing crowd control, Trilling characterizes James as a writer for whom the tension between violence and order in modern urban spaces fueled a burgeoning social imagination. Other critics have also identified the crowd as a fixture of James's early work. Mary Esteve, for instance, argues that James's attraction to the crowd – or, as he preferred to call it, following Thomas Carlyle, the "swarm" – lies equally in its resonance as an aesthetic object and in its physical, literal form, as an intermingling of anonymous individuals who, by shared proximity, become a uniquely heterogeneous collective.[49] Both sides of James's interest – the aesthetic and the sociological – share crucial affinities with the idiosyncratic portrait of the crowd developed in Gustave Le Bon's *La Psychologie des foules* (1895, published in English a year later as *The Crowd: A Study of the Popular Mind*), which emphasizes how individuals linked by physical space begin to think collectively while remaining strangers to one another. Le Bon terms this phenomenon "the law of the mental unity of crowds," whereby individuals unconsciously fall victim to mass suggestibility:

> whoever be the individuals that compose [the crowd] . . . the fact that they have been transformed into a crowd puts them in possession of a sort of collective mind which makes them feel, think, and act in a manner quite different from that in which each individual of them would feel, think, and act were he in a state of isolation.[50]

Here Le Bon alludes to the very threat that, as I will show later in this chapter, James underscores in his own treatment of political violence: namely, that crowds are extremely vulnerable to manipulation, their malleability resulting in actions that do not correspond to members' individual motives. "Little adapted to reasoning," Le Bon claims, crowds are "quick to act," their spontaneous outbursts born of a volatile collective

unconscious.[51] Once submerged in the multitude, individuals lose those
habits of discernment and self-awareness necessary for independent
thought and action, and therefore run the risk of behaving in unpredictable, even violent, ways.

It is clear, then, why Le Bon and others found the crowd so troubling. If,
as Le Bon warned, the individual within the crowd "is no longer himself,
but has become an automaton who has ceased to be guided by his will,"
then that individual no longer bears responsibility for his actions, and is
simply swept up in the passions of his group.[52] Curiously, though, James
found the renunciation of free will to be one of the most pleasurable and
productive aspects of joining a crowd, as benign receptivity to suggestion
could foster unexpected occasions of literary creativity. In his preface to
The Princess Casamassima, appended to the New York Edition of the novel
in 1909, James remarks that the book's plot and characters emerged
fortuitously, "from the habit and the interest of walking the streets."[53]
Casting himself as a kind of urban ethnographer, he describes how, observing London's crowds, "[p]ossible stories, presentable figures, rise from the
thick jungle as the observer moves, fluttering up like startled game, and
before he knows it indeed he has fairly to guard himself against the brush of
importunate wings. He goes on as with his head in a cloud of humming
presences" (*PC*, 33).

The novel that resulted from these presences is not simply a testi-
monial to the pleasures of *flânerie*, but a curiously sober melodrama
that explores the pressures that collectivity exerts on subjectivity,
embodied in the character of Hyacinth Robinson, a bookbinder turned
anarchist who, James explains, grew "out of the London pavement"
(*PC*, 34). Presenting Hyacinth as both an advocate for individual liberty
and a victim of broader forces – economic systems, political ideology,
and born criminality – *The Princess Casamassima* imagines criminal
subjectivity as defined by the conflicts among individual desire, the
dictates of a group, and the burdens of one's history, rather than
hewing to any single explanation. The illegitimate son of an English
lord and a French seamstress who murdered her lover in a jealous rage,
Hyacinth, at the novel's outset, perceives himself as a born criminal
tainted by "the inheritance which had darkened the whole threshold of
his manhood," his mother's transgression having made him "*ab ovo* a
revolutionist" (*PC*, 105, 282). Upon the death of his surrogate parent,
Amanda Pynsent, Hyacinth ruminates on the course his life might have
taken should she never have adopted him, picturing himself enduring
"[t]he workhouse and the gutter, ignorance and cold, filth and tatters,

nights of huddling under bridges and in doorways, vermin, starvation and blows, possibly even the vigorous efflorescence of an inherited disposition to crime" (*PC*, 371). While Hyacinth's imaginary past begins by echoing Mayhew's study of the urban poor, it closes with a deliberately Lombrosian invocation of inherited criminality. In Hyacinth's formulation a life of poverty begets a life of crime, not because of economic necessity but because the indignities of poverty will nurture his "inherited disposition" into being. Hyacinth does not envision committing crimes in order to survive, but fears that poverty would awaken the attraction to crime imprinted upon him at birth.

Ironically, by positing childhood experience as formative, Hyacinth admits that the scandal of his parentage and murder of his father may not be the sole determinants of his identity. These constraints certainly leave their mark, but, through the examples of other characters buoyed by industrial modernity's increased opportunities for upward mobility, James implies that they can be erased. For Millicent Henning, Hyacinth's child-hood playmate now employed in an upscale department store, Hyacinth's "base birth really made little impression . . . she accounted it an accident much less grave than he had been in the habit of doing" (*PC*, 532). By viewing Hyacinth's birthright as an accident, Millicent counters his faith in the fixity of identity, her position in a developing industry quietly asserting that the circumstances of birth can be annulled by another, this time more fortuitous event. In this manner, Millicent's social advancement not only reverses Hyacinth's gloomy fatalism, dismissing his inheritance as a single, chance occurrence liable to be overturned by others, but more thoroughly debunks the notion of predetermined subjectivity just as the novel's protagonist expresses such unreserved faith in it. Even when James describes Millicent in emblematic terms, those accounts stress her essential malleability; whereas Hyacinth casts himself as the hopeless son of criminal parents – the quintessential born criminal – Millicent's more cavalier approach to one's personal fortunes makes her the representative "daughter of London," who

> had drawn her health and strength from [the city's] dingy courts and foggy
> thoroughfares, and peopled its parks and squares and crescents with her
> ambitions; it had entered into her blood and her bone, the sound of her
> voice and the carriage of her head; she understood it by instinct and loved it
> with passion; she represented its immense vulgarities and curiosities, its
> brutality and its knowingness, its good-nature and its impudence, and
> might have figured, in an allegorical procession, as a kind of glorified
> townswoman, a nymph of the wilderness of Middlesex, a flower of the

accumulated parishes, the genius of urban civilisation, the muse of cockney-
ism. (*PC*, 93)

Molded by a lifetime of urban experience, Millicent testifies to London's
doggedness, brashness, and fostering of unquenchable ambitions, drawing
"her health and strength" from an environment that molds its citizens into
the people they evolve to become. Even as this passage characterizes
Millicent as the embodiment of a collective, general type (the lifelong
Londoner), that type is rooted in a specific environment, and privileges
sustained experience in the metropolis over the one-time event of a
metropolitan birth. Like Hyacinth, Millicent is defined by her origins
(his criminal, hers urban), but where Hyacinth sees himself as a born
criminal forever burdened by his ancestry, Millicent epitomizes new possibilities for self-representation, self-conception, and independence drawn
from her immersion in the London crowds. In her, James offers an
alternative to the notion of born criminality, and to inherited character
more generally, as Millicent embodies social and environmental forces that
transcend the circumstances of birth through prolonged processes of subjective evolution.

This exchange between the burdens of fixed character and the liberation
of environment, chance, and individual will is precisely where *The Princess
Casamassima* locates its protagonist's anarchism. For Hyacinth, Millicent's
advancement and subsequent feelings of transcendence are the products of
false consciousness, encouraged by a capitalist economy that arrests subjectivity through general categories of class. She simply trades one station
for another, moving up within but never out of class hierarchies, and
therefore never frees herself from what Hyacinth perceives as a severe
limitation on personal autonomy. As he listens to the anarchists of the
revolutionary Sun and Moon club promoting violent revolt, Hyacinth
comes to see in anarchism a way of overthrowing the systems of power
that have defined his and Millicent's lives, and thereby realizing a future
truly unencumbered by the past. At the same time, the narrative suggests
that anarchism is not a viable strategy for overcoming the tyranny of class
or any other hierarchy, but is instead a tangled rhetoric that cannot see the
paradox of its dual emphases on self-creation and economic rootedness.
Anarchism promises Hyacinth an escape from poverty and a knotty family
tree, but it also fixes him within general categories of subjectivity, both
socioeconomic and criminal. Indeed, Hyacinth's anarchism reaffirms his
status as a born criminal, in that it too compels him to accept a single,
causal explanation – economics – for his present state, and preys upon his

faith in his own criminality by encouraging him to commit the acts of violence he believes himself fated to carry out. Coming under the influence of Eustache Poupin, a French *émigré* described as "a Republican of the old-fashioned sort, of the note of 1848, humanitary and idealistic, infinitely addicted to fraternity and equality," Hyacinth feels he has little choice but to follow Poupin in a radicalism tellingly described in pathological terms (*PC*, 114). As Hyacinth grows closer to Poupin and his equally "addicted" wife, he begins to realize that he, too, "was one of the disinherited, one of the expropriated, one of the exceptionally interesting; and moreover he was one of themselves, a child, as it were, of France, an offshoot of the sacred race" (*PC*, 120). Almost as soon as he discovers it, Hyacinth recognizes his anarchism as a nationalistic duty, fulfilling the life for which he is pre-ordained. Far from an exercise in free will, his radicalism represents the unifying obligations of kinship and collective belonging.

By figuring Hyacinth's burgeoning anarchism as a family affair, James also suggests that an ethos such as anarchism can too easily veer into abstraction, signifying broad principles of collectivity, civil disobedience, and the nobility of labor rather than any tangible methodology or goal. While Amanda Claybaugh argues that, in both *The Princess Casamassima* and its contemporary *The Bostonians* (1886), social reform "relies, no less than the writing of realist novels, on the finding or creating of representative figures," in the former novel James undercuts that process by demonstrating how reform becomes peripheral to representation.[54] Rather than offering a practicable path to revolt, several anarchists in *The Princess Casamassima* perceive themselves and one another as metaphorical agents, the material embodiments of causes, rather than exerting the individual autonomy they claim as their overriding goal. For instance, Paul Muniment, a well-spoken chemist's assistant whom Hyacinth praises as a "splendid exception" to the "third-rate minds" of the working classes, personifies for Hyacinth the dream of an anarchist future in which one can overcome shameful origins through commitment to radical change (*PC*, 218, 217). But despite Hyacinth's faith in his friend's capabilities, James depicts Muniment as a general symbol of anarchism, eloquence, and the social potential of violence – "a fine embodiment of the spirit of the people" – and not as an individual with concrete plans for an anarchist revolution (*PC*, 446). In epitomizing what Hyacinth, referring to another anarchist leader, terms "the very incarnation of a programme," Muniment affirms his credibility as a revolutionary without having to do anything to maintain it (*PC*, 328); he incarnates his program for reform, but never actually follows it. And yet Muniment's ability to stand in for a larger principle is what allows Hyacinth to downplay the ambiguity of his radicalism, ignoring the fact that it reflects a nebulous ideal of collectivity and social justice rather than a plan to realize the unfettered autonomy for which Hyacinth yearns. As Hyacinth tells Muniment in admiration, "I would go by what you tell me, anywhere . . . I don't know that I believe exactly what you believe, but I believe in you, and doesn't that come to the same thing?" (PC, 446).

Here and elsewhere, Muniment symbolizes revolutionary aspiration writ large, and allows Hyacinth to forget his biological criminality and embrace the pleasures of surrendering his individuality to another broad ideal. When he speculates on the form that an anarchist insurrection might take, Hyacinth overlooks the messy particulars of political violence in favor of the phenomenological delights of abandoning himself to the archetypal revolutionary crowd that Le Bon would denounce a few years later:

> [T]here was joy, exultation, in the thought of surrendering one's self to the wave of revolt, of floating in the tremendous tide, of feeling one's self lifted and tossed, carried higher on the sun-touched crests of billows than one could ever be by a dry, lonely effort of one's own. That vision could deepen to a kind of ecstasy; make it indifferent whether one's ultimate fate, in such a heaving sea, were not almost certainly to be submerged in bottomless depths or dashed to pieces on resisting cliffs. Hyacinth felt that, whether his personal sympathy should rest finally with the victors or the vanquished, the victorious force was colossal and would require no testimony from the irresolute. (PC, 478)

Hyacinth's imaginary surrender parallels James's own immersion in the multitude described in the novel's preface, while his rendering of the crowd in metaphorical terms, as a sublime "wave of revolt" that will either lift or drown its members, echoes James's comments on the spectacular crowds of the Irish uprising. But like James's coolly detached view of Irish revolutionaries, Hyacinth's ecstatic vision of the crowd overlooks the material violence of political uprising, and remains indifferent to the "ultimate fate" that will befall scores of revolutionaries in favor of a utopian vision of collectivity. Inspired by Muniment's embodiment of political ideals, Hyacinth bases his anarchism on feeling rather than fact, and adopts an aestheticized incendiarism that prizes a collective, aestheticized pleasure over social justice.

In each of these cases, James's novel presents the anarchist in conflicting ways, refusing to adopt any single model of political criminality. Its protagonist is a self-identified born criminal who views the anarchist cause as an aesthetic experience that would negate his subjectivity, while other anarchist characters attempt to exemplify their political ideals by becoming living abstractions or argue against ideals in favor of more immediate forms of revolt (as one patron of the Sun and Moon grumbles, "if a man could see as far as he could chuck a brick, that was far enough"; *PC*, 282). We could understand these divergences as evidence of James's flimsy grasp of contemporary political philosophy; as Elizabeth Carolyn Miller has pointed out, James's interchangeable use of terms such as "*anarchism, nihilism*, and *socialism* suggests a confusion on the part of the characters – or, some would say, the author – about their motivating ideology."[55] Yet this reading assumes any discrepancy in the novel's representation of political criminality to be unintentional, rather than a deliberate decision to posit criminal motivation as necessarily varied. A more sympathetic – and, indeed, more accurate – reading might view *The Princess Casamassima* as debunking what Sarah Cole describes as the popular "near-caricature" of anarchists as "bomb-wielding maniacs" whose pathological bloodlust trumps all other forms of motivation.[56] In this reading, James imbues his anarchist characters with multiple motives in order to show how an individual's devotion to the anarchist cause could never be reduced to a single factor, pathological or otherwise. This heterogeneity of anarchist motivation also explains why James consistently foregrounds the impossibility of determining who is or is not a "true" revolutionary – for example, by highlighting Muniment as the embodiment of revolution only to cut him down as a self-interested fraud whose actual agenda is the pursuit of novelty. Hyacinth's frail personal politics evaporates for precisely this reason, as he decides to abandon the Sun and Moon after discovering that Muniment "had always thought the men who went there a pack of duffers and was only trying them because he tried everything" (*PC*, 328). Revealing the ease with which one might pass as either a born criminal or a revolutionary, James presents his characters as curious examples of both predestination and self-creation, at once affirming and disavowing both positions as valid explanations for political crime.

Perhaps the only popular perception of anarchism that *The Princess Casamassima* rejects entirely is the Lombrosian notion of the anarchist as committing crimes of passion. If, for Lombroso, the anarchist was motivated by "the lively desire to feel pain and suffer," coupled with a "fanaticism … kindled by madness and hereditary neuropathy," then James's novel deflates such a position by representing anarchism as a bureaucratic system of inefficiency and deliberation.[57] In this way, Ross Posnock argues, James follows the historical record more closely than readers versed in popular stereotypes of the terrorist might expect, as he ridicules the idea of

anarchist passion as "not only one of Hyacinth's romantic clichés but a
virtual oxymoron" that ignores the fact that the anarchist movement
depended upon networks of newspapers, clubs, and smaller meetings in
order to organize political aspiration into a workable program for reform.[58]
James alludes to this situation in his depiction of a vast anarchist conspiracy
operating in secret across the continent, which promises Hyacinth a
method for pursuing his cause independent of Muniment and the Sun
and Moon. Drawn once again to the abstraction of conspiracy, which
replaces individual agents with a broader vision of collective purpose,
Hyacinth explains this revolutionary underworld as a reservoir of potential
political energy regulated by a steely, emotionless resolve:

> Nothing of it appears above the surface; but there is an immense under-
> world, peopled with a thousand forms of revolutionary passion and devo-
> tion. The manner in which it is organised is what astonished me ... In
> silence, in darkness, but under the feet of each one of us, the revolution lives
> and works. It is a wonderful, immeasurable trap, on the lid of which society
> performs its antics. When once the machinery is complete, there will be a
> great rehearsal. That rehearsal is what they want me for. The invisible,
> impalpable wires are everywhere, passing through everything, attaching
> themselves to objects in which one would never think of looking for
> them. (PC, 330)

This conception of a Continental anarchist subculture serves a crucial
function in James's characterization of revolutionary politics, as it demonstrates how little the ardency of radicalism accomplishes absent organizing
principles. This is a crowd that values forbearance over hotheadedness, as,
according to Posnock, revolutionary passion is "engulfed by the endless
labor of preparing a 'great rehearsal' for revolution."[59] Ironically, this
deliberateness makes the clandestine anarchist network just as ineffectual
a conspiracy as the loose talk of the Sun and Moon, since nothing is ever
truly accomplished amidst a perpetual series of preparations. Through an
"immense underworld" that initially appears lifted from the pages of
popular fiction, James paints anarchism not as aestheticized abstraction,
but as surprisingly reliant upon forms of bureaucracy that stifle political
passion, its measured rehearsals for violence disputing the notion of the
Lombrosian radical as a popular fantasy.

Popular fantasy is enduring, however, and by the end of the novel James
returns to the subject of born criminality, seemingly unable to abandon its
influence. When the Continental anarchist network convinces Hyacinth to
assassinate a high-ranking political official in order to instigate a series of
attacks that will begin the process of social and governmental upheaval,

Hyacinth is again forced to reckon with the relationship between his own wavering interest in the anarchist collective and the predisposition to violence that, if acted upon, would effectively make him an exemplary instance of the Lombrosian degenerate. On the one hand, Hyacinth dreads "the horror of the public reappearance ... of the imbrued hands of his mother" should he successfully complete his mission, and is unwilling to become a general criminal type in service of a cause that no longer appeals to his political instincts (*PC*, 582). On the other hand, however, the appearance of that dread indicates a palpable shift in the novel's treatment of born criminality. Rather than being pushed to commit a crime by ancestral influence, Hyacinth is now repelled by his family's legacy of bloodshed:

> the idea of the personal stain made him horribly sick; it seemed by itself to make service impossible. It rose before him like a kind of backward accusation of his mother; to suffer it to start out in the life of her son was in a manner to place her own forgotten, redeemed pollution again in the eye of the world. (*PC*, 582–583)

Here, James reverses the traditional conception of the born criminal by characterizing Hyacinth's "personal stain" as propelling him away from crime rather than toward it. In fact, Hyacinth claims that his birthright now makes his assassination mission "impossible," paradoxically invoking both the possibility of free will and the mandates of inherited criminality. In the end, Hyacinth opts to take action against himself rather than the target of the assassination plot, and chooses suicide as a means to escape the resurrection of his mother's crime within his own person. A rejection of one violent act in favor of another, Hyacinth's death calls attention to both the shaky theoretical foundations of inherited criminality and the impossible pressures of collective identification. Just as this suicide complicates the Lombrosian explanation for criminal behavior – it asserts an individual will that rejects the fatalism of inherited criminality – it also repudiates anarchism as a strangely severe ideology, indifferent to the lives of its members and unyielding in its pursuit of a collective ideal that ignores the harsher realities of individual experience.

In its combined view of political criminality as a fixed biological trait, a conscious response to economic exploitation, and a pleasurable immersion in abstract, collective experience, *The Princess Casamassima* hints at the modernism apparent in James's later writing, using its protagonist to articulate the subjective liminality that saturates modernist fiction. According to Omri Moses, James shares with Gertrude Stein and T. S.

Eliot a dialectic of contingency and structure in his approach to character, as his fictional personages "improvise their responses to circumstance by creating open-ended patterns that reverberate on and adjust to their milieu in so many different respects that any simple causal account of their own motivation or intention ... fails to describe its nature."[60] This fundamental blurring of the link between motivation and action is precisely what makes James's treatment of criminality so indicative of his modernism; echoing Lisa Rodensky's point that "[m]oving more fully into modern novels means handling characters overtly presented as fictions," *The Princess Casamassima* dramatizes how an individual like Hyacinth copes with the unrelenting set of circumstances intent on challenging his self-conception as a subject rooted in prior circumstances, now petrified into set traits.[61] Moreover, by staging multiple sides of the argument concerning the root cause of terror, James shirks any clear political or criminological position, and in the process dismisses as illusory the promise of all ideology, social or scientific, that claims exclusive knowledge of subjective or collective experience. James takes anarchism to task for its inability to advance a feasible program of reform while satirizing the novel's revolutionaries as a ramshackle collection of the bureaucratic and self-aggrandizing, all of whom are quick to proclaim the need for violent action yet powerless to bring it into being. He likewise undercuts the validity of inherited criminality, and makes Lombroso's theory of biological deviance appear both outlandish and outmoded in a social milieu dominated by a belief in upward mobility and the conscious overcoming of one's background. Thus, when considered in light of contemporary debates about the motives for political violence and the psychology of the criminal subject, *The Princess Casamassima* reflects the failure of any system of thought to encapsulate the experience of the individual as distinct from and related to that of the group, and frames such ideologies as grave impediments to self-knowledge. To define oneself as either an anarchist or a born criminal, James argues, is ultimately to align oneself with an inflexible ideology, and thereby reduce the particularities of individual experience to oppressively general categories.

Conrad's Accidental Anarchist

Like James before him, Joseph Conrad was also skeptical of revolutionary violence's political efficacy, and even dismissed outright the philosophy of propaganda by deed. In his 1920 author's note to *Under Western Eyes* (1911), Conrad characterizes the novel's Russian revolutionaries as wedded to a misguided, violent radicalism that invariably elicits an equally violent governmental response. He excoriates his characters for carrying out acts of "senseless desperation provoked by senseless tyranny," and laments that such terrorist acts have become de rigueur in modern Russia. "The most terrifying reflection," he claims,

> is that all these people are not the product of the exceptional but of the general – of the normality of their place, and time, and race. The ferocity and imbecility of an autocratic rule rejecting all legality and, in fact, basing itself upon complete moral anarchism provokes the no less imbecile and atrocious answer of a purely Utopian revolutionism encompassing destruction by the first means to hand, in the strange conviction that a fundamental change of hearts must follow the downfall of any given human institutions. These people are unable to see that all they can effect is merely a change of names.[62]

For Conrad, terrorism only replicates the repression it seeks to overcome, normalizing the unchecked use of force and thereby blurring distinctions between rulers and the ruled. Such political violence is not "exceptional" but "general," and reflects a pervasive condition of brutality that binds citizens and despots alike in a fitful but collective whole. This state of affairs reveals what Stephen Ross calls "the close continuity between bourgeois culture and its nihilistic flip side," as "the dominant culture's techniques of biopolitical production create the very subjects it ostensibly wants to eradicate."[63] With both the government and its detractors resembling versions of the same thing, Conrad suggests that "[u]topian revolutionism" is a practical impossibility, with even the most successful terrorist attacks producing superficial alterations of the political landscape – a "change of names" rather than a lasting ideological shift.

The skepticism that Conrad evinces in his note to *Under Western Eyes*, similar to James's reservations about anarchist aims and methods in *The Princess Casamassima*, has been well documented in contemporary criticism, most notably by Mark Wollaeger, who argues that, in this and in Conrad's earlier fiction, skepticism allows one to resist "the consolations afforded by sheltered retreats."[64] The belief that terrorism never yields real reform, then, reflects Conrad's greater critique of comfortable but facile ideological positions, pursued so single-mindedly that adherents ignore the complexities of the beliefs to which they submit. The political radicals of Conrad's fiction testify to this point, their absolutism insisting upon the essential rightness of their activities and the necessity of terrorism in a world dominated by oppressive state powers. In *Under Western Eyes*, Conrad offers us Victor Haldin, a young Russian revolutionary who assassinates a reviled Minister of State by throwing a bomb at him in the midst of an excited crowd. Haldin expresses no misgivings about his actions, and maintains to Razumov, a fellow university student and the novel's protagonist, that terrorism is what allows law-abiding citizens to enjoy their liberties in peace, and advances a spirit of progress in a society starved for political change. As he tells Razumov, "[y]ou suppose that I am a terrorist, now – a destructor of what is. But consider that the true destroyers are they who destroy the spirit of progress and truth, not the avengers who merely kill the bodies of persecutors of human dignity. Men like me are necessary to make room for self-contained, thinking men like you" (*UWE*, 16). By Haldin's logic, terrorism is not a passionate explosion of force or a nihilistic negation of authority, but a pragmatic attempt to avenge crimes against individual liberty that only harms "the bodies" of tyrannical bureaucrats in order for an abiding "spirit of progress and truth" to flourish. Though the speech preaches logic and practicality, its invocation of an abstract spirit of modernity ironizes Haldin's claims; though he paints himself as a levelheaded champion of autonomous intellectuals such as Razumov, his appeals to spirit reveal a romanticized notion of revolutionary violence not unlike Hyacinth's appreciation of the crowd as the avatar of a bloodless, aestheticized utopia of collectivity. By underlining the discrepancies in Haldin's confession, Conrad, like James, highlights the contradictions within the urge to political violence more generally.

Whereas Haldin professes a tidy view of anarchism as a vehicle for cultural advancement only to have his words betray his idealism, Conrad's other fiction displays its skepticism of political violence more pointedly, using numerous characters to make plain the rifts between anarchist ideology and actions committed in its service. For instance, the earlier short story, "An Anarchist," published in *Harper's Magazine* in August 1906 and included in the 1908 collection *A Set of Six*, questions the nature of an individual's attraction to political violence. In that story, a young Parisian engineer who flees his country after becoming enmeshed in its growing anarchist movement details his escape from St. Joseph's Island, where he had been imprisoned after the Parisian police discovered him carrying a bomb as part of a plot to rob a bank and then destroy the emptied building. Rather than sharing Haldin's faith in violence as ushering in a more equitable society, the engineer describes anarchism as a blatantly self-serving enterprise, complaining that even the most intelligent anarchists are "neither more nor less than housebreakers" who boast that they "robbed the rich" in order to "[get] back their own."[65] The story's narrator, however, never warms to the engineer's protestations against anarchism, not because he believes the equation of anarchism with greed to be false, but because, as he sees it, the engineer

> was much more of an anarchist than he confessed to me or to himself; and . . . the special features of his case apart, he was very much like many other anarchists. Warm heart and weak head – that is the word of the riddle; and it is a fact that the bitterest contradictions and the deadliest conflicts of the world are carried on in every individual breast capable of feeling and passion.[66]

Here Conrad figures anarchism as an outgrowth of emotionality, typical yet inconsistent. For the narrator, motives for political violence are inseparable from the avarice that compels certain individuals to theft, but they cannot be reduced to selfishness alone. Anarchism is, instead, a riddle – a contradictory set of passions rather than the conscious choice to advocate for a change in socioeconomic conditions. Anarchism results from affects more complex and less immediately recognizable than ideology, political affiliation, or support for a cause, and thus speaks more to a universal condition of psychological paradox endemic to "every individual breast capable of feeling and passion" than to a pathological selfishness characteristic of criminal types.

The tension Conrad posits between anarchism as an illogical outgrowth of passion and as an ideology that masks self-interest under the guise of politics crackles throughout *The Secret Agent* (1907), one of modernism's most celebrated renderings of political criminality. In that novel, however, social concerns over the shortcomings of anarchism as a philosophy and terrorism as a practice yield to an exposé of the individual passions and chance occurrences that stall the transformative potential of revolutionary violence and contest the cultural and scientific purchase of criminal typology. Depicting the planning of and eventual fallout from a failed bombing of the Royal Observatory in Greenwich,[67] the novel delivers a scathing indictment of anarchism, but in a way that reserves most of its fury for those who would characterize the terrorist according to static taxonomies of criminality. In characterizing both the terrorist's motives and the concept of criminal identity as ultimately illegible, subject more to the whims of chance than to the dictates of criminal anthropology or political ideology, *The Secret Agent* illustrates the abandonment of Victorian ideas of the born criminal in favor of increasing emphases on the inherent unpredictability of the criminal subject and the foundational role of chance in acts of terror.[68] Throughout Conrad's novel, the terrorist becomes so frightening precisely because of his opacity, as criminal motivation remains obscure and acts appear random, even to the criminal himself.

The Secret Agent describes a late nineteenth-century London struggling against the influence of increasingly outmoded but still visible social and scientific beliefs, among them the physiognomic determinism of Lombroso's criminal anthropology. As William Greenslade has persuasively demonstrated, this was familiar territory for Conrad's fiction. In *Heart of Darkness* (1899), he explains, Conrad "wanted to exploit positivist science, tactically, but then to face away from the reductive and limiting psychology which it posited," a dissonance that marks that work as a bridge between late nineteenth- and early twentieth-century fiction: "In so far as [Conrad] is post-Darwinian he conceptualises with the available discourses of determinism, but as he is a modernist he urges the claims of 'consciousness' against that determinism."[69] In *The Secret Agent*, by contrast, Conrad is far more skeptical of Lombrosian positivism than he was less than a decade earlier, and forcefully asserts the representational value of individual consciousness over the strictures of criminal anthropology. As two of the novel's anarchists, Karl Yundt and Ossipon, argue over the merits of biological criminality, their bitter denunciations strongly suggest that the born criminal is, or should be, a thing of the past. When Ossipon, an "ex-medical student without a degree; afterwards wandering lecturer to working-men's associations upon the socialistic aspects of hygiene," proclaims Stevie, the mentally disabled brother-in-law of Adolph Verloc, the eponymous secret agent, "very characteristic" and "perfectly typical" of criminal degeneracy, Yundt responds bluntly that "Lombroso is an ass."[70] Alluding to Lombroso's study of criminals' bodies while working as a prison physician, Yundt complains that the anthropologist's willful ignorance of injustice undermines his empirical certainty:

> Did you ever see such an idiot? For him the criminal is the prisoner. Simple, is it not? What about those who shut him up there – forced him in there? Exactly. Forced him in there. And what is crime? Does he know that, this imbecile who has made his way in this world of gorged fools by looking at the ears and teeth of a lot of poor, luckless devils? Teeth and ears mark the criminal? Do they? And what about the law that marks him still better – the pretty branding instrument invented by the overfed to protect themselves against the hungry? Red-hot applications on their vile skins – hey? Can't you smell and hear from here the thick hide of the people burn and sizzle? That's how criminals are made for your Lombrosos to write their silly stuff about. (*SA*, 35)

While Yundt's sympathies lie with those oppressed by their government, marked by the letter of the law and the strains of poverty rather than any physical stain of criminality, his criticisms of Lombroso are just as much a reflection of changing popular attitudes toward the born criminal as they are an extension of his political and ideological affiliations. While, as Stephen Kern argues, the late Victorian public was "eager to displace the etiology of crime from current social conditions to remote human or even animal ancestral origins over which modern society had no control and for which it bore no responsibility," Yundt's outburst exposes that effort as inexcusably superficial, and deliberately blind to the complexities of individual agency.[71] The seemingly rhetorical question of "what is crime?" thus reflects a historical exasperation with Lombroso and the positivist criminology he championed, fueled by a growing sense that the characterization of crime as the instinctual reflex of a predetermined few too conveniently avoids the substance of an individual's deeds – their relationship to internal motivation, legal institutions, and environmental pressures – to be accepted as an explanation for political crime.

In place of the certainties of criminal anthropology, *The Secret Agent* proposes a variable, multifaceted criminal subject whose actions respond to a combination of interior motivation and external circumstance, but in a manner that underscores the uncertainties of fictional representation. In this way, it reflects David Herman's argument about modernist narrative – namely, that in modernist fiction, "mental states have the character they do because of the world in which they arise, as a way of responding to possibilities (and exigencies) for acting afforded by that world" – but then complicates that perspective by blurring the connections among specific situations or stimuli, the mental states that correspond to them, and the actions that might appear to result.[72] Resisting any clear causal link between the body and the mind, the mind and the world, or the mind and the deed, Conrad's novel deliberately challenges readers to determine what does or doesn't motivate a criminal act. It makes its most provocative case through the character of Stevie, whose body and actions literalize the ubiquity of chance and the inscrutability of physical impressions, ironically juxtaposed with the persistent, unpersuasive invectives of Lombrosians such as Ossipon. Stevie's disability renders him an obvious candidate for Lombrosian analysis, but few of his actions align with criminal anthropology's central tenets, or, indeed, with any explicit cause or motive. Take the layers of "concentric, eccentric" circles that Stevie draws while Verloc hosts his anarchist coterie, "a coruscating whirl of circles that by their tangled multitude of repeated curves, uniformity of form, and confusion of intersecting lines suggested a rendering of cosmic chaos, the symbolism of a mad art attempting the inconceivable" (*SA*, 34). Though Stevie's circles are uniform in shape, their random repetition across the paper creates a flurry

of interweaving, haphazard figures, a "tangled multitude" whose place-
ment on the page depends upon Stevie's private whims, and whose very
existence testifies to an interiority that Lombrosian positivism would
appear to deny or dismiss as peripheral to the core biological fact of
Stevie's degeneracy. True to form, Ossipon chalks Stevie's actions up to
pathology, maintaining that "it's enough to glance at the lobes of his ears"
to peg Stevie as a criminal type (SA, 35). The connection between physiognomy and action is obviously strained here, with Ossipon failing to forge a
plausible link between the boy's appearance and his occupations. Indeed,
the "glance" that Ossipon deems sufficient proof of Stevie's born criminality is remarkably cavalier, as it denies the agency that the drawings suggest
in favor of a blanket assertion of criminality based solely upon physical
aberration. As a result, Ossipon's unconvincing diagnosis ironically affirms
the explanatory power of the random gesture – the act whose purpose
remains obscure but whose occurrence marks an individual consciousness
capable of carrying out its desires – as a vehicle for psychological rather
than physiognomic insight. Whereas for Ossipon Stevie's circles are less
useful than the material specifics of physical appearance in determining his
character, the rest of the narrative makes a sustained case for the "cosmic
chaos" of Stevie's gestures as an indication of how apparently random
action implies an ambiguous but nonetheless potent psychology.

   In acknowledging but never plumbing the depths of an unreadable
mind, this passage also equates the difficulty of ascribing criminality to
an individual with the limitations of narrative in registering subjectivity
more broadly, and so illustrates how Conrad's novel of anarchist terror is
also a distinctively modernist formal experiment. By emphasizing the
illegibility of consciousness, Stevie's circles rebuke both criminal anthropology's positivism and traditional strategies of psychological representation, situating the enigma of criminality within the larger formal problem
of communicating interior states and individual agency through narrative.
That problem is perhaps best exemplified in Stevie's unexpected and grisly
death early in the novel, an event to which various characters allude but
that Conrad never represents directly. As Adam Parkes observes, "a typical
Conrad tale works like an orchestrated sequence of increasingly powerful
detonations or shocks," and the fact that Stevie's demise in a botched
bombing attempt occurs offstage but reverberates through characters'
thoughts and actions in later chapters registers the recurring trauma of
dynamite violence for those who experience it.[73] At the same time, the
decision not to depict the explosion is not only a statement about the
event's unspeakable violence, but also an implicit critique of narrative's

limitations in representing Stevie's consciousness during a chance occurrence. Significantly, Stevie's death is accidental, and, ironically, the novel's only instance of terrorist violence. Ordered by his brother-in-law to bomb the Royal Observatory, Stevie bungles the mission – of which he presumably has a questionable understanding – tripping over a tree root and inadvertently detonating his explosive. When a police constable picks through Stevie's remains in order to reconstruct a narrative of the accident, he deems the event an unavoidable tragedy: "I stumbled once myself, and pitched on my head, too, while running up. Them roots do stick out all about the place. Stumbled against the root of a tree and fell, and that thing he was carrying must have gone off right under his chest, I expect" (*SA*, 66). By referencing his own uneasy footing at the scene, the constable views Stevie's accident, like any chance event, as something that could not have been foreseen yet in hindsight seemed so obviously bound to happen. Verloc is even more pragmatic when he explains the blast to his wife Winnie, Stevie's sister, as "a pure accident; as much an accident as if he had been run over by a 'bus while crossing the street" (*SA*, 188). In each description, the accident is beyond human agency – no one could have attempted or prevented it – and therefore ungoverned by psychological processes: Stevie had no opportunity to think about the event as it occurred, and he cannot narrate the event to make sense of it after the fact. In this way, the refusal to depict Stevie's death acknowledges narrative's inability to represent the collision of thought, agency, and chance. If, as Christopher GoGwilt argues, Stevie's death and subsequent absence refute the traditional "narrative principle of a developing consciousness," transforming a novel of political intrigue into an uncanny modernist subversion of the *bildungsroman*, they are also stern reminders of Conrad's skepticism toward the fictional depiction of interior states, and of his mounting interest in chance as negating the certainties of positivism and narrative alike.[74]

Stevie's death is also ironic in that it undermines the meticulous planning involved in the proposed attack, which, like other dynamite outrages, was meant to intimidate through its apparent spontaneity. Far from being Stevie's own idea, the Greenwich bombing plot is the brainchild of Vladimir, a Russian ambassador who demands that Verloc – who secretly shifts the assignment onto his brother-in-law – instigate a government crackdown on England's foreign-born anarchists through an act of violence so senseless as to send the country into an indiscriminate panic. Vladimir proposes a site of cultural rather than governmental significance in order to pigeonhole the anarchists as beyond reason, thinking that a

nationwide purge of a group now seen as uncontrollably violent could clear
the way for similar measures in Russia. Coolly attempting to balance the
level of material destruction caused by a terrorist bombing with its corresponding level of public response, Vladimir's decision to target Greenwich
reflects an understanding that terrorism becomes transformative only when
it appears to lack an apparent motive; if the British are increasingly
indifferent to political violence, then a successful attack must sever ties
with rationality in order to alert them to the menace of political radicalism.
As Vladimir argues, "what is one to say to an act of destructive ferocity so
absurd as to be incomprehensible, inexplicable, almost unthinkable; in
fact, mad? Madness alone is truly terrifying" (SA, 25). By this logic, the
most frightening criminal action is the crime that defies all logic, an
inexplicable show of catastrophic force that shatters the public's false
impression of criminality as an easily discerned and containable
phenomenon.

In this way, Vladimir's model of anarchist terrorism is designed to
eradicate the concept of the criminal type, or the born criminal whose
body betrays the identity of a dangerous individual, by invoking another,
increasingly popular generalization about criminal behavior. Instead of
concocting a plan that depends on Lombrosian notions of degeneracy –
political violence as pathology – Vladimir's proposed attack exploits the
developing popular impression of the anarchist as unencumbered by any
ideological agenda other than the enactment of mass violence. Assuming
that the mad bomber's unpredictability is the only way to rattle the public
out of their complacency regarding political crime, Vladimir trades one
stereotype for another. It is ironic, then, that Stevie – who never proclaims
himself an anarchist even though he, more than any other character in the
novel, "can't stand the notion of any cruelty" – is the one to wreck
Vladimir's plan, and thereby affirms the inevitable intrusion of randomness into the most carefully orchestrated ventures (SA, 45). Through this
lens of chance we see the novel's broader theory of criminality emerge – a
conception of criminal behavior based not on inherited pathologies and
physical disfigurement, but on the ubiquity of the random act of violence
which we both always and never see coming. The fatalism of Lombroso's
born criminal here gives way to that of the chance event, whether it is a
planned action whose purpose is to shock at the moment of its occurrence
and provoke anxiety afterward, or the truly random occurrence that
trumps all planning. This is why The Secret Agent ends so ominously,
tracing the movements of "the perfect anarchist" known only as "the
Professor" as he disappears into a crowd, ready to detonate the explosives

he keeps wired to his body should the desire strike him, "unsuspected and deadly, like a pest in the street full of men" (*SA*, 227). The Professor embodies Vladimir's faith in orchestrated outrage, as he boasts of his efforts to invent "a detonator that would adjust itself to all conditions of action, and even to unexpected changes of condition," and thereby contain chance in order to conduct a seamless bombing free of human error (*SA*, 50). Yet the fact that such a detonator does not exist only reinforces the suspicion that the Professor, menacing as he is, could trip over the very same obstacles that Stevie did, succumbing to chance and leaving his grand hopes for violence unrealized. Like the novel's other characters, the Professor reveals the folly of attempting to tame a chaotic, unpredictable modernity at the same time that he epitomizes the fractures in generalized criminal types (perfect anarchists and mad bombers) as explanatory rubrics for how and why violence comes to be.

For all its emphasis on chance, however, *The Secret Agent* occasionally invokes the principles of hereditary deviance, most obviously in the figure of Winnie, who murders her husband upon realizing that Stevie's death, though accidental, would never have occurred had Verloc not corralled the boy into assuming responsibility for the bomb that destroyed him. Conrad's account of the murder focuses on the weapon that initiates it, with the narrator observing that the knife that plunges into Verloc's chest "met no resistance" before drily remarking that "[h]azard has such accuracies" (*SA*, 193). This act of violence is oddly depersonalized and hence brutally efficient; the narrator shifts agency from the actor to the weapon, and the blade strikes Verloc at precisely the right moment, in the right place, without the interference of chance. Yet the narrator complicates the certainty of the event by characterizing Winnie's actions as the result of a deviant inheritance fed by popular anxieties of the day: "Into that plunging blow, delivered over the side of the couch, Mrs. Verloc had put all the inheritance of her immemorial and obscure descent, the simple ferocity of the age of caverns, and the unbalanced nervous fury of the age of bar-rooms" (*SA*, 193). Rather than a chance occurrence, Winnie's action reflects an eruption of born criminality strikingly akin to the Lombrosian systems of criminal classification ridiculed throughout the rest of the novel. Her "inheritance" makes itself known in spectacular fashion, and the "simple ferocity" of Winnie's action arises just as much from the "cavern" as it does from the neuroses of her contemporary "age of bar-rooms."

Why, then, does Conrad invoke Lombroso at the end of a novel that so thoroughly abuses him? The answer to this question lies in Conrad's treatment of subjectivity writ large, as he pivots from the issue of

criminality to larger themes of identity and its fragmentation. Rebecca
Walkowitz, in exploring the problem of national and cosmopolitan identities in *The Secret Agent*, argues that Conrad "resists, above all, the 'fact' of
identity," and "does not imagine more inclusive or more flexible paradigms
of belonging, but neither does he allow the old paradigm to function as it
did, invisibly and timelessly."[75] While Walkowitz emphasizes the issue of
"naturalness" in Conrad's novel – a character's ability to perform gestures
associated with a national identity or set of customs in order to assimilate
into a particular cultural or national context – her argument that
Conradian subjectivity never settles into a fixed position highlights the
competing modes of identification that make Conrad's characters so
difficult to pin down as either general "types" or discrete individuals. No
single aspect of Winnie's identity can fully account for Verloc's murder, as
Conrad characterizes her actions as simultaneously atavistic, responsive to
modern anxieties, and pure revenge. When Ossipon describes Winnie,
after the murder, as "a degenerate herself of a murdering type . . . or else of
the lying type," he identifies only one possible avenue for comprehending
Winnie's actions in a move that invokes Lombroso in the manner of "an
Italian peasant recommend[ing] himself to his favourite saint" (*SA*, 212,
217). At the same time, ignoring Conrad's atavistic allusion in describing
Winnie's actions would be equally mistaken, since that decision would
reflect a certainty that Conrad's text ultimately disputes. In killing her
husband, Winnie performs an action whose motivation is never made
entirely clear, save for the fact that it cannot be placed firmly within a
chain of causation.

Like Verloc's murder, the secret agent's physiognomy also refutes generalized notions of criminal subjectivity. While the remarkable bodies of
Conrad's anarchists seem to confirm their bearers as exemplary figures of
Lombrosian criminality, and thus to support a fixed conception of identity
rooted in inherited pathologies, Verloc's body proves more elusive, troubling the infallibility of those systems of classification.[76] Allan Hepburn
has argued that "espionage creates identities," and that the body of the
fictional spy reflects the fragmentation of an individual who must, of
necessity, remain divided in his or her loyalties.[77] Vladimir voices a related
idea when he complains that Verloc, like the anarchists with whom he
associates, is too physically unfit to carry out a successful terror campaign,
or to be taken seriously as a revolutionary. "You haven't got even the
physique of your profession," he says of Verloc's corpulence. "You – a
member of a starving proletariat – never!" (*SA*, 16). By pointing out the
conflict between Verloc's body and his performative radicalism, Vladimir

offers a conception of subjectivity based on the presupposition that an individual's physical appearance should align with conventional stereotypes – that is, an anarchist, as an embodiment of poverty, is always thin – so as to mirror that individual's mind. And yet Verloc's body does little to establish his position within London's anarchist community. Rather, Verloc's secret identity is successful due to an indefinable set of characteristics. Though he initially seems "[u]ndemonstrative and burly in a fat-pig style," and so "might have been anything from a picture-frame maker to a locksmith; an employer of labour in a small way,"

> there was also about him an indescribable air which no mechanic could have acquired in the practice of his handicraft however dishonestly exercised: the air common to men who live on the vices, the follies, or the baser fears of mankind; the air of moral nihilism common to keepers of gambling hells and disorderly houses; to private detectives and inquiry agents; to drink sellers and, I should say, to the sellers of invigorating electric belts and to the inventors of patent medicines. (*SA*, 10)

Here Conrad eschews Lombrosian atavism in favor of a system of identifications closer to that of Henry Mayhew, positioning Verloc's anarchist identity in terms of his resemblance to other individuals who labor in dubious professions. Verloc, in this passage, doesn't look like anything, but rather possesses an "indescribable air" that exceeds his physical appearance. He passes for a radical, then, not because of his looks, but because of a quality more intangible, and ultimately less available for scrutiny.

By the end of *The Secret Agent*, Conrad has left the state of criminal subjectivity in a curious double bind. Throughout the book, the significance of the physical body in expressing anything fundamental about the nature of identity or the motives of the criminal mind has been disavowed, yet the body also manages to signify in profound and startling ways. Verloc's anarchist cohorts are alternately fat and skeletal, and because both states reflect a physical inability to muster an act of political violence, they counter the Lombrosian paradigm of inherited criminality, as these anarchists never seem to commit any real crimes. Consequently, the idea of the terrorist as a general type undergoes a series of affirmations and denunciations, with Conrad presenting methods for understanding the criminal only to expose them as practically unsound. In the end, Conrad retains the ambiguity of criminality just as he leaves open the question of revolutionary violence's motives and effects, looking askance on any philosophical, criminological, or political system that denies its own idiosyncrasy.

The Pure Emblem of Terror

In contrast to *The Secret Agent*, G. K. Chesterton's "The Anarchist," a 1909 installment of his weekly opinion column for London's *Daily News*, offers a more comic view of political violence. The essay describes Chesterton's bizarre encounter with a man dressed entirely in black, who identifies himself as a committed anarchist. Despite the man's sinister appearance, he does not resemble Conrad's nihilistic Professor so much as a misanthropic academic who prefers to issue prolonged explanations of anarchism's ideological history rather than perform acts of propaganda by deed. Chesterton chides the anarchist for his "blinding rapidity of syllabification" and "rapid rattling mouth," observing that, through a fog of scholarly references and citations, the anarchist can only baffle those who might otherwise share his convictions, and discourage potential revolutionaries whose attraction to anarchism has little to do with its intellectual foundations.[78] When the anarchist complains of Chesterton's stereotypical conflation of anarchism and terrorism, arguing that not all anarchists can be reduced to dynamiters, Chesterton grows exasperated, lamenting that "it's the man with the bomb that I understand!"[79]

While Chesterton lampoons anarchism as a stiflingly academic movement, that characterization was by no means widely accepted at the time. Rather, the public perception of anarchism in 1909 remained focused, just as it was for James in the 1880s and Conrad only two years before, on the movement's affinity for violence, and its attempt to enact what Bakunin, in his 1873 treatise *Statism and Anarchy*, described as "the *anarchist* social revolution, which arises spontaneously within the people and destroys everything that opposes the broad flow of popular life."[80] Far from Chesterton's vision of an impotent ideology, Bakunin's description of anarchist revolution as spontaneous and overwhelming, emerging from an organic, collective passion that compels followers to acts of public destruction, held immense influence well into the twentieth century, and shaped much of the discourse surrounding anarchism as it traversed the continent. "Most of the anarchists were neither criminals nor advocates of violence," Haia Shpayer-Makov explains, but "it was precisely through this image that anarchism penetrated public consciousness and exerted its most noticeable impact on society."[81]

This is not to imply that Chesterton's view of anarchism was naïve. On multiple occasions his essay rails against the idea of anarchism as dusty pedantry, and takes the movement to task for its caution in approaching political change. While Chesterton claims not to understand the cerebral anarchist of his essay, he identifies with the "man with the bomb," whose anarchism proceeds from a visceral desire to eradicate the symbols of a repressive social order. Chesterton remarks early on in "The Anarchist" that the sight of London's mansions towering over crowds of indigent men becomes so distasteful that it inspires in him an unexpected compulsion to violence, illustrating how extreme economic disparity can push an otherwise sober individual to advocate an explosive dissolution of authority. Though he ultimately backs away from this stance, Chesterton acknowledges the appeal of anarchist violence when faced with the sight of oppression, admitting that "[i]f one of those huddled men under the trees had stood up and asked for rivers of blood, it would have been erroneous – but not irrelevant."[82]

Because of his propensity to argue both sides of a position – for instance, ridiculing anarchism as an ideology of inaction but labeling violent revolution as "erroneous" – Chesterton's general attitude toward anarchism is frustratingly opaque. His limited interest in anarchism as a serious political philosophy compounds the problem, as does his habit of basing his opinions more on anecdotal experience than on any concentrated study of anarchist literature. Graham Greene, an admirer of Chesterton, described the author's political acumen as virtually nonexistent, claiming that he was "too good a man for politics" and consequently unable to delve "far enough into the murky intricacies of political thought."[83] In addition to his political shortsightedness, Chesterton's satirical bent has prompted critics to dismiss texts like "The Anarchist" as epigrammatic moments of comedy rather than approaching them as salient points of critique. As Marshall McLuhan put it, Chesterton's paradoxes "tickled where they should have stung."[84]

Yet Chesterton's anarchist paradox really did carry a sting. His ambivalence toward anarchism mirrors that of James and Conrad, but his critique goes further by ironizing the anarchist's popular function as an abstraction through which anxieties about political radicalism, criminal motivation, and the seeming randomness of dynamite violence are expressed. Presenting the anarchist as an overdetermined symbol rather than an individual, Chesterton ridicules perceptions of "the anarchist" as a general concept devoid of interiority or psychological acumen, and therefore easily manipulated into serving the aims of multiple, even contradictory political positions. This is where the scholarly anarchist of the *Daily News* essay obtains his force – as a caricature whose humor derives from its not resembling a more prominent caricature. The fact that this figure appears in a newspaper column ironizes Chesterton's critique even further, in that by attending to the various manifestations and deployments of anarchist stereotypes, Chesterton satirizes a popular press responsible for their longevity while at the same time acknowledging the near impossibility of abandoning stereotype entirely. What emerges from this layered engagement with anarchism is an unexpectedly modernist Chesterton, who upends the conventional wisdom regarding political criminality through some of his most experimental writing. If, as Deaglán Ó Donghaile maintains, Chesterton "reads [anarchism's] revolutionary character both as a symptom of political modernity and as a generator of literary modernism," then the effects of that reading defy more traditional accounts of Chesterton as the self-proclaimed organ of popular English sensibility.[85] Given his stolid Catholicism, political conservatism, and longstanding equation of experimental aesthetics with cant and dissimulation, Chesterton is easy to characterize as an antimodernist, or, at the very least, as skeptical of modernism's defining features. Yet his work on anarchism weds an assertive political critique with an appreciably avant-garde aesthetic, and serves as an undeservedly neglected instance of modernism's response to political criminality.

The most celebrated of Chesterton's writings on anarchism is, not coincidentally, also his most modernist. His short, surreal novel, *The Man Who Was Thursday*, published the year before the anarchist essay appeared in the *Daily News*, offers a madcap vision of anarchism as at once a global conspiracy, a widespread fraud, and a mode of self-identification that invariably segues into existential estrangement. Its narrative centers on Gabriel Syme, a poet-turned-detective who infiltrates a secret society known as the Central Anarchist Council, whose members take their names from the days of the week. Initiated into the group as Thursday, Syme discovers that each of his fellow conspirators is, like himself, an undercover policeman attempting to sabotage the Council and thereby stop the spread of anarchism. The ruse is so complete that anarchists and detectives become versions of the same thing, and by the novel's end every character evinces a radical skepticism of his prior convictions in the fixity of good, evil, and subjectivity, uncertain of his political goals as well as his identity. Throughout, the novel undermines the model of the political criminal as a legitimate category of identification by asserting that a policeman's penchant for order and rationality mirrors the anarchist imperative to destroy, making notions of the anarchist criminal type a dangerous abstraction that only impedes the public's understanding of political violence.

Chesterton shrugged off some of the book's more radical implications in his *Autobiography* (1936), where he belittles his novel as an example of "groping and guesswork philosophy."[86] Yet *The Man Who Was Thursday* remains a significant modernist satire of criminal classification, which gleefully skewers any notion of the anarchist as either a stable subjective descriptor or a mode of identification that attends to the quirks of individual psychology. That satire pivots on a belief that art, terrorism, and the law arise out of similar habits of mind, apparent at the novel's outset when Lucian Gregory, an "anarchic poet" who invites Syme to his first anarchist meeting, characterizes artistic production and political crime as interchangeable:

> An artist is identical with an anarchist . . . The man who throws a bomb is an artist, because he prefers a great moment to everything. He sees how much more valuable is one burst of blazing light, one peal of perfect thunder, than the mere common bodies of a few shapeless policemen. An artist disregards all governments, abolishes all conventions.[87]

Just as Gregory claims that the poet and the anarchist share an appreciation for shock, the circumstances of Syme's initiation into the London police force complicate distinctions between terrorists and detectives. A dedicated but unsuccessful poet, Syme is recruited by a mysterious agent who explains that his devotion to his art makes him an ideal "philosophical policeman," an undercover detective who ferrets out anarchist terror plots through a systematic study, or close reading, of the movement's propaganda. As the recruiter explains, the work of the philosophical policeman is "to trace the origin of those dreadful thoughts that drive men on at last to intellectual fanaticism and intellectual crime . . . We say that the dangerous criminal is the educated criminal. We say that the most dangerous criminal now is the entirely lawless modern philosopher" (*MWWT*, 45). The novel's anarchists offer a similar assessment of their methods, comparing the work of dynamite to the destructive potential of the mind. As the Secretary of the Anarchist Council proclaims, "[d]ynamite is not only our best tool, but our best method. It is as perfect a symbol of us as is incense of the prayers of the Christians. It expands; it only destroys because it broadens; even so, thought only destroys because it broadens. A man's brain is a bomb" (*MWWT*, 64–65).

In presenting anarchism as the preferred ideology of the educated classes and the perfect representation of the destructive powers of thought, Chesterton probes one of the chief tensions within anarchist thought and practice at the turn of the century: the effort to realize a utopian vision of individual freedom through acts of mass violence. His novel does not simply suggest that anarchism forfeits its intellectual ideals by advocating material destruction, but instead links the philosophical goals of anarchism to the physically disruptive work of the bomb in order to assert that the two cannot exist independently. A brain is not *like* a bomb in *The Man Who Was Thursday*, but rather *is* a bomb, and the only limit to anarchist violence lies in the imaginations of those who commit it. From a historical perspective, the comparison is apt; as Robert Caserio explains, while "anarchism stands for a liberation of social order from single-minded determinations; for a generous break-up of the pieces of the whole into a productive decentered multiplicity of elements," and thus represents "the promise of an ever-metamorphic non-hierarchic social form," for the fulfillment of that promise "the famous propaganda of the deed – terrorism – came to seem indispensable."[88]

Ironically, the popular equation of anarchism and terrorism meant that, in the public estimation, anarchists pursued an "ever-metamorphic" social landscape but could themselves be understood in static terms, pigeonholed by their unwavering commitment to force. This is where the poignancy of Chesterton's satire begins to surface, as it undercuts popular notions of anarchism as a general category of identification by revealing how limited those notions actually are in classifying anarchists according to overly restrictive parameters of belief and behavior. For instance, the anarchists in *The Man Who Was Thursday* display a disciplined brand of fanaticism, propelled by violent ideas rather than the brute, unthinking passion that Lombroso defined as the primary impetus for political crime. More significantly, unlike those who call for universal equality or freedom from a tyrannical government, they work toward the annihilation of humanity, practicing a nihilistic form of terror with no political aim other than material and political erasure. As Syme's recruiter contends, "[w]hen [anarchists] say that mankind shall be free at last, they mean that mankind shall commit suicide. When they talk of a paradise without right or wrong, they mean the grave. They have but two objects, to destroy first humanity and then themselves" (*MWWT*, 47). Here Chesterton reveals in anarchism's philosophical underpinnings a compulsion to self-destruction, as adherents commit acts of terror in order to achieve a liberation that removes both aggressors and bystanders from the world.

On the one hand, the idea of anarchism as a form of nihilism was perfectly commensurate with the popular view of anarchist practice as senseless or chaotic, yet, on the other, Chesterton's reduction of anarchism to its basest and most terrifying caricature serves the more immediate purpose of exposing how ideologies are so often understood in terms of abstract ideals rather than the idiosyncrasies of their individual expression. Chesterton ironizes that process through the figure of the secret policeman, whose attempts to mimic the behavior of an anarchist are based largely on general understandings of political criminality, but whose own attraction to the law develops out of an individual passion strikingly akin to that of the revolutionary. Indeed, Syme's impetus for becoming a policeman is reactionary, as his "respectability was spontaneous and sudden, a rebellion against rebellion" (*MWWT*, 41). Growing up in a household of political and cultural radicals, Syme cultivates a fanatical affinity for order, unaware that he does so in precisely the same fashion as the anarchist who rails against the order of government. Describing himself as a "poet of respectability," Syme argues for the aesthetic and cultural force of logic (*MWWT*, 11). He contrasts his views with those of the anarchist-poet Gregory, claiming that "[t]he rare, strange thing is to hit the mark; the gross, obvious thing is to miss it. We feel it is epical when man with one wild arrow strikes a distant bird ... [T]ake your books of mere poetry and prose, let me read a time-table with tears of pride" (*MWWT*, 12–13). Though he argues on behalf of an exact and orderly world, Syme's tears betray the fervor with which he approaches his cause. For him, the pleasures of logic parallel the pleasures of aesthetics, and his status as a poet of respectability proves that the two can be combined. He appears soberly spontaneous, "subject to spasms of singular common sense, not otherwise a part of his character. They were ... poetic intuitions, and they sometimes rose to the exaltation of prophecy" (*MWWT*, 113). Overlooking the impulsiveness with which he embraces this aestheticized orderliness, Syme develops a passionate distaste for anarchism, which he perceives as an ugly and unthinking ideology. After witnessing a dynamite attack, Syme "did not regard anarchists, as most of us do, as a handful of morbid men, combining ignorance with intellectualism. He regarded them as a huge and pitiless peril, like a Chinese invasion" (*MWWT*, 42). Syme's paranoid conception of anarchism depends upon a fundamentally reactionary mode of thought, akin to the cultural anxiety concerning reverse colonization and Yellow Peril. To him, anarchism appears not only as a form of global conspiracy, but also as an abstract force rather than a collection of motivated individuals.[89] Syme bases his impressions of anarchism not on the material specifics of the bombing he

survived or on firsthand knowledge of those who identify themselves
with the movement, but on a generalized, metaphorical conception
of anarchism as a depersonalized threat.

This attitude permeates *The Man Who Was Thursday*, as Chesterton
depicts the anarchist movement as an abstract, ubiquitous secret society
rather than a scattered collection of "morbid men." As Evelyn Waugh
claimed, Chesterton employs this notion of an anarchist conspiracy not
only because it addresses a "conspiracy-mania which is latent in most of
us," but also because it emphasizes the "deep moral truth that men in
association are capable of wickedness from which each individually would
shrink."[90] By this logic, Chesterton's invocation of an anarchist conspiracy
echoes James's concerns regarding the insidious influence of the crowd, as
it reflects an anxiety concerning the destructive powers of collective
thought, and a suspicion, parallel to Le Bon's theory of crowd psychology,
that even rational individuals are swayed by the irrationality of the groups
to which they belong. These fears swell to comic proportions when all the
members of the Anarchist Council except for Sunday, the leader of the
group, reveal their official identities, and begin to concoct elaborate
narratives of Sunday's anarchist plot. Believing that Sunday has conspired
to isolate them in England while he travels to Paris to assassinate both the
Russian czar and the French president, Wednesday acknowledges the dim
prospects for intervention, because, as he suspects, Sunday has "bought
every trust . . . captured every cable, [and] has control of every railway line"
(*MWWT*, 123).

Such paranoia is not without merit, however, as the detectives understand that their most potent impressions of anarchism were obtained by
observing one another during their earlier Council meetings, and so they
have no empirical evidence of how an anarchist conspiracy operates.
Realizing that they have unwittingly created a fiction of anarchist practice,
the detectives now distrust their prior conceptions of both anarchism and
themselves. One, echoing Lombroso, laments the fact that because he
could never form a concrete impression of Sunday's identity based on
the defining features of his face, he now doubts the existence of faces
altogether. As he complains to Dr. Bull, formerly known as Saturday,
Sunday's inscrutable face has

> made me, somehow, doubt whether there are any faces. I don't know
> whether your face, Bull, is a face or a combination in perspective. Perhaps
> one black disc of your beastly glasses is quite close and another fifty miles
> away . . . My poor dear Bull, I do not believe that you really have a face. I
> have not faith enough to believe in matter. (*MWWT*, 168)

To pursue the logic of the conspiracy is to invite an existential crisis, turning one's brain into a bomb that shatters the stability of the subject.[91] According to Ó Donghaile, such radical indeterminacy shows how, "for Chesterton, true anarchy lies in its uncertainty: as the complexities and contradictions of modern and metropolitan existence radically alter the terms upon which subjective consciousness is experienced, they also shift experiential focus away from the norm of a stable British identity and re-orient the subject in the direction of a disrupted, decentred and profoundly fractured identity."[92] What the anarchist conspiracy achieves in Chesterton's novel is not the dissolution of the state – or, for that matter, of the world – but rather the dissolution of the self. In imagining the conspiracy's infinite reach, the detectives' minds succumb to the anarchist's bomb, their stereotypical perceptions of a general anarchist threat overwhelming their autonomy.

Such radical critique represents Chesterton's most nuanced criticism of anarchism, and of the patterns of abstract thought it engenders. When he reveals that Sunday is not only the leader of the global anarchist conspiracy but also the mysterious policeman who hired the detectives who constitute the Anarchist Council, Chesterton shows how law-abiding individuals fall prey to suspicion, paranoia, and fanaticism when placed within a group of like-minded reactionaries. His most troubling suggestion is not the prospect of a global anarchist revolution, or even the idea that thinking, writing, and bombing amount to roughly the same thing. Rather, *The Man Who Was Thursday*'s most nightmarish argument is that human behavior, however deliberate it may appear, is both profoundly impulsive and entirely susceptible to suggestion.[93] Thus, for Chesterton, the problem of anarchism is also the problem of the crowd, or what Le Bon described as the condition in which "the heterogeneous is swamped by the homogeneous."[94] Chesterton makes an identical point near the novel's end, where he depicts a mob of townspeople who pursue the Anarchist Council's detectives under Sunday's influence. Looking upon the crowd as it charges toward him, Syme characterizes the group as a single-minded entity:

> He could see them as separate human figures; but he was increasingly surprised by the way in which they moved as one man. They seemed ... like any common crowd out of the streets; but they did not spread and sprawl and trail by various lines to the attack, as would be natural in an ordinary mob. They moved with a sort of dreadful and wicked woodenness, like a staring army of automatons. (*MWWT*, 130)

Unlike the isolated philosopher of "The Anarchist," who appears more laughable than threatening, this "army" represents an aggressive conflagration of human impulse, blindly obeying another's commands. This tendency to align oneself with the movements and mindset of the crowd was, for Chesterton, the most unsettling aspect of anarchism, which terrifies not through acts of violence, but through the virulent habits of mind that allow violence to occur, and that allow outside observers to pigeonhole it as the exclusive provenance of abstract, even inhuman, entities.

Yet if Chesterton's problem with the crowd lies in its habit of generalizing the individual, replacing subjective agency with a leveling collectivity, then his generalized portrayal of the anarchist presents an important contradiction. Indeed, Chesterton depicts anarchists not as distinct individuals, but as embodiments of revolutionary sentiment. As Deak Nabers notes, subjectivity in the novel "is defined in terms of standardization, not a resistance to it," as characters identify themselves by their respective abilities to fit into a crowd.[95] Consequently, Chesterton avoids mentioning specific brands of anarchism, and instead offers an impression of the anarchist as a general symbol of modern violence, and as a general type of criminal. His characters thus exemplify and play upon Sarah Cole's contention that "the person of the anarchist bomber was typically figured in stylized terms – a repository, we might say, for a certain literary zeal."[96]

Partly, this generalization of anarchism is due to Chesterton's lack of interest in the particulars of anarchist thought and his profound interest in "literary zeal." Though he devoted his later years to the promotion of distributism, believing that England would thrive under an economic system under which property is parceled out equally among all individuals, Chesterton's study of anarchism as a political philosophy was remarkably shallow.[97] This fact is all the more surprising since, as Heather Worthington points out, "Chesterton's own concept of the perfect society was, in the positive sense, anarchical: one in which government is unnecessary, where individuals would deal fairly and rationally with each other without recourse to a system of imposed laws."[98] However, Chesterton's politics were "anarchical" in the sense that distributism remained suspicious of government intervention into property, but not in the same way as French anarchist Pierre-Joseph Proudhon's famous claim that "property is theft."[99] Instead, Chesterton's perfect society was more attuned to the promise of collective well-being than to individual liberty, as distributism aspired to a faintly socialist system wherein the means of production are equally disbursed among the people, leading to mutual cooperation among smaller communities. It also rebuffed conventional political categories; as Chesterton explained in a 1908 editorial for *The New Age*, while he possesses "a great tenderness for revolution," he "stand[s] outside the movement commonly called Socialism."[100] Resistant to characterizing distributism in traditional terms, Chesterton shirked common markers of political ideology in favor of an opaque system of national collectivity.

For all his devotion to a politics of equality that refused tidy categorization, Chesterton showed little concern for anarchism's efforts toward the same goal. His fictional treatment of anarchism as an abstract form of terrorism reflects his antipathy to ideological and historical nuance, yet in *The Man Who Was Thursday* he satirizes impressions of anarchism derived from the sensationalistic accounts of riots, demonstrations, and acts of terror found in the popular press, as when Lucian Gregory complains that people "learn about anarchists from sixpenny novels; they learn about anarchists from tradesmen's newspapers; they learn about anarchists from *Ally Sloper's Half-Holiday* and the *Sporting Times*" (*MWWT*, 33). Here Chesterton takes aim at himself, a prominent journalist and comedic editorialist who cannot see beyond the stereotype of the dynamite fiend to ascertain the individual motives for political violence. Aligning the practice of journalism with sensationalism, Chesterton acknowledges his role as a proprietor of generalized accounts of the anarchist movement, making a joke that is no less pointed for its humor. Instead of providing a more accurate depiction of anarchism's ideological foundations, Chesterton populates his novel with the caricatures of anarchism featured in mass-market publications of the day, alluding to his own complicity in perpetuating anarchist stereotypes while reifying those stereotypes at every turn.

Though Chesterton exposes himself to critique by pointing out the origins of his anarchists within the popular press, his novel advances the more unorthodox claim that anarchists are also responsible for their own generalization, as both the anarchists and the undercover detectives conceive of themselves in deliberately abstract terms. When Professor de Worms, also known as Friday, explains the success of his anarchist disguise, he characterizes himself as both an artist and a work of art: "I am a portrait painter. But, indeed, to say that I am a portrait painter is an inadequate expression. I am a portrait" (*MWWT*, 89). Referring to an extensive make-up job that rendered him a frail old man, de Worms also gestures toward a larger argument – that he exists wholly as the representation of an idea. His statement echoes those of other characters in the novel, most notably Syme, who, to bolster his chances at being elected to the Central Anarchist Council, proclaims "I am not a man at all. I am a cause" (*MWWT*, 36). By casting himself as the most blood-thirsty anarchist in Europe, claiming that he does not "go to the Council to rebut that slander that calls us murderers" but rather goes "to earn it," Syme knowingly embodies a general type of criminal, a vicious and unscrupulous avatar who lends credibility to stereotypes of anarchist terror (*MWWT*, 36). In other words, Syme becomes a living stereotype, devoid of individual, material characteristics and existing purely as ideology.

Ironically, the idea of the anarchist as a pure emblem of terror makes little impression on public consciousness in the world of the novel. Echoing the sentiments of Vladimir in *The Secret Agent*, who complains that the English take a blasé approach to terrorism, Chesterton's anarchists are undermined by public apathy toward their mission of radical change. Sunday, however, argues that such low expectations create opportunities for propaganda and violence. When Gregory, despairing after multiple arrests for anarchist agitation, asks Sunday what disguise will allow him to propagandize and remain free from police interference, the reply is simple: "You want a dress which will guarantee you harmless; a dress in which no one would ever look for a bomb? . . . Why, then, dress up as an *anarchist*, you fool! . . . Nobody will ever expect you to do anything dangerous then" (*MWWT*, 25). As Sunday argues, the stereotype of the anarchist is twofold; while the anarchist is traditionally figured as a tireless zealot, there also exists a competing perception of the anarchist as fundamentally lazy, unable to enact plans for political upheaval. In simultaneously characterizing the anarchist as deadly and ineffectual, violent and complacent, Chesterton highlights the manner in which stereotypes work against one another, and suggests that anarchism, in attempting to live up to a general standard of criminality, loses any claim it might have to effecting political change. Just as individual anarchists lose themselves to the sway of the collective, they also abandon their political agency by hewing to an overly general conception of revolutionary politics. As in James, these anarchists become ideas, unable to bring themselves to material fruition.

With this fluctuation of stereotypes in mind, one wonders why Chesterton continues to depict the anarchist as a general symbol of terror throughout the novel. One possible explanation lies in his autobiography, in a passage that voices larger concerns about the aesthetics of violence in fiction compared to its realization in practice. Describing his Father Brown mysteries, Chesterton distinguishes between fictional and actual crime:

> Some time ago . . . I calculated that I must have committed at least fifty-three murders, and been concerned with hiding about half a hundred corpses for the purpose of the concealment of crimes; hanging one corpse

on a hat-peg, bundling another into a postman's bag, decapitating a third and providing it with somebody else's head, and so on through quite a large number of innocent artifices of the kind. It is true that I have enacted most of these atrocities on paper; and I strongly recommend the young student, except in extreme cases, to give expression to his criminal impulses in this form; and not run the risk of spoiling a beautiful and well-proportioned idea by bringing it down to the plane of brute material experiment, where it too often suffers the unforeseen imperfections and disappointments of this fallen world.[101]

Though comic in tone, Chesterton's remarks on the "beautiful and well-proportioned idea" of violence debased by "brute material experiment" hint at a larger, not exclusively literary proposition: violence, in theory, can be a positive thing, but only "disappoints" in practice. Here Chesterton denounces physical violence not as a matter of ethics, but of aesthetics. If violence cannot be committed without suffering "imperfections and disappointments" when transferred from thought to fact, then it should never leave the realm of ideas in the first place. By this formulation, Chesterton's anarchists are most effective when they represent in aesthetic terms the abstract notion of violence, and fail to persuade when they attempt to act upon their convictions. Here again anarchism serves as another form of crowd behavior, since, like the crowd, the anarchist becomes an aesthetic object that persuades only when it makes a spectacle of itself. Anarchism may be a general concept, Chesterton argues, but like James and Conrad before him, he admits that it remains powerful in its abstraction, and uncomfortably attractive in its aesthetics.

Notes

1. Michael Bakunin, *Statism and Anarchy*, trans. and ed. Marshall S. Shatz (Cambridge: Cambridge University Press, 1994), 133.
2. Daniel Pick, *Faces of Degeneration: A European Disorder, c.1848–c.1918* (Cambridge: Cambridge University Press, 1989), 120.
3. Paul Topinard, quoted in Stephen Jay Gould, *The Mismeasure of Man*, revised edition. (New York: W. W. Norton, 1996), 164.
4. For overviews of Lombroso's career, see Mary Gibson, *Born to Crime: Cesare Lombroso and the Origins of Biological Criminology* (Westport: Praeger, 2002), 19–30; and David G. Horn, *The Criminal Body: Lombroso and the Anatomy of Deviance* (New York: Routledge, 2003).
5. On degeneration's literary history, see William P. Greenslade, *Degeneration, Culture and the Novel, 1880–1940* (Cambridge: Cambridge University Press, 1994).

6. Cesare Lombroso, *Criminal Man*, trans. Mary Gibson and Nicole Hahn Rafter (Durham: Duke University Press, 2006), 53.

7. Ibid., 43.

8. Mary Gibson and Nicole Hahn Rafter, editors' introduction to Lombroso, *Criminal Man*, 3.

9. Nicole Rafter, *The Criminal Brain: Understanding Biological Theories of Crime* (New York: New York University Press, 2008), 86.

10. Nicole Hahn Rafter, *Creating Born Criminals* (Urbana: University of Illinois Press, 1997), 113.

11. Pick, *Faces of Degeneration*, 116.

12. See Henry Mayhew, *London Labour and the London Poor*, vol. IV (New York: Dover, 1968), 23–27.

13. David Taylor, "Beyond the Bounds of Respectable Society: The 'Dangerous Classes' in Victorian and Edwardian England," *Criminal Conversations: Victorian Crimes, Social Panic, and Moral Outrage*, ed. Judith Rowbotham and Kim Stevenson (Columbus: Ohio State University Press, 2005), 8.

14. Martin J. Wiener, *Reconstructing the Criminal: Culture, Law, and Policy in England, 1830–1914* (Cambridge: Cambridge University Press, 1990), 229.

15. Greenslade, *Degeneration, Culture and the Novel*, 88.

16. Kevin Bell, *Ashes Taken for Fire: Aesthetic Modernism and the Critique of Identity* (Minneapolis: University of Minnesota Press, 2007), 3, 4.

17. Sarah Cole, *At the Violet Hour: Modernism and Violence in England and Ireland* (Oxford: Oxford University Press, 2012), 84.

18. Ibid., 94.

19. Michael Levenson, *Modernism and the Fate of Individuality: Character and Novelistic Form from Conrad to Woolf* (Cambridge: Cambridge University Press, 1991), 31.

20. Among the most prominent assassinations: Russian emperor Alexander II was killed by bombs thrown into his carriage (March 1881); failed politician Charles J. Guiteau shot American president James Garfield (July 1881); Lord Frederick Charles Cavendish, England's chief secretary for Ireland, was stabbed in Phoenix Park (May 1882); Italian anarchist Sante Geronimo Caserio stabbed Sadi Carnot, the President of France (June 1894); Italian anarchist Luigi Lucheni murdered Empress Elizabeth of Austria (September 1898); American anarchist Gaetano Bresci shot Umberto I, King of Italy (July 1900); American president William McKinley was shot by Polish–American anarchist Leon Czolgosz (September 1901); and the assassination of Austria's Archduke Francis Ferdinand and his wife, Countess Sophie Chotek (June 1914), culminated in the First World War.

21. Paul Avrich, *The Haymarket Tragedy* (Princeton: Princeton University Press, 1984), 215, 216, 217.

22. Richard Bach Jensen, *The Battle against Anarchist Terrorism: An International History, 1878–1934* (Cambridge: Cambridge University Press, 2014), 52.

23. Ibid., 52.

24. On the Fenian dynamite campaign of the 1880s, see Niall Whelehan, *The Dynamiters: Irish Nationalism and Political Violence in the Wider World, 1867–1900* (Cambridge: Cambridge University Press, 2012).

25. Deaglán Ó Donghaile, *Blasted Literature: Victorian Political Fiction and the Shock of Modernism* (Edinburgh: Edinburgh University Press, 2011), 97.

26. Richard D. Sonn, *Anarchism* (New York: Twayne, 1992), 50.

27. Jeffory A. Clymer, *America's Culture of Terrorism: Violence, Capitalism, and the Written Word* (Chapel Hill: University of North Carolina Press, 2003), 71.

28. Ibid., 71.

29. Alex Houen, *Terrorism and Modern Literature, from Joseph Conrad to Ciaran Carson* (New York: Oxford University Press, 2002), 25.

30. On the relationship between modernism and anarchism, see Allan Antliff, *Anarchist Modernism: Art, Politics, and the First American Avant-Garde* (Chicago: University of Chicago Press, 2001); Cole, *At the Violet Hour,* 83–129; David Kadlec, *Mosaic Modernism: Anarchism, Pragmatism, Culture* (Baltimore: Johns Hopkins University Press, 2000); Arthur Redding, *Raids on Human Consciousness: Writing, Anarchism, and Violence* (Columbia: University of South Carolina Press, 1998); Marilyn Reizbaum, "Yiddish Modernisms: Red Emma Goldman," *Modern Fiction Studies* 51.2 (Summer 2005): 456–481; and David Weir, *Anarchy and Culture: The Aesthetic Politics of Modernism* (Amherst: University of Massachusetts Press, 1997).

31. Paul Sheehan, *Modernism and the Aesthetics of Violence* (Cambridge: Cambridge University Press, 2013), 2.

32. On British anarchism during the period, see Matthew Thomas, *Anarchist Ideas and Counter-Cultures in Britain, 1880–1914: Revolutions in Everyday Life* (Aldershot: Ashgate, 2005).

33. W. M. Phillips, *Nightmares of Anarchy: Language and Cultural Change, 1870–1914* (Lewisburg: Bucknell University Press, 2003), 15.

34. Mikhail Bakunin, quoted in Paul Avrich, *Anarchist Portraits* (Princeton: Princeton University Press, 1988), 6.

35. Cole, *At the Violet Hour,* 84.

36. George Woodcock, *Anarchism: A History of Libertarian Ideas and Movements* (Peterborough: Broadview, 2004), 11.

37. Pick, *Faces of Degeneration,* 131.

38. Lombroso, *Criminal Man,* 313.

39. Ibid., 313.

40. Ibid., 314.

41. Henry James, *Letters,* vol. II, 1875–1883, ed. Leon Edel (Cambridge, MA: Harvard University Press, 1975), 334.

42. Ibid., 334.

43. Ibid., 334.

44. On the novel's relationship to English politics, see Christine DeVine, *Class in Turn-of-the-Century Novels of Gissing, James, Hardy and Wells* (Aldershot: Ashgate, 2005), 47–75, and Margaret Scanlan, "Terrorism and the Realistic Novel: Henry James and *The Princess Casamassima,*" *Texas Studies in*

Literature and Language 34.3 (Fall 1992): 380–402. For an influential Foucauldian reading of the novel, see Mark Seltzer's *Henry James and the Art of Power* (Ithaca: Cornell University Press, 1984), 25–58.

45. Barbara Arnett Melchiori, *Terrorism in the Late Victorian Novel* (London: Croom Helm, 1985), 12–18.
46. Roy Porter, *London: A Social History* (Cambridge, MA: Harvard University Press, 2001), 253.
47. On nineteenth- and twentieth-century literature's fascination with the crowd, see *Crowds*, ed. Jeffrey T. Schnapp and Matthew Tiews (Stanford: Stanford University Press, 2006); John Plotz, *The Crowd: British Literature and Public Politics* (Berkeley: University of California Press, 2000); and Michael Tratner, *Modernism and Mass Politics: Joyce, Woolf, Eliot, Yeats* (Stanford: Stanford University Press, 1995).
48. Lionel Trilling, "The Princess Casamassima," *The Moral Obligation to Be Intelligent: Selected Essays*, ed. Leon Wieseltier (New York: Farrar, Straus, Giroux, 2000), 150.
49. Mary Esteve, *The Aesthetics and Politics of the Crowd in American Literature* (Cambridge: Cambridge University Press, 2003), 62.
50. Gustave Le Bon, *The Crowd: A Study of the Popular Mind* (Mineola: Dover, 2002), 2, 4.
51. Ibid., xi.
52. Ibid., 8.
53. Henry James, *The Princess Casamassima* (London: Penguin, 1987), 33. Hereafter cited parenthetically, as *PC*.
54. Amanda Claybaugh, *The Novel of Purpose: Literature and Social Reform in the Anglo-American World* (Ithaca: Cornell University Press, 2007), 148.
55. Elizabeth Carolyn Miller, *Framed: The New Woman Criminal in British Culture at the Fin de Siècle* (Ann Arbor: University of Michigan Press, 2008), 156.
56. Cole, *At the Violet Hour*, 84.
57. Lombroso, *Criminal Man*, 314, 315.
58. Ross Posnock, *The Trial of Curiosity: Henry James, William James, and the Challenge of Modernity* (New York: Oxford University Press, 1991), 270.
59. Ibid., 271.
60. Omri Moses, *Out of Character: Modernism, Vitalism, Psychic Life* (Stanford: Stanford University Press, 2014), 36.
61. Lisa Rodensky, *The Crime in Mind: Criminal Responsibility and the Victorian Novel* (Oxford: Oxford University Press, 2003), 216.
62. Joseph Conrad, *Under Western Eyes* (London: Penguin, 2002), lxxxv. Hereafter cited parenthetically, as *UWE*.
63. Stephen Ross, *Conrad and Empire* (Columbia: University of Missouri Press, 2004), 150.
64. Mark A. Wollaeger, *Joseph Conrad and the Fictions of Skepticism* (Stanford: Stanford University Press, 1990), 170.
65. Joseph Conrad, "An Anarchist," *A Set of Six* (Garden City: Doubleday, Page, and Co., 1925), 149.

66. Ibid., 161.
67. The novel is loosely based on actual events. On February 15, 1894, French anarchist Martial Bourdin accidentally detonated a bomb near the Observatory and died from his wounds shortly thereafter. For connections to Conrad's novel, see Norman Sherry, *Conrad's Western World* (Cambridge: Cambridge University Press, 1971), and Ian Watt, "The Political and Social Background of *The Secret Agent*," *Essays on Conrad* (Cambridge: Cambridge University Press, 2000), 112–126.
68. On Conrad and chance, see Leland Monk, *Standard Deviations: Chance and the Modern British Novel* (Stanford: Stanford University Press, 1993), 75–109.
69. Greenslade, *Degeneration, Culture and the Novel*, 113.
70. Joseph Conrad, *The Secret Agent* (New York: Oxford University Press, 2004), 34–35. Hereafter cited parenthetically, as *SA*.
71. Stephen Kern, *A Cultural History of Causality: Science, Murder Novels, and Systems of Thought* (Princeton: Princeton University Press, 2004), 33.
72. David Herman, "1880–1945: Re-minding Modernism," *The Emergence of Mind: Representations of Consciousness in Narrative Discourse in English*, ed. David Herman (Lincoln: University of Nebraska Press, 2011), 253.
73. Adam Parkes, *A Sense of Shock: The Impact of Impressionism on Modern British and Irish Writing* (Oxford: Oxford University Press, 2011), 100.
74. Christopher GoGwilt, *The Fiction of Geopolitics: Afterimages of Culture, from Wilkie Collins to Alfred Hitchcock* (Stanford: Stanford University Press, 2000), 177.
75. Rebecca L. Walkowitz, *Cosmopolitan Style: Modernism Beyond the Nation* (New York: Columbia University Press, 2007), 37.
76. On anarchists' bodies in Conrad's political satire, see James F. English, "Anarchy in the Flesh: Conrad's 'Counterrevolutionary' Modernism and the *Witz* of the Political Unconscious," *Modern Fiction Studies* 38.3 (Autumn 1992): 615–630.
77. Allan Hepburn, *Intrigue: Espionage and Culture* (New Haven: Yale University Press, 2005), xiii.
78. G. K. Chesterton, "The Anarchist," *Alarms and Discursions* (London: Methuen, 1924), 76–77.
79. Ibid., 77.
80. Bakunin, *Statism and Anarchy*, 133.
81. Haia Shpayer-Makov, "Anarchism in British Public Opinion 1880–1914," *Victorian Studies* 31.4 (Summer 1988): 487.
82. Chesterton, "The Anarchist," 75.
83. Graham Greene, "G. K. Chesterton," *G. K. Chesterton: A Half Century of Views*, ed. D. J. Conlon (Oxford: Oxford University Press, 1987), 59.
84. Herbert Marshall McLuhan, introduction to Hugh Kenner, *Paradox in Chesterton* (New York: Sheed and Ward, 1947), 4.
85. Ó Donghaile, *Blasted Literature*, 104.
86. G. K. Chesterton, *The Collected Works of G. K. Chesterton*, vol. 16, ed. George J. Marlin et al. (San Francisco: Ignatius Press, 1988), 105.
87. G. K. Chesterton, *The Man Who Was Thursday: A Nightmare* (London: Penguin, 1986), 12. Hereafter cited parenthetically, as *MWWT*.

88. Robert L. Caserio, "G. K. Chesterton and the Terrorist God outside Modernism," *Outside Modernism: In Pursuit of the English Novel, 1900–30*, ed. Lynne Hapgood and Nancy L. Paxton (New York: St. Martin's, 2000), 71.

89. On conspiracy in Chesterton and others, see Adrian S. Wisnicki, *Conspiracy, Revolution, and Terrorism from Victorian Fiction to the Modern Novel* (New York: Routledge, 2008).

90. Evelyn Waugh, "The Man Who Was Thursday," *G. K. Chesterton: A Half Century of Views*, ed. D. J. Conlon (Oxford: Oxford University Press, 1987), 73.

91. Notably, such radical skepticism also affirms the novel's modernism. That affirmation can appear ironic, given the book's earlier account of Impressionism as "another name for that final scepticism which can find no floor to the universe" (*MWWT*, 127), yet the satire of *The Man Who Was Thursday* strongly indicates that such skepticism models a useful critique of commonsense notions of anarchism and the political criminal.

92. Ó Donghaile, *Blasted Literature*, 107.

93. Ironically, a common critique of Chesterton was that his popularity made him overly enamored with the crowd. In a 1917 letter to John Quinn, Ezra Pound complained that "Chesterton *is* so much the mob, so much the multitude." *The Letters of Ezra Pound, 1907–1941*, ed. D. D. Paige (New York: Harcourt, Brace, 1950), 116.

94. Le Bon, *The Crowd*, 6.

95. Deak Nabers, "Spies Like Us: John Buchan and the Great War Spy Craze," *Journal of Colonialism and Colonial History* 2.1 (Spring 2001): par. 16.

96. Cole, *At the Violet Hour*, 94.

97. On Chesterton's promotion of distributism in *G. K.'s Weekly*, the magazine he edited from 1925 until his death, see Michael Coren, *Gilbert: The Man Who Was G. K. Chesterton* (London: Jonathan Cape, 1989), 234–239.

98. Heather Worthington, "Identifying Anarchy in G. K. Chesterton's *The Man Who Was Thursday*," *"To Hell with Culture": Anarchism and Twentieth-Century British Literature*, ed. H. Gustav Klaus and Stephen Knight (Cardiff: University of Wales Press, 2005), 22.

99. Proudhon advances this claim in *What Is Property?: An Inquiry into the Principle of Right and of Government* (1840).

100. G. K. Chesterton, "Why I Am Not a Socialist," *The New Age* 2.10 (January 4, 1908): 189.

101. Chesterton, *The Collected Works of G. K. Chesterton*, 312.

CHAPTER 3

The Modernist Crime Novel
Popular Literature and the Forms of Experiment

> "All the same," said Elinor after a long silence, "I wish one day you'd write a simple straightforward story about a young man and a young woman who fall in love and get married and have difficulties, but get over them, and finally settle down."
> "Or why not a detective novel?" He laughed. But if, he reflected, he didn't write that kind of story, perhaps it was because he couldn't. In art there are simplicities more difficult than the most serried complications.
> — Aldous Huxley, *Point Counter Point* (1928)[1]

As I have argued in the preceding chapters, starting in the late nineteenth century a significant number of British and American authors began paying sustained attention to the representation of the criminal, and tested multiple forms through which the medium of fiction might account for, explain, or at least illuminate the connections between individual motivation and acts of crime. Necessarily, these experiments produced a range of effects. While detective novelists such as Sayers reinvigorated the formal and thematic devices of their genre by combining them with social, philosophical, and aesthetic concerns traditionally classified as modernist, authors like James, Conrad, and Chesterton turned a skeptical eye toward subjects such as criminal anthropology and anarchist terrorism in their efforts to understand the individual causes of criminality and the corresponding pressure to credit them to social or biological forces. Other modernists went even further in probing the vagaries of the criminal mind by trying their hands at the genre of crime and detective fiction, composing texts that not only took seriously the problem of criminal representation, but also aimed to appeal to popular audiences and thereby subsidize other projects with less potential for commercial success.[2] These works did not simply adapt discrete elements of genre fiction to more "serious" enterprises; rather, they were immersed in the generic mandates of crime fiction, combining an avant-garde spirit of aesthetic invention with a refusal to

123

dismiss the categorical boundaries of genre as necessarily antithetical to modernism.

Writers who pursued this challenge knew well that any venture into the crime genre carried with it a sizeable risk to one's reputation, since to categorize oneself as both a serious author and a crime novelist has always been a fraught and professionally uncertain business. Critics tend to dismiss as mere diversions the generic efforts of established authors, ascribing their desire to write crime fiction to an uncomplicated interest in formal constraint, while genre writers who attempt more "literary" fare are often pigeonholed as unsophisticated sensationalists whose ambitions exceed their abilities. Such perceptions operated in full force during the early decades of the twentieth century, when many writers with loftier literary aspirations opted to publish their genre pieces under a pseudonym, or else struggled to prevent their popular reputations from predisposing critics against their other, more ostensibly highbrow projects. Willard Huntington Wright, who served as an editor for *The Smart Set* from 1912 to 1914, published detective fiction as S. S. Van Dine, though that nom de plume did not protect him from becoming inextricably linked with his fictional sleuth Philo Vance, as the title of his 1928 essay, "I Used to be a Highbrow, but Look at Me Now," attests.[3]

Although the choice to author a work of crime fiction could have deep and lasting consequences for one's career, especially for those who aspired to positions of prominence in critical or avant-garde circles, a number of authors took the plunge, producing works whose depictions of criminality, while relatively neglected today, provide crucial context for our under- standing of modernism and its alternate dismissal of and fascination with popular forms. This chapter examines two of those authors – Wyndham Lewis and Gertrude Stein – and how their experiments with the conven- tions of crime fiction, initially conceived as way of broadening the formal parameters and potential audiences of their work, establish them as pivotal figures in modernism's long history of engagement with popular, com- mercial authorship.[4] Specifically, the chapter analyzes Lewis's *Mrs. Dukes' Million* (1908–1909; published posthumously in 1977) and Stein's *Blood on the Dining-Room Floor* (1933; published posthumously in 1948), exploring how both texts represent a form of modernist practice that has received scant critical attention: the modernist crime novel. In asking how the experimental possibilities of genre fiction might enrich the pop- ular possibilities for modernism, Lewis and Stein's depictions of crimin- ality pose a remarkable challenge to long-held, stereotypical notions of generic form as resolutely opposed to variation, modernist elitism and abstention from the literary marketplace, and the unfeasibility of formal innovation within the restrictions of genre. Indeed, their novels trouble accounts of modernism that conceive of the period as a reaction against the encroachment of mass culture, and illustrate precisely how modernism and crime fiction could inflect one another in compelling and productive ways. In these works, the criminal not only serves as an ideal vehicle for pressuring the limits of psychological representation, as that figure does for Conrad, James, and Chesterton, but also, and more importantly, reveals a surprising and underexplored symmetry between modernist experiment and generic formula.

Highbrow, Lowbrow, Middlebrow, Modernism

In pairing Lewis and Stein in this manner, I do not wish to imply that, in writing crime fiction, they somehow erased the barriers between highbrow and lowbrow art that thwarted their contemporaries, or that they disavowed an aesthetic of complexity in their attraction to a popular genre. Such a claim would be misleading, and, considering the trajectory of recent modernist criticism, overly dependent upon a high/low binary that has already lost much of its critical purchase. The "great divide" that Andreas Huyssen posited between high modernism and mass culture has by now been traversed so many times as to constitute a critical straw man, invoked only to be dismissed. Huyssen's claim that "[m]odernism constituted itself through a conscious strategy of exclusion, an anxiety of contamination by its other" – an other, Huyssen suggests, defined by "an increasingly consuming and engulfing mass culture" – has borne the brunt of repeated critique over the last few years, as critics advocate a fresh conception of modernism that does not exclude mass and commercial culture, but instead utilizes such a culture for its own ends.[5] Lawrence Rainey, for example, contends that modernism, far from being antagonistic to mass culture, "marks neither a straightforward resistance nor an outright capitulation to commodification but a momentary equivocation that incorporates elements of both in a brief, necessarily unstable synthesis."[6] By Rainey's formulation, modernism does not fall so neatly into either its conventional stereotype – an elitist cadre of highbrow intellectuals – or its lowbrow opposite – an entirely commercial venture dedicated to sales, marketability, and self-promotion above any aesthetic concerns.

More recent critics have extended Rainey's account of modernism's wobble between high and low by aligning the period with the middlebrow, or those twentieth-century fictions made possible by the proliferation of mass-market paperbacks, lending libraries, and book-of-the-month clubs and characterized by their adherence to popular forms just as they promote new opportunities for intellectual engagement to an increasingly literate mass audience.[7] Though the precise definition of middlebrow writing remains in dispute, most critics characterize it as both an aspirational form for readers – designed to admit middle-class audiences into artistic and cultural debates from which they were formerly excluded – and an economic boon for producers. To Pierre Bourdieu, middlebrow art thus represents "the product of a productive system dominated by the quest for investment," and as such must target "the widest possible public."[8] Others focus on the formal qualities of the middlebrow as they inflect a text's reception among diverse readerships. According to Nicola Humble, one of the middlebrow's most distinguishing features is its status as "a hybrid form, comprising a number of genres, from the romance and country-house novel, through domestic and family narratives to detective and children's literature and the adolescent Bildungsroman."[9] In a similar vein, Ina Habermann contends that the "most important aspect of mid-dlebrow writing is an accessibility unhindered by either high sophistication or an alienating reliance on cliché."[10] Highlighting the middlebrow's indeterminacy, Humble defines it as "an essentially parasitical form, dependent on the existence of both a high and a low brow for its identity, reworking their structures and aping their insights, while at the same time fastidiously holding its skirts away from lowbrow contamination, and gleefully mocking highbrow intellectual pretensions."[11] To be a middlebrow author is thus to move between two opposites – the intel-lectual rigor of the highbrow novel on the one hand, and the entertainment value of lowbrow fiction on the other – borrowing elements of both without conforming too decisively to either.

Such elusiveness drew, and continues to draw, its fair share of criticism. As Melissa Sullivan and Sophie Blanch contend, to write or read middlebrow fiction entails a form of self-exposure, an admission that one aspires to an intellectualism that one does not possess, even as mass audiences do not recognize such an aspiration as revealing the failure to reach its desired result. Consequently, middlebrow "practi-tioners and audiences … repeatedly faced three main charges: that their allegedly second-rate entertaining tastes usurped the power of the highbrow, that their miscegenation of high and lowbrow cultures lacked substance or distinction, and that they succumbed to aesthetic ideals deemed necessary for sales or popularity by publishers or agents."[12]

In light of such arguments, it becomes easier to see just how fraught the modernist appropriation of crime fiction was, since that genre was widely held as, at worst, a crassly commercial form of lowbrow art, or, at best, a duplicitous middlebrow effort to delight readers while fooling them into thinking that such fiction represents a respectable aesthetic choice. Modernists who wrote crime fiction might expect to be accused of pandering to the tastes of a mass audience, profiting from the public's enthusiasm for formulaic narratives and sensational violence, or duping readers into believing that consuming genre fiction by a celebrated author might endow them with cultural capital that such fiction simply cannot provide. While several prominent modernists affirmed their admiration for popular culture – most notably T. S. Eliot, who made little secret of his interest in detective fiction, telling a reporter in 1950 that he no longer read contemporary fiction save "the works of Simenon concerned with Inspector Maigret" – few were willing to identify themselves as popular genre writers, with all the stereotypes that such a position entailed.[13] Admitting to one's reading of genre fiction was a very different thing than writing it.

In addition to understanding the professional stakes of identifying oneself as a crime fiction writer, one should also note that the genre looked quite different in 1933 than it did in 1908; thus, any critical account of Stein and Lewis's efforts to work within its confines must situate their books within two distinct historical moments. Lewis, for instance, began *Mrs. Dukes' Million* during the heyday of the Edwardian detective, a period marked by the re-emergence of the most famous Victorian detective. After angry readers of the *Strand Magazine* demanded a sequel to Doyle's "The Final Problem" (1893), which infamously concludes with Sherlock Holmes falling to his death at Switzerland's Reichenbach Falls, Doyle responded by resurrecting Holmes in *The Hound of the Baskervilles*, serialized in *The Strand* from 1901 to 1902, and in a new spate of short stories published in the magazine between 1903 and 1904 and collected a year later under the triumphant title *The Return of Sherlock Holmes*. At the same time that Doyle was reclaiming his position as the preeminent figure in British detective fiction, authors such as G. K. Chesterton began to carve out their own niches within the genre while remaining faithful to its foundational tenets of intrigue and fair play. Chesterton's Father Brown mysteries, the first of which appeared in 1910, carry on the tradition of the amateur detective but introduce the element of theology; as crime fiction critic T. J. Binyon remarked, Chesterton's mysteries made a sizeable contribution to the genre by "reveal[ing] themselves as parables, in which moral theology is presented as detection," but did not significantly depart from the traditions of Doyle and his predecessors.[14] Lewis's foray into crime fiction, then, occurred at a peculiar time in the genre's history. While its fundamental features were remarkably resilient, the possibility for change was gradually beginning to surface.

Stein, meanwhile, ventured into crime fiction just as the genre was undergoing a rapid set of transformations, as a new generation of authors reconsidered what such fiction should and could represent. While traditional clue-puzzle mystery writers such as Sayers, Agatha Christie, and Margery Allingham still commanded the lion's share of critical and popular attention in England and America – a dominance of the market that led historians to dub the period between the World Wars the "Golden Age" of detective fiction[15] – by the early 1930s Dashiell Hammett's hard-boiled style of detection had risen to prominence in the United States, where cheap detective magazines and pulp paperbacks made Hammett's aggressive and action-driven brand of fiction readily available. More than any other practitioner of the detective genre, Stephen Knight argues, Hammett was the author most responsible for "bringing the independence and isolated rectitude of the old frontier hero into conflict with urban crime of modern America," and he instituted a clear division between the grittiness of hard-boiled detective fiction and the "calm spell of the clue-puzzle."[16] At the time Stein wrote *Blood on the Dining-Room Floor*, the trademarks of crime fiction no longer seemed self-evident, as authors on both sides of the Atlantic waged a fierce debate as to how the genre should evolve, or else remain the same.[17] Unlike Lewis, Stein entered the genre when the very concept of crime fiction seemed stretched to its breaking point, and consequently was able to sample a variety of crime fictions whose existence was unthinkable just a few decades prior.

Perhaps because they were conceived at such opposite moments in the history of crime fiction, *Mrs. Dukes' Million* and *Blood on the Dining-Room Floor* have little in common, at least at first glance. Lewis's text is filled with its author's trademark venom, and gleefully satirizes the familiar tropes of crime fiction while also questioning the definition of criminality. Stein's novel, meanwhile, bears all the markers that readers have come to expect of Stein: a narrative whose ambiguity frustrates any attempts at description, long digressions into the histories of characters only distantly related to the mystery at hand, and pages of twisting, grammatically recalcitrant sentences that repeat questions and phrases until they become narrative refrains. Yet for all their differences, both novels reflect their authors' attempts to absorb key tropes of the crime genre while simultaneously manipulating those generic mandates in ways strikingly akin to other modernist experiments with literary form. By interrogating the limits of crime fiction – exposing to ridicule its most distinctive conventions in Lewis's case, while placing intense epistemological pressure on others in Stein's – these two novels offer vigorous appraisals of genre fiction's narratological potential for modernism, suggesting how works of popular fiction might influence other, more experimental literary endeavors.

By examining Lewis and Stein in tandem and considering the avenues by which they alternately satirized, refined, and reconfigured the formal and thematic conventions of the crime genre, this chapter argues that the two authors pose distinct challenges to both genre fiction and modernism, and ultimately destabilize commonsense notions of experimental literary production and its relation to popular forms. If, as Aaron Jaffe contends, the "key ingredient of modernist reputation is not merely the demonstration of high literary labor through extant literary texts, but the capacity to frame this work in reference to the contrastingly lesser work of certain contemporaries," then Lewis and Stein's crime fiction offers a crucial instance of the modernist negotiation between "high literary labor" and "lesser work," as well as the professional and cultural value assigned to either category.[18] Though Lewis and Stein faced myriad complications in their efforts to produce crime fiction – their own prejudices for and against the genre, misgivings about aligning themselves too closely with popular literary forms, and the problem of innovation within generic categories – such complications did not prevent either from challenging the conventions of the genre in provocative ways, pointing to the role that formal experimentation within a circumscribed set of generic constraints could play in modernist literary production. Consequently, both of their novels open up a fresh set of possibilities for understanding modernism's relationship to popular literature, and, concurrently, popular literature's under-appreciated place within the modernist canon.

Wyndham Lewis and the Modernist Potboiler

Early in his career, before the publication of the first issue of *BLAST* in 1914 made him a national symbol of literary rebelliousness, Wyndham Lewis needed money, and turned to crime fiction in the hope of earning the funds he so desperately lacked. That Lewis, an unfailingly antagonistic presence on the British art and literary scenes from his first publications in Ford Madox Ford's *English Review* to his death in 1957, would deign to work within a popular genre may come as a surprise, especially considering his loudly professed opposition to formal conventions. In that inaugural issue of *BLAST*, Lewis characterizes his magazine as "an avenue for all those vivid and violent ideas that could reach the Public in no other way," and attacks movements such as Impressionism, Naturalism, and Futurism as insufficiently attuned to the brash individualism of artistic creation.[19] Proclaiming Vorticism, his own avant-garde movement, as an uncompromising alternative to those other "–isms," Lewis contends that "great artists in England are always revolutionary," and that Vorticism represents both a fundamental disavowal of competing artistic enterprises and a concentrated effort to initiate an aesthetic revolution within the placid cultural landscape of prewar Britain.[20] The stakes of the project were high, and left little room for distractions like popular literature or financial necessity.

Given the single-mindedness of his *BLAST* manifestoes, Lewis would appear an unlikely candidate for a crime novelist, or, for that matter, for a writer with any particular concern for a popular audience. Indeed, largely because of the legendary bitterness he aimed at his rivals, coupled with his infamous attraction to fascist politics during the early 1930s, Lewis has become modernism's misanthrope par excellence, seemingly indifferent to public sentiment.[21] He extended that reputation in his contempt for various forms of popular culture, which included a pronounced disdain for the producers and consumers of detective fiction. In the fragmentary essay "Berlin Revisited" (composed circa 1937), Lewis recounts a recent trip to the capital in which he marvels at inhabitants' earnest attempts at social and economic respectability. Stopping at a bookshop to see if Berliners' reading tastes match their outward appearance of bourgeois striving, Lewis explains to the store's clerk that on a visit to the city two years prior he was "greatly distressed to see nothing but detective stories in the windows of German shops," but now wonders if tastes have improved, since he can find no such works on display.[22] The clerk confirms that detective fiction now plays a reduced role in the German literary marketplace, but laments that such a change deprives readers of their favorite works, since "intelligent people all liked detective stories."[23] Lewis, with far more deference than one might expect, responds that "for a very intelligent man it might be an excellent thing to read a crime story, but for the multitude crime stories and nothing else was not the most suitable fare."[24] Notably, Lewis does not dismiss the crime genre as a form, but instead doubts its appropriateness for a mass audience, which he views as too likely to read genre fiction to the exclusion of all other types of literature. By his logic, one should not avoid detective fiction due to any inherent deficiencies in form or content, but rather to the threat it poses to the "multitude," which it distracts from other, more edifying artistic expressions.

Despite this antipathy toward genre fiction and its consumption, Lewis was not entirely opposed to popular forms, or to popularity more generally. As Scott Klein points out, in his memoir *Blasting and Bombardiering* (1937) Lewis describes the Vorticist as "the predecessor of the film star, a kind of 'comedian' before the arrival of the cinematic comedians from the world of the music hall."[25] Similarly, Michael North has written persuasively on Lewis's lifelong enthusiasm for animation and his respect for Walt Disney as a "great artist."[26] In spite of his persona as an aggressive outsider suspicious of popular works that prey upon an audience's naïveté, Lewis was not averse to the idea of reaching an audience, or to popular forms like film that he came to view as innovative in their own right. In fact, Lewis saw his early work as something that could be popular, provided that one subscribed to his definition of the term. As he writes in *BLAST*, popular art is not the art of the masses, but instead "the art of the individuals."[27] The Vorticist aesthetic has "nothing to do with 'the People,'" yet *BLAST* "will be popular, essentially. It will not appeal to any particular class, but to the fundamental and popular instincts in every class and description of people."[28] In other words, one does not need to speak to the concerns of a mass public in order to be popular, but must instead express those individualistic ideas that resonate across a wide spectrum of potential audiences, cutting across class distinctions and instilling a sense of urgency in all who share viewpoints similar to one's own.

The popular serves a pivotal function for Lewis, as it represents the goal to which all revolutionary art aspires, provided that such work does not attempt to ingratiate itself to the public by conforming to popular tastes. It is precisely this issue that complicates Lewis's relationship to popular fiction. To appeal to "the People" is, essentially, to reify prevailing trends by aligning one's work with the conventions of commercially successful art, giving an audience what it expects rather than what it needs. Lewis's denunciation of Chesterton, who relished his position as a mouthpiece for English popular sentiment, arises from this antagonism to authors who court readers' favor instead of challenging them with new ideas. In his essay "Futurism and the Flesh" (1914), Lewis takes Chesterton to task for mocking Italian Futurism rather than delivering a more nuanced critique of its methods, arguing that through his "dialectical ogling" Chesterton "gives you . . . simple entertainment, and expects the good-humour and titivation resulting will make you swallow his clumsy ideas."[29] For Lewis,

Chesterton's work is a sophomoric vehicle for "simple entertainment" – slight, jocular, and insulting to readers' intelligence.

In light of his idiosyncratic conception of popularity as, on the one hand, divorced from popular sentiment, and, on the other, imbued with an individualism that traverses demographics, Lewis's turn to crime fiction seems all the more curious, given that such a move would appear to indicate a shift away from the experimental aesthetics for which he advocated and toward a more conventional and purposefully commercial style of writing. However, as was the case for many authors who attempted crime fiction, Lewis's motives for writing *Mrs. Dukes' Million* were more material than ideological. He began his potboiler in 1908 when he was desperate for money to support work on *Tarr*, a novel he viewed as wholly superior to its counterpart and that Ezra Pound characterized as "a *serious work*" fundamentally unlike "the average successful commercial proposition at 6s. per 300 to 600 pages."[30] Whereas *Tarr* explores topics typically associated with "serious" fiction – nationality; physical, sexual, and psychological violence; the function of art in bourgeois society – the aims of Lewis's potboiler are more obscure. The plot centers on a mean-spirited lodging house keeper named Mrs. Dukes, who inherits a million pounds from her estranged husband only to be kidnapped by a gang of actors and replaced by Evan Royal, one of the gang's most successful mimics. The substitution works at first – Mrs. Dukes's son, Cole, is the only one who senses that something is amiss, and he quickly loses interest in the matter – but when Royal is abducted by the Actor-Gang's enemies, a complication that forces the gang to replace him with his understudy Hercules Fane, the plan unravels. After his escape and return to Mrs. Dukes's lodging house, Royal conspires with Fane and Lucy (another member of the gang as well as Fane's love interest) to steal most of the inheritance for themselves. Though the novel's frantic plot hints that Lewis's hopes of commercial success were ill-founded, as *Mrs. Dukes' Million* is remarkably difficult to follow in its feverish substitution of characters and roles, it nonetheless draws upon several of the crime genre's most significant elements: a stolen inheritance, kidnapping plots, unreliable characters, and, in the form of Raza Khan, the leader of the Actor-Gang, a criminal mastermind whose villainous ambition the novel's protagonists must thwart.

Perhaps to avoid the stigma of being publicly identified as an author of genre fiction – or at least of this particular example – Lewis intended to publish the book under the pseudonym "James Sed." He also seems never to have settled on a title for the project, proposing *The Three Mrs Dukes,*

Khan & Company, and *A Will Happily Revised* as possibilities. Though much of the text's composition history remains unknown, confined to a few letters between Lewis and his literary agent, J. B. Pinker, we know that the manuscript failed to impress, as Pinker informed Lewis that he would be hard pressed to find an audience for it. Lewis agreed with Pinker's assessment, and conceded that the novel would serve as "a lesson showing the futility of pot-boiling."[31] He put the manuscript aside and it remained undisturbed until the late 1950s, when it was rediscovered in a London junk shop.[32] A limited edition of 2,000 copies finally appeared in 1977, twenty years after Lewis's death, as *Mrs. Dukes' Million*.

The novel met a lukewarm reception upon its release, much of which indicates that readers were just as conflicted as Lewis as to how to categorize such a peculiar, genre-bending work. In his review for the *Times Literary Supplement*, eminent crime fiction critic Julian Symons acknowledges that *Mrs. Dukes' Million* seems like "a thriller without serious purpose," and laments both the editorial decision not to annotate the text and the amazing awkwardness of the title, which might have been improved with the more grammatically comfortable *Mrs. Duke's Millions*, or, for that matter, *Khan and Company*, which is the title of the manuscript on which the 1977 edition is based.[33] At the same time, Symons praises the novel for its deft manipulations of plot and character, arguing that the narrative's ingenuity demonstrates Lewis's pleasure in writing it. Though Lewis's claim to have begun a potboiler only to support work on *Tarr* suggests that the project was more of a financial necessity than a labor of love – as he put it in a letter to Pinker, "the only thing of which there is question as far as this book is concerned is money-making"[34] – Symons characterizes the author as an amused puzzle-maker not unlike the traditional detective novelist, excited by the narrative possibilities that genre writing affords. As he puts it, Lewis "creates difficulties for the pleasure of solving them."[35]

While Symons's professional regard for crime fiction might have predisposed him toward a view of Lewis's novel that privileges its generic elements, no less exacting a modernist critic than Hugh Kenner offered much the same assessment, accounting for the strangeness of Lewis's potboiler by situating it within the cultural milieu of *fin-de-siècle* genre fiction. Citing as the novel's ancestors "a tale by Stevenson or Chesterton, of intrigue, romance, and jolly disguise," Kenner contends that *Mrs. Dukes' Million* arose out of a particular strain of late nineteenth-century adventure fiction, and so establishes the novel's debts to popular literature.[36] His allusion to Chesterton – whom Symons also notes in his review – is especially germane, since for all Lewis's disgust at Chesterton's outsized public persona, the sprawling and uproarious plot of his potboiler mirrors the comic bombast of *The Man Who Was Thursday*, published in the same year that Lewis began work on *Mrs. Dukes' Million*. Lewis may have eviscerated his rival elsewhere, but here, where increasingly frantic criminal plots are hatched, foiled, and hatched again in a dizzying frenzy of activity, the spirit of Chesterton looms large.

Yet these accounts of Lewis as either a proto-Golden Age detective writer or a devotee of popular adventure do not fit their subject all that comfortably, since *Mrs. Dukes' Million* is less an homage to than a radical critique of those genres. Just as the novel subscribes to several tropes characteristic of popular crime fiction, it also satirizes them in a manner that reflects Lewis's enduring crusade against convention, and in so doing constitutes one of Lewis's earliest experimental texts. This impression of the novel as more akin to Lewis's other work than critics have acknowledged would appear to conflict with the author's dismal view of the book, although, as Douglas Mao points out, "disparaging the premises of his own unsuccessful projects was one of [Lewis's] trademark strategies."[37] Even if Lewis intended *Mrs. Dukes' Million* as an investment in what he considered an unrelated project, and so could never divorce his attitude toward the manuscript from Pinker's low opinion of its marketability, the novel still features many of the same formal provocations that characterize his most celebrated experimental works, a fact that leads Paul Edwards to label *Mrs. Dukes' Million* a "proto-Modernist vision" defined by a sophisticated model of the artist as a fierce iconoclast, rousing readers "from the hypnotic sleep of 'normality' by making the normal seem strange."[38]

One can also locate the novel's modernism in its depiction of criminality, specifically the degree to which its representation of the criminal serves as an early manifestation of Lewis's career-long attack on interiority. In practically every chapter, *Mrs. Dukes' Million* interrogates the concept of criminality by undermining crime fiction's faith in individual agency, insisting that crime, rather than an illegal action performed by a discrete subject, is actually a much more complicated negotiation between intention and deed. As Raza Khan asks in an impassioned speech on the gap between violent thoughts and criminal actions, "[w]hat is crime? The man that kills his sweetheart because she is unfaithful, the man that gains a fortune that necessitates the starving of many, Napoleon – all are criminals! It is only the sordid intention that makes the really despicable criminal" (*MDM*, 67). Khan's outburst sets the tone for the rest of the novel, as it posits a diffuse model of criminality based on motivation rather than action. For Khan, the worst crimes are defined solely by intention; if one does not believe that one's actions harm another, or is convinced that those actions are in some way beneficial, such actions cannot be considered criminal. Though the majority of the novel's characters share Khan's theory of criminal motivation, their opinions are so obviously self-serving that no concrete definition of criminality emerges from them. Evan Royal does not "regard himself as a criminal, but as a disinterested adventurer," and so feels little remorse for his duplicitous performance as Mrs. Dukes (*MDM*, 248). When his devotion to the Actor-Gang begins to waver, Royal argues that he possesses no real interest in financial gain, but instead finds his motivation in the pursuit of pleasure. "I don't do this for money," he claims in a statement that speaks to and against Lewis's own motivations for writing a potboiler, "but for fun – not innocent fun, because I am not a particularly honest man, anyway, but fun all the same; a funny sort of fun of my own" (*MDM*, 280). Hercules Fane adopts an identical notion of crime when he and Lucy agree to help Royal defraud the Actor-Gang by stealing a handsome portion of Mrs. Dukes's inheritance for themselves, leaving enough for Mrs. Dukes to live comfortably plus £50,000 to satiate Khan and the rest of the gang. Fane, like Royal, "did not look upon this new adventure as a criminal act at all, somehow. It seemed too much an adventure to be a mean theft" (*MDM*, 284).

This labile definition of criminality serves a fitting purpose, in that the chief activity of the Actor-Gang is the process of imitation, as Royal and, briefly, Fane, attempt to hide the evidence of Mrs. Dukes's kidnapping by usurping her identity. While, from a legal standpoint, the capture of Mrs. Dukes and the theft of her inheritance are the novel's most obvious crimes, the bulk of the narrative is devoted to the act of forgery: a theft and subsequent recreation of identity whose criminal status is never entirely resolved. Rather than classifying the Actor-Gang's performances as crimes, Lewis presents them as adventurous exercises in subjective uncertainty, in which the aesthetic and the epistemological merge to unsettle the reader's conception of what identity can or cannot be. If early twentieth-century crime fiction takes as one of its primary goals the definitive identification of the criminal – the detective's act of discovering the culprit behind a crime and exposing that individual to the judgment of both the public and the law – then Lewis's potboiler takes the opposite approach by refusing to establish identity as a fixed concept, and thereby casting doubt on what, precisely, makes forgery a criminal act. Crime, in this context, cannot be identified with any degree of certainty, but then again, neither can the individual.

Exemplifying Lewis's well-known fascination with exteriority and multiplicity, *Mrs. Dukes' Million* displays a pronounced investment in the body that can mimic in elaborate detail the traits, behaviors, and habits of numerous individuals, accumulating what Sean Latham sees in *Tarr* as the "endless and chaotic jumble of social and psychic forces that coalesce as publicly staged identities."[39] Several of the novel's characters pressure the limits of subjectivity so strongly that it becomes almost impossible to understand any individual as a unique entity.[40] Raza Khan claims that he was forced to abandon acting because he felt too deeply the emotions he performed on stage, noting that "[a]ll my greatest feelings … possessed me only when I was feigning" (*MDM*, 62). Evan Royal expresses a similar sentiment when he explains his processes of imitation. Asked if his devotion to the portrayal of Mrs. Dukes might arouse suspicion, since the riotous mannerisms and habits of speech that he adopts occasionally rise to the level of farce, Royal replies that the work of acting can never be overdone, as full commitment to a role eliminates any trace of the performer. As he puts it, to

> draw people's attention, to play the eccentric old woman, to get talked about and be much in evidence, all this takes people further away from finding out the *real* person I am, and the fraud that is being practised on them. The more I impose myself on them as a tiresome, whimsical old woman, the less they would ever guess that I was anything else. (*MDM*, 269)

By this logic, Royal can exaggerate Mrs. Dukes's already prominent eccentricities because, paradoxically, the more distinctive his performance becomes, the more improbable it seems that he is anyone other than who he pretends to be.

This is not to suggest, however, that the transformation of identity occurs in a simple or straightforward fashion. Rather, Royal's method of studying Mrs. Dukes in order to reinvent himself as a passable likeness of her is a meticulous, occasionally contradictory, process. Before the Actor-Gang kidnaps Mrs. Dukes, Royal rents one of her rooms and presents himself as Ernest Nichols, an avant-garde painter who takes his new land-lady as the subject of his work. Approaching Mrs. Dukes from a variety of angles and perspectives, each of Nichols's studies yields new insight into the woman Royal will eventually become:

Several diagrams rather than drawings of her head were pinned in a row on the wall. Each peculiarity, the exact position of her limbs, the relaxed muscles, the lines of the forehead were registered. The painting on which he was engaged was rather like a *plan* of her head than a painting. It was very wooden, and could an artist have watched him at work he would have said that Mr. Nichols was making, not a painting, but an exact copy in colour of Mrs. Dukes' face. (*MDM*, 13)

The fact that Royal copies rather than paints reflects the degree to which identity in the novel has become a replicable, physical commodity, as Royal's process of endless repetition allows him to become an accomplished imitator of Mrs. Dukes's poses, gestures, and expressions. Planning his subject instead of painting her, Royal produces a series of minute observations that, rather than expressing their subject's individuality, constitute a mathematical diagram of her physical form, which a sufficiently diligent student can adopt.

Besides assuming Mrs. Dukes's habits of expression, Royal also spends a good deal of time practicing her handwriting, and develops a method of forgery so precise that it becomes its own peculiar language. Royal, we find, "had made a typical alphabet of 'Duke letters,' as he called them: a typical Duke A, a typical B, etc." (*MDM*, 137). Such intricate preparations make for a highly successful Mrs. Dukes, but they pale in comparison to the minutiae of Fane's research. As Fane gleefully explains,

> I've got kind of a system now for studying Mrs. Dukes, and can reel off Duke-like sayings by the score. Her conversation is quite original, always extravagant and whimsical, and therefore, like all strong mannerisms, is more or less easy to imitate. All her quaint sayings and ways of putting things follow one or two very simple rules, once you've observed them closely and compared a certain number with each and all of the others. As far as that goes, I flatter myself I have the secret, and am master of the part. As to the tone of the voice. *That* I think I've got also, but haven't yet practised enough working them together – the tone and the matter – *what* she says, that is, and the way she says it. That will soon come. As to her attitudes. I can't say that I have penetrated the secrets of her physical structure. That would be a feat indeed. And of course the peculiarity of anyone's attitudes depends a good deal on the peculiarity of their physique. But I think by twisting my spine into such a curve as to form a sort of platform of the top part of my back, and then by resting the back of my head on this platform – by keeping my knees slightly bent, and moving my arms as though they were made of wood, as she always does, that I could impersonate her very well. (*MDM*, 155)

The philosophical problem of Fane's description arises from its focus on Mrs. Dukes's exceptionality, her "quite original" conversation and "peculiar" physique that, for all their uniqueness, are entirely repeatable.[41] What the Actor-Gang's performance accomplishes – besides making money – is a troubling of the distinction between originality and forgery, as their work undermines the observer's ability to distinguish between the authentic and the copy, and threatens to overwhelm any coherent model of discrete subjectivity. Although the original Mrs. Dukes is always characterized as a unique individual, even her most minute characteristics appear so easily imitated that it becomes difficult to take seriously any assertion of originality in the novel. Lewis uses the paradox as fodder for comedy, as when a character asks Fane, after introducing him to Royal (who is disguised as Mrs. Dukes), "what do you think of the old woman? She's an original isn't she? You'll soon get hold of the part, and be able to imitate her to perfection" (*MDM*, 96).

While the novel muddies the concept of identity, it also leaves open the possibility that certain traits might remain unique. After Royal decides to betray his employers and take Mrs. Dukes's fortune for himself, Fane, and Lucy, his typically impeccable impersonation "became trenchant, more sarcastic than ever, overbearing, and recklessly energetic. It was a new Mrs. Dukes, verily; yet another!" (*MDM*, 235). Royal's new manner is not quite an imitation of the original Mrs. Dukes, but rather, after Fane's brief substitution, "the fourth Mrs. Dukes," who is "disposed to comport herself for the rest of the piece in a very different manner from any of her predecessors" (*MDM*, 235). Even here, though, subjectivity is never wholly distinctive. This Mrs. Dukes is distinguished from her antecedents while at the same time conforming to a general type, evincing a form of individuality yet also functioning as one further instance of a continuing, numbered sequence. Even before he becomes this "fourth Mrs. Dukes," Royal starts to forget which attitudes belong to Mrs. Dukes and which belong to his own character, as the act of imitation becomes less a crime of forgery and more an encroaching subjective state. Royal complains at this point that he is "losing the trick," as he has been forced "to do so *much* talking, that I'm afraid I have substituted a tone of my own for Mrs. Dukes'. I can't say for certain, anyway" (*MDM*, 113–114). Royal's problem is not that he can no longer access the real, genuine article, who might help him to remember the exact tone of her voice, but rather that he has performed the part so often that he is unable to recall those traits unique to Mrs. Dukes and those he invented in order to inhabit his role more fully. He and the woman he imitates are now one and the same, an idiosyncratic union of subject and object.

Like Royal, Lucy also faces the problem of her own subjectivity as it threatens to intrude upon her performance, further undermining the notion of identity theft as an assertion of individual agency. Boasting of her imitative abilities, Lucy deems her role as the charwoman, Mrs. Beechamp, remarkably close to perfection. As she tells Fane, she has "almost become, body and soul, the charwoman," and now "Mrs. Beechamp's own mother wouldn't know me from her daughter!" (*MDM*, 110). For all her efforts, however, Lucy has a particular manner of speaking that threatens to give her away – an almost imperceptible foreign accent that announces her identity whenever she attempts the Queen's English: "When disguised as the charwoman, she spoke the purest Cockney. She could speak Cockney without a trace of anything but Cockney, or even affect a very thorough American accent, but in speaking English, the slight foreign accent was always noticeable" (*MDM*, 107). Crucially, Lucy can disguise her accent by putting on another regional dialect, but when attempting to speak without an accent her foreign origins betray her. Thus, Lewis presents the idea of a national character as an innate characteristic that one can never entirely overcome, yet he also stresses the fact that Lucy's foreignness only emerges when she attempts to speak without a discernible pattern of dialect, as her performance is impeccable when adopting a different vernacular. Here one finds a clear echo of *Tarr*, which, as Paul Peppis argues, excoriates conceptions of nationality and racial identity as "reductive, simplifying, and inadequate to explain the disorderly facts of human identity and activity."[42] While nationality marks the individual in some sense, it is so easily hidden or cast aside that its influence never constitutes a serious impediment to a talented actor. Nationality, in other words, can identify a character as originating from or belonging to a particular location, but its revelatory power remains limited given the ease with which it can be disguised.

While hints of their own characteristics occasionally imperil the work of the Actor-Gang, their performances are so thoroughly convincing that they persuade even the most suspicious observers. Royal's impersonation is so consuming, in fact, that it entirely upends the original Mrs. Dukes's conception of self. As her captors transfer her to a new location, Mrs. Dukes spies the disguised Royal from across a train platform and immediately experiences an existential panic: "she felt that it was probably *she* who was the ghost, and this other woman the reality ... Yes, she thought, that other old woman was the *real* Mrs. Dukes. She was

Mrs. Dukes no longer" (*MDM*, 257). In this, the sole moment in which Mrs. Dukes comes face to face with the reality of what has happened to her, there is no mention of a crime. Instead, Mrs. Dukes believes that she has made some kind of existential mistake, and that the woman she sees is actually the "real" Mrs. Dukes come to dissuade her of her claims to that title. In this manner, what could have been the most pivotal scene of the novel passes with little fanfare, inverting the traditional logic of the crime novel by characterizing the book's most consequential crime as simply an established and mundane fact. Whereas one might expect that, in a crime novel focused upon a case of stolen identity, the chance encounter of the original individual with her imposter would lead to a crisis, or at least heighten the narrative's suspense, Lewis defies those expectations by resisting the appeal of an easy twist of plot. The novel's animating crime is forgotten the moment it is discovered, and its significance for the victim is left maddeningly unresolved.

Perhaps a more remarkable feature of *Mrs. Dukes' Million* than its depiction of criminality, however, is its peculiar method of narration, which routinely emphasizes its alternating divergences from and adherences to the traditions of crime and detective fiction, taking pains to assert that this potboiler both is and is not a fitting representative of its genre. Lewis's narrative makes repeated references to a rhetorical persona dubbed "a person of certain penetration," a figure with no relation to the plot who can comment upon events for which the novel's main characters are not present, as well as being a kind of omniscient narrator who provides insight into others' motivations. As the narrator asserts, no author of sufficient modesty could disregard such an important rhetorical device, since "[w]hen the author feels that it would be conceited to claim so much penetration for himself, he just ushers in this person of certain penetration" (*MDM*, 14). Though Lewis's tone is decidedly flippant, making quick work of both the artificiality of generic constraint and authorial egotism, the individual of certain penetration draws attention to the conventional mechanisms of the crime genre by satirizing the ubiquitous bursts of insight usually proffered by an equally penetrative detective. This and other rhetorical devices mock the seemingly omniscient detectives popularized by Poe and Doyle, as when Lewis draws the reader's attention to the narrative's reliance upon two young men who wander through a party for the sole purpose of offering convenient commentary on its attendees:

> [L]et me hasten to explain that we are not following these young men round because they interest us in the least. On the contrary, they are very tiresome –

although charming – young men. We are merely using them as a convenience. As we have not been invited ourselves to this reception, and there is no one that we know, except the host, we are using the eyes of these young gentlemen – and even we have condescended to make use of their voices – in the imparting of a little information. For this reception is of great interest and of importance in the progress of our story. This is merely said in case the reader should imagine he was expected to pay any attention to them – glance at them, give them a smile. No, he can be as rude as ever he pleases with them. They are people of no interest or consideration. Mere conveniences. (*MDM*, 191)

With this direct appeal to the reader – singling out those parts of the scene that should prove inherently interesting (the plot and "progress of our story") and those one can dismiss as inessential (the personalities of the two men, who are "people of no interest or consideration") – Lewis lampoons the artifice of narration and perspective, troubling the relationship between generic form and the vicissitudes of identity by presenting his two young men as "mere conveniences" without interiority, while at the same time alluding to the potential for psychological complexity in other, more pertinent individuals.

Characters as purely structural as the two partygoers, emptied of subjectivity so fully that the narrator only deems them useful for the work of their eyes, illustrate the preference for the mechanics of the body over psychological experience that defines so much of Lewis's art. Jessica Burstein describes this concern with the exterior over the interior as Lewis's "routine dislocation of character," which produces "moments when character becomes unhinged, when the most literal aspects of 'integrity' ... not so much dissolve ... as unfasten."[43] For Lewis, the body's material breakdowns gesture to other splits in characterization, as individuals become defined by the unruly bodies they struggle to preserve and protect against outside influence, and not by the subjective experiences which, in other characters created by other authors, might emerge from the depths of the psyche. As Andrzej Gąsiorek argues, Lewis "resisted conceptions of identity that construed it in terms of a self-liberation that would permit some authentic nonrational kernel of being to burst through," and consequently "defended an external aesthetic that stressed clarity and structure."[44] Michael Levenson affirms such an approach when he locates Lewis's attitude toward the mind/body divide in *Tarr* within a desire to rebuke those authors too enamored with the interior lives of their characters. As he asserts, the "assault which Lewis made on character was at the same time an assault on modernist orthodoxies. To a movement that located the value of personality in the mind, that conceived identity in terms of psychological states, that pursued the intimacies of introspection, and that sought a language for the unconscious – to this movement Lewis responded with the body."[45] At the same time, he explains, "Lewis did not regard the body as possessing an inherent dignity, as revealing the mystery of creation, or as offering hope for individual and social renewal. For Lewis the body is not a source of value but a rebuttal to every moral valuation; it confronts luminous morality with opaque matter; it is *absurd*."[46] The two partygoers in *Mrs. Dukes' Million* serve as a unique case in point in that Lewis renders both as physical props of convenience, disembodied eyes that become instantly absurd because they offer no powers of reflection, introspection, or intimacy. The two men epitomize convention, representing nothing save the artifice of the genre in which they exist.

Besides identifying specific characters as conventions, *Mrs. Dukes' Million* also addresses the pronounced and unwanted effects that crime fiction can produce in its readers, signaling the suspicion of public taste Lewis would display almost thirty years later in "Berlin Revisited." Alluding to the improbability of readerly expectations, especially those that arise in readers of crime fiction, Lewis's potboiler derides the genre as one that lulls its devotees into accepting ludicrous situations and twists of plot. Some of these moments occur almost imperceptibly, as when the narrator points out the ominous exterior of a particularly filthy house, only to reprimand the reader for making assumptions about what resides inside by explaining that "dirt does not constitute tragedy or mystery" (*MDM*, 152). Other references are less subtle. The narrator describes Mr. Higginbotham, a repressed young curate who rents a room from Mrs. Dukes, as fascinated by stories of criminality that expose a world of vice and sin that he can only observe at a distance:

> Like many men sworn to a peaceful and saintly life, mysterious occurrences, scenes of violence, chapters of criminal life in which he could not participate, had a great fascination for him. And he was in the habit of relieving himself of his inclination for these forbidden things by entering very fervently into the lives of others for whom they were *not* forbidden, and who lived in them. At times he lived his parishioners' lives with far more gusto than they themselves. (*MDM*, 33–34)

Like the excitable Higginbotham, whose penchant for scandalous, criminal gossip pushes him to prurient excess, Mr. Truman, a partner in the firm of solicitors that holds Mrs. Dukes's fortune, becomes an object of ridicule because he "happened just then to be reading some detective stories in a new sixpenny magazine, and he determined to do a little investigation on his own account," clearly brought under the sway of his literary influences (*MDM*, 207). The firm's clerk receives a similar treatment, as his habitual nervousness is exacerbated by "detective stories" that, ironically, lead him to suspect the plot to steal Mrs. Dukes's inheritance when others remain skeptical (*MDM*, 212). The clerk fears that Hillington, a member of the Actor-Gang posing as Mrs. Dukes's financial representative, "was keeping the poor old woman locked up ... and was doing her to death. His familiarity with cases of this sort – everyday occurrences in the literature that he most affected – made it very easy for him to divine this" (*MDM*, 214). While the clerk is ultimately vindicated in his suspicions of foul play, his taste in literature is never validated as either useful or enviable, but instead faces harsh critique for its tendency to instill in readers an overly liberal view of their own critical acumen, making armchair detectives out of even the most slow-witted individuals.

The problem with such literature, Lewis's novel suggests, is not only that it encourages unsophisticated readers to believe the improbable, finding nefarious plots and assuming strained connections among characters and events, but also that it inflects popular journalism, which in the world of the novel has become just as lurid and melodramatic as works of crime fiction. Lewis plainly sees little distinction between the two, as both represent the triumph of material gain over artistic expression. While scouring a set of newspapers in hopes of stumbling upon some hint of the murders that Khan has commissioned, Royal encounters a parody of crime reportage, which the narrator chastises as a "swamp of malarial eloquence" (*MDM*, 252). After providing a lengthy excerpt from the beginning of the article, the narrator pauses to address the sensationalism that blights publications specializing in the tawdry details of crime:

> The reporter up till now had been observing an admirable restraint. The material was so rich, the opportunity so magnificent, that almost incredulously he had remained calm for the moment ... We have of course been the gainers by this. At this point he suddenly loses all self-control, however, and breaks out into the most fulsome jargon of his trade. (*MDM*, 251)

The narrator's attitude toward the prurience of the article is a mixture of hyperbole and derision, and alludes to Lewis's own position working within the confines of the crime genre, with all the financial and popular expectations that such a position entails. Any restraint on the part of the crime reporter or novelist is "admirable," considering that "the

opportunity" for attracting attention – and, concurrently, for selling papers
and books by appealing to the public interest in sensationalism – is
a "magnificent" one. Lewis invokes this ideological struggle between the
responsibilities of art and the draw of the marketplace in another scene,
when he describes how Royal becomes increasingly bitter over the circumstances that led him to participate in the Actor-Gang's plot to defraud
Mrs. Dukes, and complains – in a moment that obviously speaks to Lewis's
own frustrations in having to write a novel like *Mrs. Dukes' Million* in the
first place – that "[w]hat we are doing now need not be a pot-boiler, but it
is. What a terrible thing poverty is!" (*MDM*, 117).

The parallels that Lewis posits between the crime novelist and the crime
reporter further the book's broader implication that genre fiction knowingly misleads its consumers, soliciting their money through the implication that reading such work will somehow allow them to become, in their
daily lives, the kind of heroic protagonists that one meets in the pages of
a crime novel. The example par excellence of such foolhardy generic
consumption is Hatchett, the solicitor responsible for the safe-keeping of
Mrs. Dukes's fortune who serves as a caricature of the crime novels with
which Lewis's, had it been published immediately after its completion,
would have found itself competing. While the members of Hatchett's firm
"could have imagined each other as figuring in one of the detective stories
they lost themselves in every night, but only as incidental characters,"
Hatchett "was a different spirit":

> Sherlock Holmes, for them the most romantic character in fiction, might
> have looked like him! As we spoke of a man as representing a class or an
> abstract idea, such as the idea of gout – we would say that this Mr. Hatchett
> appeared to them evidently of the class of heroes, the class of heroes of
> novels. Certainly he would not make the hero of a love story. But there are
> heroes and heroes. He had in his veins, yes that was it indubitably, the blood
> of the great race of amateur-detective-heroes. There was something vague,
> sensational, and romantic about him and his co-partners. (*MDM*, 332)

Here Lewis takes aim at the most famous of all literary detectives, damning
Holmes by awarding him the superlative of "the most romantic character
in fiction." Even the character that most resembles Holmes is "vague,
sensational, and romantic," and, despite his potential as a heroic figure,
could only live up to such potential in a very particular kind of novel.
The irony here is that Hatchett, as the heir apparent to Holmesian mastery,
plays an extremely minor role in the plot of *Mrs. Dukes' Million*, another
deluded amateur detective hoping to resemble his fictional idol. His
intellectual prowess is only sufficient to alert him – at the end of the

novel, no less – to the fact that something has been vaguely amiss in his dealings with Mrs. Dukes and her associates. Through Hatchett and the esteem with which his detective-fiction-obsessed colleagues view him, Lewis delivers a scathing rebuke of the traditional detective protagonist and his adherents as romantic and ultimately useless figures, personifying characteristics that, in practice, offer no defense against the criminal.

Though we might understand *Mrs. Dukes' Million* as a spoof of the crime genre and its most prominent attributes, Lewis's potboiler nonetheless offers one sobering moment in which the subject of criminality becomes more than a rhetorical or existential problem. Near the end of the novel, as a German marching band performs through the city streets, the narrator pauses to consider the circumstances of its squalid surroundings: "The poor do not understand the causes and the meaning of things. [The band was] gazed on sombrely and with a pathetic perplexity. Why the wife was beaten by her husband she did not know. A young man who that morning took his life accounted naively for the act in a letter attributing his despair to love" (*MDM*, 359). What initially seems like another ironic jab at a particular group quickly becomes a more penetrating observation about the futility of crime and the processes of victimization that it creates. The anonymous wife has no explanation for her abuse, while the young man can leave no cogent rationale for his suicide beyond a conventional overture to desire. While these two figures may serve as further examples of Lewis's satirical streak – the dead man's amorousness is dismissed as "naïve," while the beaten wife falls in with the rest of "the poor" in that she fails to "understand the causes and meanings of things," which, in this case, refer to her own abuse – it is more productive to understand the passage as a moment where Lewis's irony deliberately undercuts itself. Turning from the formal constraints of genre fiction to the lived experience of suffering, Lewis counters Royal's "adventurous" crime of impersonating Mrs. Dukes with a recognition of domestic violence that dims the novel's lighthearted obfuscation of crime's consequences. Much like Douglas Mao's assessment that Lewis, while inarguably "brutal and paranoid" in his conception of humanity, can occasionally dilute his venom with "some complex lessons about the value of otherness and the perils of what can look like love," this moment of sympathy in a novel predominantly concerned with formal experiment and the evisceration of individuality absorbs the blow of satire to admit the more serious presence of a social problem.[47] While *Mrs. Dukes' Million* may intrigue as an experiment with generic form, its most surprising aspect is not that Lewis deigned to write it, or its unsettling implication that identity is entirely fungible, but rather the fact that beneath Lewis's satire exists a kind of moral vision, or an ethics that, if not wholly unprecedented, is at least highly unexpected from this particular modernist.

Crime, for Stein

Whereas *Mrs. Dukes' Million* initially seems like a departure from the majority of Lewis's writing, an anomalous dalliance with a popular genre, Gertrude Stein's attraction to crime and detective fiction has been well established. She wrote numerous essays on the subject, openly proclaimed her enthusiasm for traditional mysteries, hard-boiled detective stories, and journalistic accounts of violent crime, and quipped in her 1937 *Harper's Bazaar* essay "Why I Like Detective Stories" that the genre was, simply, "what I can read."[48] The reasons behind this attraction, however, are more opaque. On the one hand, Stein's absorption in genre fiction would seem to follow from her abiding interest in literary form. As Ellen Berry has argued, part of detective fiction's allure for Stein was its status as "pure" narrative: "Stylized, ritualized, indifferent to deep characterization or significant theme, the genre apparently exists solely to answer the question 'what happened,' to fulfill the reader's expectation that an enigma will be solved."[49] On the other hand, the detective genre's emphasis on rational solutions to seemingly unfathomable events, which Maria DiBattista describes as an assurance that "reality will yield its secrets and that good and evil will definitely declare themselves," stands in stark opposition to Stein's own writing, in which little is definitely declared and secrets rarely offer up their mysteries.[50] Finally, there is also a third option for understanding Stein's formal attraction to detective fiction, if, following the example of Sayers and other, equally innovative practitioners, we accept the genre's characteristic style as mediated by an intense self-scrutiny that refuses to take its customs for granted. If, as Gabrielle Dean contends, the detective story is "always in the process of analyzing itself, for it is a plot about a plot, and more generically, about plot itself," then Stein's passion for it would seem to arise from a concern with narrative complexity rather than simplicity, and thus to further her abiding interests in the disruption of literary convention.[51]

In addition to viewing Stein's motivations for writing in and about a popular genre in formal terms, we should also consider how her investment in modernist experimentation directly informs her notions of popular authorship. Stein maintained on multiple occasions that successful works of genre fiction should be both entertaining and aesthetically complex if they aim to reach a sizeable audience. Describing her admiration for hard-boiled pioneer Dashiell Hammett in *Everybody's Autobiography* (1937), she distinguishes her interest in detective fiction from what she regards as more trivial forms of entertainment, explaining that "I never was interested in cross word puzzles or any kind of puzzles but I do like detective stories. I never try to guess who has done the crime and if I did I would be sure to guess wrong but I like somebody being dead and how it moves along and Dashiell Hammett was all that and more."[52] Though brief, Stein's account illustrates her view of the genre as a blend of intellectual engagement and narrative pleasure. As she observes, all detective stories begin with the structural necessity of a corpse, but only the most engrossing proceed to more inventive plotlines that absorb the reader in their difficulty. Stein does not venture any guesses as to "who has done the crime," not because she is uninterested in the solution to the mystery, but because the pleasures of detective fiction, unlike those of a crossword puzzle, arise from a process of narrative deferral, a continued suspense that comes when one resists the urge to predict a plot's outcome and instead follows the twists of a complex, unfolding narrative. Stein's other critical writings on detective fiction reflect a similar attitude, as they are all preoccupied in one way or another with the connections among generic convention, formal difficulty, and popular appeal, and maintain that while detective fiction may be a formulaic brand of entertainment, part of its popularity derives from its unexpected devotion to the complexities of literary form, and to the reader's resultant immersion in them.

As an exemplary figure of successful generic authorship, Stein offers Edgar Wallace, the British-born novelist most famous for helping to create King Kong, and whose work "uses the old melodrama machinery and ... makes it alive again."[53] Echoing Pound's challenge to "make it new," Stein advocates a kind of detective fiction that, inspired by Wallace's example, can breathe new life into old forms, as "it is much better to make an old thing alive than to invent a new one."[54] For Stein, the reformulation of the traditional "melodrama machinery" that authors like Wallace undertake marks a significant improvement over what she deems "the Sherlock Holmes super-detective" style of fiction, which, while still incredibly popular among readers, had by the 1930s become a static structure promising simple escapism rather than formal ingenuity. In the Holmes style, Stein complains, "the crime and the criminal is nothing but something for the unreal hero to conquer."[55] By contrast, Stein argues that in melodramatic detective fictions such as Wallace's, the hero, heroine, and villain – the three primary character types that Stein identifies within a melodramatic narrative – are equally necessary to the story, and as such contribute to a subtler and more engrossing plotline. Such fiction reverses the trend of the "super-detective," where all characters but one grow "too dependent and eventually the hero detective having really to exist all by himself ceases to exist at all."[56] In this way, the problem with "super-detective" fiction is one of self-negation. The "super-detective" protagonist is wholly implausible in his exploits, which predictably result in a too-tidy conclusion, and so the narrative in which he appears loses that sense of liveliness promised by more dynamic literary forms that refuse to mine unvarying conventions.

Stein's quarrel with the impossibility of "super-detective" fiction also extends to the role of evidence and motivation within a text's narrative economy. She claims to prefer English to American detective novels because the former "are more long winded which is better and money is more real in them which is very much better."[57] To illustrate the latter point, she maintains that the idea of financial gain as a criminal motive enhances detective fiction as a fundamentally "interesting" genre, since such a motive arouses readers' curiosity without leading them to doubt the plausibility of the narrative that unfolds:

> You see that is the reason why money has to be, otherwise a detective story could not be interesting. Edgar Wallace makes it mysterious but it is always money, it is a disappointment when it is drugs or an international conspiracy, you always have the feeling that all the struggle is not worth while because by the time the real war comes all that diplomacy will have been forgotten and so what is the use and drugs that is the same, just about the same quantity of drugs get in anyway, but money that is different, twenty guineas is different, money is different and English people do feel that money is more real than Americans feel it is and that is why their detective stories are so much more soothing.[58]

Here Stein observes that detective fiction's use of money as a motivation for crime proves effective largely because alternative explanations such as drugs or conspiracy seem unrealistic by comparison. The drug trade is so prevalent that it could never be all that shocking to readers as a motive, while the specter of a vast government conspiracy fails to satisfy because it is too shocking to be believed. Stein's implication is that money, as an integral aspect of everyday life, possesses a popular vitality that other criminal motivations cannot match, and compels readers in part because of its ubiquity in contemporary social interaction.[59] Thus, the detective genre is most captivating when it grounds its mysteries in the circumstances of everyday life, avoiding hyperbole in favor of a grittier, more naturalistic depiction of the world as it currently exists.

How, then, to explain Stein's characterization of detective fiction as "soothing," since the representation of a world rife with crime would seem to make for an anxious rather than pacified audience? Though it might appear oxymoronic, the idea that genre fiction placates its readers through the same formal devices that hook them into a suspenseful narrative is vital to understanding Stein's argument about what detective fiction can and should be, and to appreciating the links between that genre and modernism. What Stein does not mean here is a reiteration of the traditional model of detective fiction as maintaining, through the affordances of generic convention, a reader's comfort in the triumph of good over evil, or what W. H. Auden describes as the genre's defining "dialectic of innocence and guilt" in which the guilty party is definitively expelled from a community once a detective declares that individual responsible for a narrative's central crime.[60] Stein's view of detective fiction as soothing does not arise from the narrative restoration of order that D. A. Miller refers to as a mode of "repair," wherein the identification of the criminal yields a broader recognition that the world in which this narrative occurs now has no need of criminological methods, settling once again into a safe haven for its characters.[61] Rather, what Stein finds soothing in the detective genre is its insistence that even the most obscure and banal events, objects, and experiences play integral roles within a complex narrative, which forces readers to assume that even the minutest of details can prove crucial in solving the mystery at hand. Because the plot of a detective story advances through a series of small but never inconsequential clues, it reveals the centrality of what Roger Caillois described as "the reduction of the impossible to the possible" by proffering a variety of evidence in order to elicit from readers the "pleasure [that] comes from toying with the difficulties, from enumerating the obstacles which one sets out to overcome."[62] Flipping Peter Wimsey's jaundiced claim that detective fiction captures its readers through the routine deployment of convention, Stein's argument regarding the genre's comforts champions generic form as a game, an occupation whose enjoyments result from "toying with" the difficult situations manifested through recognizable tropes.

By demanding that readers piece together fragmentary clues in order to arrive at a comprehensible storyline, detective fiction comes to resemble an overtly modernist narrative that encourages active reading and narrative engagement. As Stein explains, this kind of reading practice can take on a life of its own outside the pages of a novel, lending excitement to the otherwise mundane tasks of daily life:

> I like detecting there are so many things to detect, why did somebody say what they said, why did somebody cut out a paragraph in the proof I was correcting, why did the young man we were to meet at the station and whom we have never seen before not turn up and why did they telephone to somebody else that he was still at the station waiting for us and why when we got there could nobody find him neither the fat porter nor the thin one and certainly it was a very small station and finally why when we had all given him up and we were starting for home did I find him on the other side of the station and where had he been.[63]

The everyday detection that Stein advocates echoes the amateurish problem solving that Lewis vigorously opposes in *Mrs. Dukes' Million*. Yet for Stein, contra Lewis, the pleasures of such detection come not from passively immersing oneself in the world of popular fiction, or from viewing oneself as the infallible protagonist of a detective novel in the mold of Sherlock Holmes; rather, Stein's enjoyment arises out of detection's defamiliarization of everyday life, which is also the central objective of her poetic and fictional experimentalism. Just as Deborah Mix contends that the confounding of readerly expectations in Stein's oeuvre is "potentially liberating, as it exposes our expectations as constructions . . . and opens up the possibility for other 'vocabularies' of reading and thinking," Stein's characterization of detective fiction as simultaneously soothing and realistic alerts us to new frameworks for exploring the mysteries of the everyday through generic form.[64]

If the link Stein establishes between detective fiction and the epiphanies of the everyday makes the work of a popular genre appear far more modernist than one might suspect, so too does her purposely nebulous approach to crime. In her essay "American Crimes and How They Matter," published in the *New York Herald Tribune* in 1935, Stein contends that "crime if you know the reason if you know the motive if you can understand the character if it is not a normal one is not interesting," and proceeds to argue that "crime in itself is not interesting it is only there."[65] Following upon her interest in detective fiction that remains soothing yet suspenseful, innovative yet grounded in convention, Stein dismisses most criminal acts as tedious episodes that are "only there," and thus do not demand more active forms of attention or even register themselves upon a reader's consciousness, while at the same time arguing against the kind of generic formulae that lend detective fiction its distinctive character. For Stein, the explainable crime cannot be interesting because it has an explanation, much as one's understanding of a criminal's motivation displaces any sense of mystery or intrigue created by the crime committed. By this logic, most fictional representations of crime fail because they provide readers with a sense of closure, whereas those that succeed do so because they are able to maintain and heighten the reader's uncertainty as to who committed a crime and why. Stein's vision of the criminal act thus upholds one element of Franco Moretti's critique of detective fiction – his claim that the genre utilizes the clue as metonymical form of uncertainty, "a signifier that always has several signifieds and thus produces *numerous* suspicions" – but wholly rejects Moretti's notion that the genre "does not permit alternative readings" because it must finally provide "one solution that is valid for all."[66] Consequently, it becomes easier to see why Stein regarded detective fiction as a potentially revelatory genre too often mired in outmoded habits of thought, and instead sought out representations of crime that attend to the shock and mystery of violence without alleviating or minimizing its obscurity.

As an example of the formal and cultural power of inexplicable violence, and of the uncertainty characteristic of true crime, "American Crimes and How They Matter" recounts the story of an evening Stein spent riding along with a Chicago homicide detective while enjoying a break from her American lecture tour, which had successfully capitalized upon the commercial and critical success of *The Autobiography of Alice B. Toklas* (1933).[67] During the course of the night, Stein asks her police escort for insight into how he would investigate a murder in an unfamiliar city, wondering whether or not he could identify that city's criminals by sight alone:

> We talked together a lot about not crime but whether any one would know a criminal if one saw one in another place than where one was accustomed to see them I asked the sergeant could he tell in a town he had never been in which ones were men who could commit crimes. He said very likely he could but he also very possibly would be mistaken, then he went on, police he said almost always know why a crime has been done, they mostly always know who has done the crime at least they can they often do find out but, and then he became very silent although he went on talking, sometimes they don't and it worries them.[68]

By the sergeant's admission, the Lombrosian idea that criminality can be read on the body – that is, that an individual with no particular knowledge of an area could still identify potential criminals as physiognomic others – is at best an intellectual gamble, and at worst an outright mistake. Crime, therefore, cannot be determined according to superficial standards of

judgment, and so can surprise even an experienced police officer in one of
the largest cities in America.

Just as true crime captivated Stein's imagination, catering to her fascination with the inexplicability of violence and the motivation for it, it also
gave her a solid sense of how and where detective fiction might improve.
As she claims in *Narration* (1935), while "[i]n the newspaper it is the crime
it is the criminal that is interesting," in fiction "it is the story about the
crime that is interesting."[69] Proposing that journalistic and fictional
accounts of crime captivate their audiences in fundamentally different
ways, Stein lays out a program for combining the essential aspects of
each, fusing the ineffability of the criminal mind and "the story about
the crime" in a manner that might propel detective fiction in unprecedented though necessary directions. The crux of the problem with most
detective fiction, Stein maintains in "American Crimes and How They
Matter," is definitional. Instead of opening themselves to other representational possibilities, detective novelists remain limited by their focus on
a heroic protagonist, and by their reliance upon narrative closure in
asserting that protagonist's infallibility. Both habits lead Stein to believe
that "detective fiction," as a descriptor, fatally restricts the work an author
might produce. She complains that when authors insist on referring to
their work as "detective stories instead of crime stories . . . that is in a way
the trouble with them they are detective stories instead of crime stories in
real life they are crime stories instead of detective stories."[70] For Stein,
stories of true crime, as opposed to fictional accounts, are ultimately a more
stimulating cultural phenomenon, in that their narratives, unlike those of
the detective story, are often unresolved. She contends that "in the real
crime it is more interesting if you do not know the answer at all . . . or if
there is a mystery behind the answer," and elaborates by explaining that
"however exciting the story if they find out all about who did it, and
finding out who did know all about how and why he did it then nobody
really can remember later about it at all about that crime and it does not go
on in the common memory."[71] By this logic, the problem with most
detective fictions is that they provide too easy a resolution to the mysteries
they represent, focusing on detectives rather than crimes and solutions
rather than problems. As a result, their narratives of crime and violence fail
to "go on in the common memory," descending into anonymity without
making any significant impact on either their readers or the genre as
a whole. Thus, for Stein the goal of detective fiction should not be to
present clever solutions to crime, but rather to redefine itself as crime
fiction, which represents the experience of and motivations for crime as

disturbing and inscrutable problems rather than neatly packaged enigmas that a detective explains away.

Though she makes no mention of it in "American Crimes and How They Matter," Stein had attempted to carry out her prescriptions for detective fiction by writing her own crime novel, *Blood on the Dining-Room Floor*, a short murder mystery that, for all its formal significance, has never found its place in modernist literary history. One might blame its neglect on the longstanding critical prejudice against genre fiction, since, as Brooks Landon observes, early critics registered Stein's passion for detective fiction yet mostly "treated it as just another of her many incidental idiosyncracies [*sic*] – akin to her fascination with automobiles and garages."[72] Those who reviewed the novel upon its 1948 release may have played an equal role in diminishing its impact, as they disagreed about whether the book was intentionally confounding in its fusion of modernism and the detective genre or, simply, unreadable.[73] *Time* magazine declared the novel "a curious fling at mystery-story writing by the late expatriate mumbo-jumboist," while a largely positive review in the *New York Times* diluted its praise with the claim that Stein's "reconstruction and resolution of the crime are wonderfully complicated," hinting that the work was too opaque to fit within neatly delineated generic categories.[74] Perhaps taking their cue from such ambivalence, contemporary critics waver between views of the novel as either a continuation of Stein's formal experimentalism – another attempt to speculate on the potential for innovation within poetic and narrative form, or to plumb what Caroline Levine describes as the affordances of literary form, "the potential uses or actions latent" within it – or an underdeveloped oddity impoverished by Stein's more canonical works.[75] Harriet Scott Chessman has argued for the novel's primacy in Stein's oeuvre, as it "addresses in complex and illuminating ways the situation at the heart of writing with which Stein always grapples: the communication between an 'I' and a 'you,' between an author (or a work) and a reader"; yet biographer James R. Mellow refers to *Blood on the Dining-Room Floor* as "a meager production," upholding the longstanding view that modernism and genre fiction are mutually exclusive categories.[76]

The novel came at a tumultuous moment in Stein's career, born from a mix of personal and professional frustrations. After the remarkable success of *The Autobiography of Alice B. Toklas*, which brought her the commercial and critical validation she had long pursued, Stein found herself unable to write anything, paralyzed by a case of writer's block that threatened to derail her burgeoning celebrity. As she later explained in *Everybody's Autobiography*, fame had a curiously depersonalizing effect. Almost immediately after *The Autobiography of Alice B. Toklas* became a sensation, she wrote, "it was all different, what I did had a value that made people ready to pay, up to that time everything I did had a value because nobody was ready to pay."[77] To continue her transformation from a writer whose work accrues cultural capital as the result of its commercial neglect to one with real financial viability, and at the same time to overcome the resulting anxiety of such an abrupt professional change, Stein immersed herself in the details of a familiar domestic tragedy.

In August 1933, the village of Belley, France, located just to the east of Stein and Toklas's summer home in Bilignin, was shaken by the unexplained death of Madame Pernollet, the wife of a local hotelier, who was found seriously injured on the cement walk just outside the hotel after falling from an upstairs window. The police offered several possible explanations for the incident after Pernollet died of her injuries five days later, including suicide, murder, and accident – Pernollet was a sleepwalker – but the mystery was never solved.[78] Stein describes the incident in *Everybody's Autobiography*, where, after summarizing the history of the Pernollet family and their establishment, she recounts the chain of events following Madame Pernollet's fall from the hotel window: "Then one day, it was that summer, she was found early in the morning on the cement where she had fallen, and they picked her up and took her to the hospital and no one staying in the hotel knew anything had happened to her and then she was very religious she always had been and then she was dead."[79] Stein attended the funeral, and soon after began to take the details of Pernollet's death and the rumors swirling around it as the subject of a crime novel, which she hoped might alleviate her writer's block while also extending the financial rewards she had recently begun to reap.

The result was a crime novel that, as a genre piece, seems almost entirely out of place. For one, the book does not feature a detective, replacing that traditionally capable hero with a narrator palpably uncertain about the events of the novel and frustrated that, as a result, the narrative may not be sufficiently clear to its readers. Also, Stein presents a sizeable cast of characters identified only by their first names, their familial relationships ("a brother," "a wife"), or their professions, describing and redescribing those characters in an anxious loop that deters readers from seizing upon any one individual as a potential suspect. Perhaps most importantly, the novel's narrative structure undermines the chronological organization typical of detective fiction, presenting instead a series of loosely connected chapters written in a dense stream-of-consciousness style. Some chapters deal with specific, if ill-defined events – a phone line being cut, a young man dying in the Great War, a family acquiring wealth in the war's aftermath – while others contain only the narrator's alternately clipped and meandering ruminations on the inability to express the causal relationships between characters and the actions of the novel, as well as the difficulty of imparting information to a reader who may struggle to penetrate such a sketchily drawn mystery.

Many chapters combine these two preoccupations, with the narrator recounting a series of portentous events and then seguing into an elaborate deconstruction of the process of writing a crime narrative. Stein's opening chapter, for example, begins with a hallmark of detective fiction by presenting a crime to be solved – in this case, the bizarre death of a hotel proprietor's wife, who "fell upon the pavement of cement in the court and broke her back but did not die nor did she know why. In five days she was dead."[80] However, from this initial death, around which the majority of the novel revolves, the narrator proceeds to a self-conscious parody of the traditional structure of detective fiction, drawing attention to just how strongly a narrator can influence a reader's perception of events within the narrative economy of genre fiction, and hinting at the kind of formal manipulation yet to come: "How did she die. Now I will try to tell. How she fell" (*BDRF*, 7). Stein's rhyme offers an immediate sense of the novel's playfulness even in the face of tragedy, and of its insistence that a violent death can affect readers at a visceral level while still serving as a formal device, illustrating how generic conventions are at once essential to a narrative's clarity and impediments to the gravity of its subject.

Like most of Stein's writing, then, *Blood on the Dining-Room Floor* adheres to none of the traditional criteria for the genre in which it putatively participates: it is a mystery without distinct suspects, a detective story with no detective, and a crime fiction that, in addition to being nonfictional, may in fact contain no crime, since the death of the hotel proprietor's wife is never definitively characterized as a murder. Even the novel's title is misleading in that it refers to a piece of evidence, a material statement of past violence traditionally utilized as the detective's means of piecing together a coherent, orderly narrative of a crime's occurrence and resolution. By any apparent logic, this is not a work of genre fiction that readers at the time of its composition would have recognized as such.

At the same time, though, the knowing allusions to and dismissals of convention that Stein's text displays do not override the fact that its author definitely thought of her book as a crime novel, but of the type that she would later cast in opposition to Poe and Doyle's "super-detective" fiction, with its fixation on the protagonist's ironclad methods of deduction and the resolution they inevitably achieve. Far from a formalistic failure, as the novel's early reviewers claimed, *Blood on the Dining-Room Floor* exemplifies Stein's contention that mystery exists most emphatically in the inexplicable events of the everyday, and that crime fiction should not simply guide passive readers to narrative resolution, but instead draw them into a more active process of engagement with a text in which concepts such as agency, crime, and meaning are never fixed. To achieve this aim, Stein either discards or reconfigures traditional generic elements such as detectives, suspects, and clues, and replaces them with more unsettling abstractions relatively neglected by most genre fiction yet undeniably present in real crime: irrationality, chance, and affect. In characterizing her meandering and fragmentary text as a crime novel, Stein draws a sharp parallel between the objectives of both modernist and genre fiction, and in so doing reveals not only a remarkable affinity between these seemingly disparate forms, but also a host of potential problems that arise amidst the fusion of the two.

Fundamental to the novel's emendation of the detective genre is its insistence that crime is fundamentally a chance occurrence, and is most unsettling when its motivations are left unresolved. As the narrator asserts, "nothing is surprising but a coincidence. A fact is not surprising, a coincidence is surprising and that is the reason that crime is surprising. There is always a coincidence in crime. There are so many ways in which there is no crime" (*BDRF*, 34). By this definition, detective fictions in the vein of Holmes concern "no crime" in that they rely upon facts – discrete events that the detective sews together through logical processes of deduction, removing any elements of surprise from what initially appeared to be coincidental. In other words, a mystery is only surprising (i.e., a mystery) until the detective, through powers of deduction and rational thinking, transforms coincidence into fact, and explains away any sense of randomness in the crime committed by narrating events in a coherent, chronological manner. In this respect, *Blood on the Dining-Room Floor* is most concerned with revealing what crime is not – logical, orderly, and transparent – and instead maintains that the motivations for and methods of crime are often just as unknowable as the identities of those who commit it. Stein's narrator, in exposing the traditional narrative patterns of detective fiction, alludes to the situation by instructing the reader to "[p]lease remember everybody's name. But nobody had given the names away. They never do when there is only a crime, that is to say a background for a crime. And you see the thing to remember is that when there is a background for a crime there is no crime" (*BDRF*, 27–8). For Stein, in order to be surprising, and consequently to qualify as a crime, an event must have no history, no specific background that, if uncovered, would remove the element of coincidence by framing that event within a logical narrative of causes and effects. The principle applies equally to her characters, as a complex and fully articulated psychology would provide unwanted insight into an individual's motives, shedding light on circumstances that, for the sake of surprise, should remain in darkness. Avoiding such revelations, Stein's narrator describes the novel's characters primarily through decontextualized anecdotes, and refuses to situate them within a larger pattern of actions and their consequences. In so doing, the narrator resists any coherent narrative of events while also obscuring the identities of potential suspects. In this case, to discover the history of a crime or the thoughts of those who committed it is to negate the crime itself.

Stein's deliberate resistance to traditional narrative forms in her treatment of crime is hardly unexpected when examined in light of her other work, as critics have long equated her proclivity for formal experimentation with larger epistemological imperatives. Jennifer Ashton contends that in *The Making of Americans* (1925), Stein's famous process of repeating certain phrases ad infinitum performs "a function much like character development … except that character itself does not develop in any transformational sense, but rather the 'whole' of the character emerges through successive repetitions."[81] Lisi Schoenbach describes this narrative practice as exemplifying the workings of "habit made visible through sheer exaggeration," a pragmatic psychology that reveals itself and intensifies through an arduous and excessive accretion, "a snowballing logic of repetition and amplification."[82] Where Stein's crime fiction diverges from these accounts, however, is in its manipulation of generic convention in order to accentuate its potential as a form of aesthetic experiment. In *Blood on the Dining-Room Floor*, narrative embodies the coincidental character of crime by revealing how a kaleidoscopic narrative structure with few defining events or central characters can reflect the status of crime as a chance phenomenon, in effect adopting a modernist formal perspective in order to suit the thematic demands of a popular genre.

The connection is especially apparent when placing Stein's unorthodox crime fiction alongside traditional notions of the detective novel's epistemological concerns. Take, for example, Ronald R. Thomas's characterization of the detective as close reader: "The conventions of the form generally require the detective to explain what seems to be his uncanny act of second sight as the simple application of a technique, or even a technology, to the variables of the present occasion. The literary detective's power ... is consistently represented as a new kind of reading."[83] While Stein clearly plays upon this notion of the detective as reader, she upends the paradigm by eliminating the figure of the detective and imploring readers to resist the impulse to make sense of her narrative's ambiguity. If, as Gabrielle Dean argues, Stein understood that "to read a detective novel is to participate dramatically in narrative presence, an experience of continually uncertain, contingent currency that is distinguished from and marked against the partial, isolated, and dissonant pieces of the past event," then Stein's crime writing might be said to demand a new kind of reading, or a new kind of reader who can tolerate the uncertainty of crime and its narration.[84] Such a reader is neither a Holmesian "super-detective" nor one of Lewis's deluded amateurs, but rather the ideal modernist reader, who remains open to the prospect of never achieving narrative resolution, preferring instead to enjoy Stein's emphases on coincidence, surprise, and linguistic play.

By jettisoning the expected tropes of the popular detective novel, Stein leaves readers fumbling to get their bearings within a territory that, by all accounts, should be utterly familiar. Instead of a conventional detective novel containing all the usual signposts – detectives, suspects, and clues – readers must contend with the scattered bits of information proffered by the narrator, a figure who, like the rumors that circulate throughout the text, remains eerily ill-defined. While the narrators of Stein's other works often play the role of "everybody," or the voice of a collective, this narrator is more of a "nobody" that parallels the psychological emptiness of the novel's characters. Such hollowness not only rejects the authority of omniscient narration, but also casts doubt upon the appropriateness of psychological representation in a genre traditionally populated by stock characters and other conventions. Eliminating the typical indicators of genre fiction, Stein challenges readers to accept the contingencies of crime, and, as a result, to acclimate themselves to uncertainty or grow increasingly agitated by its presence.

Just as important as the novel's narrative ambiguity is its focus on emotion and the indeterminacy of affect within a popular genre. Indeed, to understand the role of affect in genre writing is to understand the modernism of Stein's crime fiction, as well as the potential complications inherent in that pairing. Its function within *Blood on the Dining-Room Floor* is both clearly stated and utterly ambiguous, most notably in the narrator's account of the hotel keeper's wife as she learns of her husband's affair: "She tried to be while she cried. Oh dear yes. She tried and once when she tried, do you remember once when she tried she cried. She could not try and not cry. She could smile and take things in and take things out. But if she were to try she would be obliged to cry" (*BDRF*, 12). Here emotion serves as a contrast to existence, as the wife "tried to be" in the midst of her tears. Yet the narrator also speculates that "if she were to try she would be obliged to cry," implying that emotion is perhaps a duty of being, if not an affirmation of it. Ultimately, affect's function remains uncertain, as it represents either an automatic response to an unforeseen situation or unsolvable crime – adding another element of existential complexity to a popular genre – or a melodramatic device that makes manifest and even mocks the easy sensationalism of earlier genre fictions.

Affect, then, may be the most difficult of Stein's subjects to pin down, as it refutes the conventional model of the logical and, in certain texts, practically omnipotent detective – the narrator complains that "I feel I do not know anything if I cry" (*BDRF*, 17) – and smirks at the overt sentimentality of the emotive response to murder – "How do you cry about a crime" (*BDRF*, 32). This juxtaposition of modernist and popular literary conventions brings the reader to an epistemological impasse. On the one hand, Stein admits that affect can inhibit the clarity necessary for the detective to function, and her elimination of that character from the novel, as well as the stress she places on surprise as crime's defining characteristic, may concede a space for affect within the text. On the other hand, Stein's shallow characterization and withholding of a definite plot point to the superficiality of the detective genre as a whole, and so the question of how one can cry about a crime also becomes a thinly disguised taunt to readers too immersed in a conventional and even clichéd literary form to notice the manipulative quality of its conceits. The problem extends to the issue of subjectivity, as Stein's sketchy and broken narrative reflects an understanding of the individual as either a self-contained consciousness resistant to representation or an airy nonentity with little interiority to represent. How, Stein asks, does any reader feel for characters or narrators who betray no feelings, or have no feelings to betray?

The problem with such a reading, though, is that it refuses to take Stein literally. "How do you cry about a crime" is not an accusatory question (it is not even a question, as the sentence ends without a question mark), but rather a more sympathetic inquiry into the place of affect within the reading of genre fiction, and into the affective pull of fiction more generally. In pausing over the ties between fiction and emotion, Stein speculates on how the crime novel, riven from its more procedural and necessarily predictable counterpart the detective novel, can provoke an empathetic response in its readers separate from the feelings of suspense and titillation that the latter genre typically elicits. Can random acts of violence compel us to feel for those whom we do not know, and whose characters remain just as elusive as the circumstances of their deaths? Or, conversely, does an unsolved and inexplicable death somehow steel us against the empathy we might feel over the death of an individual with whom we are familiar? Is Stein's goal to inflect a literary genre with an affective purchase different than the escapist sentimentalism and vicarious terror that critics of popular, lowbrow, and middlebrow forms decry? Or is it to explain to a desensitized reading public how to be surprised again, guiding readers to rediscover that uneasy feeling of coincidence that exemplifies the unsolvable crime and thereby respond to violence with an empathy nearly extinct in modern society?

The fact that Stein never arrives at a definitive answer to such questions speaks to the problem of blending modernism and a popular genre, since the resulting combination may well be a text that is neither popular nor modernist enough to meet the demands of its potential audiences. Such was the case with Stein's novel. Like *Mrs. Dukes' Million*, it was published posthumously due to its perceived lack of commercial prospects, as Stein balked at agent William A. Bradley's observation that such a difficult, deliberately obscure crime novel seemed more appropriate to a literary magazine like *Story* than to a mass-market venue specializing in popular genres.[85] Discouraged by the text's incapacity to replicate the financial achievements of *The Autobiography of Alice B. Toklas* while maintaining that the book was, essentially, a genre fiction, Stein deemed the work a failure. In "Why I Like Detective Stories," written four years after she completed the novel, she takes a decidedly pessimistic view of her attempt at crime fiction, lamenting that although *Blood on the Dining-Room Floor* "had a good name," it failed because "there was no corpse and the detecting was general."[86] For Stein, the primary hurdle to the novel's success was its departure from narrative convention, which frustrated the expectations of readers conditioned by texts that participate more obviously in the genre. As she puts it, the book "was all very clear in my head but it did not get natural":

> the trouble was that if it all happened and it all had happened then you had to mix it up with other things that had happened and after all a novel even if it is a detective story ought not to mix up what happened with what has happened, anything that has happened is exciting exciting enough without any writing, tell it as often as you like but do not write it not as a story.[87]

Stein's description suggests a work doomed to fail by virtue of having been written. Because, Stein warns, "anything that has happened" is sufficiently exciting to stand on its own, without augmentation or fictionalization, the act of writing a novel based on an actual crime will by the nature of mediation dispel some of that excitement. A novel like Stein's, which aims to elicit an affective response through formal representation, will therefore fall victim to its contradictory insistence that the novelty, surprise, and coincidence that characterize everyday life can be captured in writing without losing something essential.

This paradox of *Blood on the Dining-Room Floor* reveals a profound dissonance between modernism and any literary genre, and raises serious doubts about the ability of a text to embody elements of both while still meeting its formal goals and attracting its intended audience. At the same time, critics would be better served by acknowledging that in Stein's case – and in Lewis's – the effort is more important than the outcome, and by turning their attention away from questions of success or failure in adhering to established formal conventions and expectations for the kinds of writing authors can produce, and toward the varying degrees of compatibility and disconnect between modernism and genre fiction as distinct yet related forms of literary production. If Stein and Lewis have written truly hybrid texts in *Blood on the Dining-Room Floor* and *Mrs. Dukes' Million*, creating works that are neither strictly modernist nor entirely generic, then these modernist crime fictions expose the strengths and limitations of their narrative components in a way that forces critics to revise prior notions of modernist and popular authorship, and to reconsider the possibility for innovation within seemingly rigid confines. This is why it is so crucial to understand the posthumous nature of these novels not as an indisputable marker of canonical irrelevance or generic ineptitude – a perception that privileges the market in determining a work's value as modernist or generic – but as the function of a literary marketplace in which a text's inability to exist within demarcated formal boundaries could derail its opportunities for publication. Stein and Lewis's novels are important not only for demonstrating how modernism and crime fiction might inform one another in mutually productive ways, but also for exposing how the fluidity of generic categories posed an unmistakable threat to the conceptions of cultural capital and literary value that circulated during the early twentieth century.

In their methodical reworking of the hallmarks of genre fiction, *Mrs. Dukes' Million* and *Blood on the Dining-Room Floor* illustrate the surprising connections between modernist experimentation and generic formulae, and show how the current critical emphasis on uncovering modernism's investment in popular culture can expand its purview to include works like the crime and detective stories that so engrossed Stein and her contemporaries. Far from lying on the periphery of modernism, genre fiction is central to our understanding of the period, not simply because modernist authors like Stein were intrigued by both factual and fictional accounts of the criminal, nor because avant-gardists such as Lewis took up the challenge of genre fiction in order to fund other works more central to their professional reputations, but because their understanding of what it was possible to achieve in narrative and in one's career emerges just as readily through the formal mandates of popular fiction. In Lewis and Stein's novels, we can trace the intricacies of experimental narrative as it strives to represent the causes and effects of crime – whether in the minds and bodies of criminals or in the vagaries of chance and circumstance – in unfamiliar yet accurate ways. In the process, these two works illuminate the aesthetic practices modernism could employ through the affordances of a popular genre. Both novels illustrate the fact that the history of modernist fiction is also bound up in the history of crime fiction, providing contemporary critics with a new way of understanding modernism within a longer and more complicated narrative of popular forms, commercial authorship, and aesthetic experiment.

Notes

1. Aldous Huxley, *Point Counter Point* (Normal: Dalkey Archive, 2001), 193.
2. I use "crime fiction" more often than "detective fiction" in this chapter, as the terms reference different yet related things. Crime fiction typically focuses on the criminal and the crime rather than the steps taken in their apprehension, and need not feature a detective. Consequently, I apply that term to works by Lewis and Stein, which deal with criminality rather than any detective figure. For overviews of the term, see John Scaggs, *Crime Fiction* (London: Routledge, 2005) and Charles J. Rzepka, "Introduction: What Is Crime Fiction?," *A Companion to Crime Fiction*, ed. Charles J. Rzepka and Lee Horsley (Malden: Wiley-Blackwell, 2010), 1–9.
3. For an excellent account of how Wright's highbrow aspirations conflicted with his view of detective fiction as irredeemably lowbrow, see Mark McGurl, *The Novel Art: Elevations of American Fiction after Henry James* (Princeton: Princeton University Press, 2001), 158–162.
4. Other prominent authors who worked in the genre include Cecil Day-Lewis, who wrote twenty mystery novels under the pseudonym Nicholas Blake; A. A. Milne, who published *The Red House Mystery* in 1922; and Kenneth Fearing, who is perhaps better known today for his thriller *The Big Clock* (1946)

than for either his poetry or his founding of the *Partisan Review*. Modernist composer George Antheil also wrote a crime novel, *Death in the Dark* (1930), as well as *Every Man His Own Detective: A Study of Glandular Criminology* (1937).

5. Andreas Huyssen, *After the Great Divide: Modernism, Mass Culture, Postmodernism* (Bloomington: Indiana University Press, 1986), vii. For other seminal accounts of modernism's relationship to popular culture and the marketplace, see Kevin J. H. Dettmar and Stephen Watt, eds., *Marketing Modernisms: Self-Promotion, Canonization, Rereading* (Ann Arbor: University of Michigan Press, 1996); Aaron Jaffe, *Modernism and the Culture of Celebrity* (Cambridge: Cambridge University Press, 2005); Mark S. Morrisson, *The Public Face of Modernism: Little Magazines, Audiences, and Reception, 1905–1920* (Madison: University of Wisconsin Press, 2001); Michael North, *Reading 1922: A Return to the Scene of the Modern* (Oxford: Oxford University Press, 1999); and Lawrence Rainey, *Institutions of Modernism: Literary Elites and Public Culture* (New Haven: Yale University Press, 1999).

6. Rainey, *Institutions of Modernism*, 3.

7. On middlebrow literature in England and America, see Erica Brown and Mary Grover, eds., *Middlebrow Literary Cultures: The Battle of the Brows, 1920–1960* (Basingstoke: Palgrave Macmillan, 2011); Faye Hammill, *Sophistication: A Literary and Cultural History* (Liverpool: Liverpool University Press, 2010), 113–163; Jaime Harker, *America the Middlebrow: Women's Novels, Progressivism, and Middlebrow Authorship between the Wars* (Amherst: University of Massachusetts Press, 2007); Lise Jaillant, *Modernism, Middlebrow and the Literary Canon: The Modern Library Series, 1917–1955* (Abingdon: Routledge, 2016); Kate Macdonald, ed., *The Masculine Middlebrow, 1880–1950: What Mr. Miniver Read* (Basingstoke: Palgrave Macmillan, 2011); Tom Perrin, *The Aesthetics of Middlebrow Fiction: Popular US Novels, Modernism, and Form, 1945–75* (New York: Palgrave Macmillan, 2015); Janice A. Radway, *A Feeling for Books: The Book-of-the-Month-Club, Literary Taste, and Middle-Class Desire* (Chapel Hill: University of North Carolina Press, 1997); and Joan Shelley Rubin, *The Making of Middlebrow Culture* (Chapel Hill: University of North Carolina Press, 1992).

8. Pierre Bourdieu, *The Field of Cultural Production: Essays on Art and Literature*, ed. Randal Johnson (New York: Columbia University Press, 1993), 126.

9. Nicola Humble, *The Feminine Middlebrow Novel, 1920s to 1950s: Class, Domesticity, and Bohemianism* (Oxford: Oxford University Press, 2001), 4.

10. Ina Habermann, *Myth, Memory and the Middlebrow: Priestley, du Maurier and the Symbolic Form of Englishness* (Basingstoke: Palgrave Macmillan, 2010), 35.

11. Humble, *The Feminine Middlebrow Novel*, 11–12.

12. Melissa Sullivan and Sophie Blanch, "Introduction: The Middlebrow – Within or Without Modernism," *Modernist Cultures* 6.1 (May 2011): 2–3.

13. T. S. Eliot, quoted in David E. Chinitz, *T. S. Eliot and the Cultural Divide* (Chicago: University of Chicago Press, 2003), 56.

14. T. J. Binyon, *"Murder Will Out": The Detective in Fiction* (Oxford: Oxford University Press, 1989), 65.

15. On Golden Age detective fiction and the problems of that designation, see Stephen Knight, *Crime Fiction since 1800: Detection, Death, Diversity*, second ed. (Basingstoke: Palgrave Macmillan, 2010), 84–101.

16. Stephen Knight, *Form and Ideology in Crime Fiction* (London: Macmillan, 1980), 135.

17. One sees this debate most clearly in the many essays and manifestoes composed by prominent practitioners of the crime genre that appeared during the late 1920s, which aim to establish a set of foundational principles by which any participating text in the genre must abide. Of these, the most influential American contribution has been S. S. Van Dine's "Twenty Rules for Writing Detective Stories," published in the *American Magazine* in 1928, which outlines the forms of plot, characterization, and point of view that foster the necessary conditions of "fair play" between a text and its readers. In the British context, Ronald Knox's "Decalogue," included as a preface to *The Best Detective Stories of 1928–29*, offers a briefer and more idiosyncratic list of dos and don'ts, whereas Dorothy Sayers's introduction to *The Omnibus of Crime* (1929) proposes a number of criteria, many of which are remarkably flexible, for authors looking to propel the crime genre into the future.

18. Jaffe, *Modernism and the Culture of Celebrity*, 101.

19. *BLAST 1*, ed. Wyndham Lewis (Santa Rosa: Black Sparrow Press, 2002), 7.

20. Ibid., 7.

21. On the relationship between Lewis's writing and his sociopolitical views, see Fredric Jameson, *Fables of Aggression: Wyndham Lewis, the Modernist as Fascist* (Berkeley: University of California Press, 1979); and Vincent Sherry, *Ezra Pound, Wyndham Lewis, and Radical Modernism* (Oxford: Oxford University Press, 1993). On Lewis's antagonism to the audience, see Lisa Siraganian, *Modernism's Other Work: The Art Object's Political Life* (Oxford: Oxford University Press, 2012), 51–78.

22. Wyndham Lewis, "Berlin Revisited," *Modernism/modernity* 4.2 (April 1997): 177.

23. Ibid., 178.

24. Ibid., 178.

25. Scott W. Klein, "Modern Times against Western Man: Wyndham Lewis, Charlie Chaplin and Cinema," *Wyndham Lewis and the Cultures of Modernity*, ed. Andrzej Gąsiorek, Alice Reeve-Tucker, and Nathan Waddell (Surrey: Ashgate, 2011), 137.

26. Michael North, *Machine-Age Comedy* (Oxford: Oxford University Press, 2009), 113.

27. *BLAST 1*, 7.

28. Ibid., 7.

29. Wyndham Lewis, "Futurism and the Flesh: A Futurist's Reply to G. K. Chesterton," *Creatures of Habit and Creatures of Change: Essays on Art, Literature and Society, 1914–1956*, ed. Paul Edwards (Santa Rosa: Black Sparrow Press, 1989), 35.

30. Ezra Pound, quoted in Ann L. Ardis, *Modernism and Cultural Conflict, 1880–1922* (Cambridge: Cambridge University Press, 2002), 102.

31. Wyndham Lewis, letter to J. B. Pinker, circa 1909–1910, *The Letters of Wyndham Lewis*, ed. W. K. Rose (London: Methuen, 1963), 44. On the novel's composition, see Paul O'Keeffe, *Some Sort of Genius: A Life of Wyndham Lewis* (London: Jonathan Cape, 2000).

32. Lewis, *The Letters of Wyndham Lewis*, 44n1.

33. Julian Symons, "A Master of Disguise," *Times Literary Supplement* 30 (30 June 1978): 726–727. Oddly, Symons never addresses the text's most curious feature: in a note at the end of the novel, editor Frank Davey explains that in chapter XV he "hypothetically reconstructed" a two-page gap in Lewis's manuscript. See Wyndham Lewis, *Mrs. Dukes' Million* (Toronto: Coach House Press, 1977), 368. Hereafter cited parenthetically, as *MDM*.

34. Lewis, *The Letters of Wyndham Lewis*, 43.

35. Symons, "A Master of Disguise," 726.

36. Hugh Kenner, "*Mrs. Dukes' Million*: The Stunt of an Illusionist," *Wyndham Lewis: A Revaluation*, ed. Jeffrey Meyers (London: Athlone, 1980), 90.

37. Douglas Mao, *Solid Objects: Modernism and the Test of Production* (Princeton: Princeton University Press, 1998), 92.

38. Paul Edwards, *Wyndham Lewis: Painter and Writer* (New Haven: Yale University Press, 2000), 32.

39. Sean Latham, *The Art of Scandal: Modernism, Libel Law, and the Roman à Clef* (Oxford: Oxford University Press, 2009), 106.

40. On metamorphosing bodies and identities in *Mrs. Dukes' Million*, see Anne Quéma, *The Agon of Modernism: Wyndham Lewis's Allegories, Aesthetics, and Politics* (Lewisburg: Bucknell University Press, 1999), 47.

41. As Scott W. Klein notes, even Fane's name puns on the notion of "feigning" an identity. Klein, *The Fictions of James Joyce and Wyndham Lewis: Monsters of Nature and Design* (Cambridge: Cambridge University Press, 1994), 27–28.

42. Paul Peppis, *Literature, Politics, and the English Avant-Garde: Nation and Empire, 1901–1918* (Cambridge: Cambridge University Press, 2000), 136.

43. Jessica Burstein, *Cold Modernism: Literature, Fashion, Art* (University Park: Pennsylvania State University Press, 2012), 68.

44. Andrzej Gąsiorek, "War, 'Primitivism,' and the Future of 'the West': Reflections on D. H. Lawrence and Wyndham Lewis," *Modernism and Colonialism: British and Irish Literature, 1899–1939*, ed. Richard Begam and Michael Valdez Moses (Durham: Duke University Press, 2007), 94.

45. Michael Levenson, *Modernism and the Fate of Individuality: Character and Novelistic Form from Conrad to Woolf* (Cambridge: Cambridge University Press, 1991), 124.

46. Ibid., 124.

47. Mao, *Solid Objects*, 139.

48. Gertrude Stein, "Why I Like Detective Stories," *How Writing Is Written: Volume II of the Previously Uncollected Writings of Gertrude Stein*, ed. Robert Bartlett Haas (Los Angeles: Black Sparrow Press, 1974), 146.

49. Ellen E. Berry, *Curved Thought and Textual Wandering: Gertrude Stein's Postmodernism* (Ann Arbor: University of Michigan Press, 1992), 146.
50. Maria DiBattista, "The Lowly Art of Murder: Modernism and the Case of the Free Woman," *High and Low Moderns: Literature and Culture, 1889–1939*, ed. Maria DiBattista and Lucy McDiarmid (New York: Oxford University Press, 1996), 176.
51. Gabrielle Dean, "Grid Games: Gertrude Stein's Diagrams and Detectives," *Modernism/modernity* 15.2 (April 2008): 326.
52. Gertrude Stein, *Everybody's Autobiography* (Cambridge, MA: Exact Change, 1993), 2.
53. Stein, "Why I Like Detective Stories," 149.
54. Ibid., 149.
55. Ibid., 149.
56. Ibid., 149.
57. Ibid., 146.
58. Ibid., 147.
59. For an incisive account of Stein's conception of money in modern social systems, see Michael Szalay, *New Deal Modernism: American Literature and the Invention of the Welfare State* (Durham: Duke University Press, 2000), 87–90.
60. Auden, "The Guilty Vicarage," *The Complete Works of W. H. Auden: Prose, Volume II, 1939–1948*, ed. Edward Mendelson (Princeton: Princeton University Press, 2002), 262.
61. D. A. Miller, *The Novel and the Police* (Berkeley: University of California Press, 1988), 3.
62. Roger Caillois, "The Detective Novel as Game," *The Poetics of Murder: Detective Fiction and Literary Theory*, ed. Glenn W. Most and William W. Stowe (San Diego: Harcourt Brace Jovanovich, 1983), 3.
63. Stein, "Why I Like Detective Stories," 147.
64. Deborah M. Mix, *A Vocabulary of Thinking: Gertrude Stein and Contemporary North American Women's Innovative Writing* (Iowa City: University of Iowa Press, 2007), 23.
65. Gertrude Stein, "American Crimes and How They Matter," *How Writing Is Written: Volume II of the Previously Uncollected Writings of Gertrude Stein*, ed. Robert Bartlett Haas (Los Angeles: Black Sparrow Press, 1974), 105.
66. Franco Moretti, *Signs Taken for Wonders: Essays in the Sociology of Literary Forms* (London: Verso, 1988), 146, 144.
67. While Stein never identifies the date of the excursion, her observation that "Baby Face" Nelson (Lester Joseph Gillis) was captured and killed that same night, just outside of Chicago, puts the date at November 27, 1934. On Stein's trip to Chicago and its significance for her American tour, see Liesl Olson, "'An invincible force meets an immovable object': Gertrude Stein comes to Chicago," *Modernism/modernity* 17.2 (April 2010): 331–361.
68. Stein, "American Crimes and How They Matter," 101.

69. Gertrude Stein, *Narration: Four Lectures* (Chicago: University of Chicago Press, 2010), 40. Stein advances a similar claim in "What Are Master-pieces and Why Are There So Few of Them" (1936) when she states that "In real life people are interested in the crime more than they are in detection, it is the crime that is the thing the shock the thrill the horror but in the story it is the detection that holds the interest." Gertrude Stein, *Selections*, ed. Joan Retallack (Berkeley: University of California Press, 2008), 312.

70. Stein, "American Crimes and How They Matter," 101.

71. Ibid., 103.

72. Brooks Landon, "'Not Solve It But Be In It': Gertrude Stein's Detective Stories and the Mystery of Creativity," *American Literature* 53.3 (November 1981): 488.

73. On the history of critics dismissing Stein's work as unreadable, see Natalia Cecire, "Ways of Not Reading Gertrude Stein," *ELH* 82.1 (Spring 2015): 281–312.

74. "A Crime Is a Crime," *Time* (June 14, 1948): 106; Anne Freemantle, Review of Gertrude Stein, *Blood on the Dining-Room Floor, New York Times* (August 1, 1948): BR13. Clippings of these and other early reviews of the novel are preserved in the Gertrude Stein and Alice B. Toklas Collection, Yale Collection of American Literature, Beinecke Rare Book and Manuscript Library, YCAL MSS 77, Box 25, Folder 446.

75. Caroline Levine, *Forms: Whole, Rhythm, Hierarchy, Network* (Princeton: Princeton University Press, 2015), 6.

76. Harriet Scott Chessman, *The Public Is Invited to Dance: Representation, the Body, and Dialogue in Gertrude Stein* (Stanford: Stanford University Press, 1989), 137; James R. Mellow, *Charmed Circle: Gertrude Stein and Company* (New York: Owl Books, 2003), 364.

77. Stein, *Everybody's Autobiography*, 46. Despite these objections, Stein relished the attention her celebrity brought her. See Mark Goble, *Beautiful Circuits: Modernism and the Mediated Life* (New York: Columbia University Press, 2010), 85–148; Jonathan Goldman, *Modernism Is the Literature of Celebrity* (Austin: University of Texas Press, 2011), 81–110; and Karen Leick, *Gertrude Stein and the Making of an American Celebrity* (New York: Routledge, 2009).

78. This is the account of the accident provided in Ulla E. Dydo, *Gertrude Stein: The Language That Rises, 1923–1934* (Evanston: Northwestern University Press, 2003), 564–570.

79. Stein, *Everybody's Autobiography*, 55.

80. Gertrude Stein, *Blood on the Dining-Room Floor* (Mineola: Dover, 2008), 6–7. Hereafter cited parenthetically, as *BDRF*.

81. Jennifer Ashton, *From Modernism to Postmodernism: American Poetry and Theory in the Twentieth Century* (Cambridge: Cambridge University Press, 2005), 34.

82. Lisi Schoenbach, *Pragmatic Modernism* (Oxford: Oxford University Press, 2012), 51.

83. Ronald R. Thomas, *Detective Fiction and the Rise of Forensic Science* (Cambridge: Cambridge University Press, 1999), 3.

84. Dean, "Grid Games," 326.

85. Dydo, *Gertrude Stein: The Language That Rises*, 570.

86. Stein, "Why I Like Detective Stories," 148.

87. Ibid., 148.

CHAPTER 4

Cases of Identity
Late Modernism and the Life of Crime

Murder didn't mean much to Raven. It was just a new job.
— Graham Greene, *A Gun for Sale* (1936)[1]

Tom Ripley had never really been despondent, though he had often
looked it. Hadn't he learned something from these last months? If you
wanted to be cheerful, or melancholic, or wistful, or thoughtful, or
courteous, you simply had to *act* those things with every gesture.
— Patricia Highsmith, *The Talented Mr. Ripley* (1955)[2]

Both modernism and crime fiction had altered dramatically by the time
Gertrude Stein began writing *Blood on the Dining-Room Floor* in 1933, their
aesthetics and audiences shifting through a combination of historical
change, developments in the publishing industry, and readers' evolving
tastes. Crime fiction especially had experienced a profound crisis of identity, pressured by hard-boiled American authors who rejected many of the
genre's traditions. Writers such as Dashiell Hammett, who by 1933 had
published all but one of his five novels, and Raymond Chandler, whose
first story for the pulp magazine *Black Mask* debuted in December of
that year, defied the thematic and stylistic conventions of the classic
mystery in what Will Norman describes as "a purge of outdated mannerisms and rejuvenation through the American vernacular rough-house."[3]
They and other hard-boiled novelists reinterpreted the crime genre by
taking as their subject an ethically ambiguous, violent society in which
a detective struggles to maintain both the rule of law and his personal ethos
without becoming a criminal himself. In contrast to the frantic amateurism
of Lord Peter Wimsey and the dispassionate analysis of Sherlock Holmes,
hard-boiled detectives were dogged professionals, and signaled a new type
of protagonist (and, by extension, new types of antagonists) immersed in
the naturalism of contemporary American fiction.

Just as crime novelists reckoned with their genre's past in order to chart
its future, so too did those writers who made their reputations as early

twentieth-century avant-gardists, or who were now beginning their careers by responding to modernism's example. With novels such as *Ulysses* (1922), *The Great Gatsby* (1925), *The Sun Also Rises* (1926), *To the Lighthouse* (1927), and *The Sound and the Fury* (1929) cementing modernism's reputation in the 1920s, novelists of the 1930s and after re-examined the formal, political, and philosophical aims of their predecessors (and, in some cases, of their own, earlier work) through an emergent late modernism. Adapting early modernist aesthetics to a new sociopolitical environment, these writers alternately critiqued and extended the formal innovations of early twentieth-century fiction while also registering the effects of extraordinary historical shifts.[4] As Thomas Davis explains, late modernism reveals how "the accumulating world-systemic distress of the decades after the roaring twenties migrated into the aesthetic theories and formal structures of modernism," as authors "renovate[d] established modernist techniques" without abandoning them entirely.[5] Tyrus Miller makes a similar point in positioning late modernism between postmodernism and earlier aesthetic experiments. Late modernism, he posits,

> mark[s] the lines of flight artists took where an obstacle, the oft-mentioned "impasse" of modernism, interrupted progress on established paths . . . The cultural products of this period both are and are not "of the moment." Precisely in their untimeliness, their lack of symmetry and formal balance, they retain the power to transport their readers and critics "out of bounds" – to an "elsewhere" of writing from which the period can be surveyed, from which its legitimacy as a whole might be called into question.[6]

By this account, late modernism fulfills the early modernist imperative of self-reflexivity, but by interrogating modernist aesthetics in order to judge their utility for a contemporary world. Hammett and Chandler perform similar functions in adapting crime fiction's traditions to new ends. Just as they abandon the "established paths" of Poe, Doyle, and Sayers, they also reimagine some of their genre's most notable conventions in ways timely and untimely, mirroring the situation of late modernist authors who adjusted early modernism's experimental aesthetics to respond to budding historical conditions.

　　As a liminal concept whose name suggests belatedness or an impending end, late modernism poses significant challenges to the idea of literary periodization. Indeed, several late modernist texts bear little formal resemblance to their early modernist predecessors, and respond to a culture far different than that of modernism's formative years. As Jed Esty observes, "[w]hile many of the stylistic hallmarks of high modernism continued to appear in various experimental and nonmimetic literatures well after World War II, the broader cultural conditions of metropolitan modernism ended rather sharply during the mid-century."[7] This apparent rift is precisely why the concept of late modernism denotes an uncanny moment in literary history, during which modernism became an increasingly mutable aesthetic phenomenon. In fact, several critics regard late modernism's untimeliness as its greatest conceptual asset; to Marina MacKay, by underscoring historical circumstance as a catalyst for aesthetic development, late modernism counters those who fetishize modernism's beginnings:

> To speak of late modernism is to signal unambiguously a move away from the manifestos of the 1910s and the climactic year of 1922, a shift that allows us to reconsider what modernism means as a description of distinctive aesthetic modes that were not monolithic or static but capable of development and transformation. Focusing on late modernism is a way of reading modernism through its longer outcomes rather than its notional origins.[8]

For MacKay and others, late modernism furthers modernism's legacy by applying its aesthetics to new aims, and prevents modernism's formal ingenuity and cultural perspicacity from ossifying as times change.

That process of renovation also produced new ways of theorizing the criminal. With the scientism of criminal anthropology now decades past its heyday, Lombroso's notion of criminality as an anomaly within the social order seemed even less convincing to both natural and social scientists, ignoring as it did the apparent fact of crime as a routine presence in everyday life, as well as the many other circumstances that could conceivably lead an individual toward criminal acts. By the 1930s, critics increasingly understood criminality as ebbing and flowing according to various social, economic, and educational pressures, rather than corresponding to physical degeneracy, and so the concept of born criminality suffered a marked decline in both the public and the professional estimation. As a result, late modernists resisted even more dramatically than their predecessors representations that couched the criminal in pathological terms. This is not to suggest that popular equations of criminality with degeneracy had disappeared; as William Greenslade points out, the continued stereotyping of Britain's working poor "still relied on an unthinking application of biological models of 'fitness' derived from a value-laded social Darwinism," and the multiple eugenicist programs of the 1930s sought to contain what supporters perceived as a pervasive criminality within the country's least educated, most economically disadvantaged members.[9] Late modernists, however, saw criminality as something different, and potentially much more useful as a template for understanding modern forms of subjectivity as negotiating between specific and general categories of personhood. They followed their modernist precursors in viewing criminals as experiments in psychological representation, but took a different path by deconstructing the motivations that lead individuals to couch their senses of self within a broader criminal identity, drawing upon established tropes of criminality in order to present themselves as singular examples of the type. Instead of adopting the tenets of positivist criminology or challenging them as directly as James or Conrad, late modernists asked how the criminal might actually be a self-styled instance of identity formation, an individual who mines the conventions of criminality in order to earn a unique signifying power within a specific social milieu. Their fictional criminals were less pathological than professional types, playing upon Mayhew's theory of criminality as an unwillingness to work by suggesting that a criminal identity could afford its bearer a powerful sense of self that paradoxically affirms individual agency by locating that individual within a broad category of persons. Rather than retreating from general criminal typologies, then, late modernists explored how such typologies provide unexpected opportunities for identification.

To accomplish that aim, late modernists built upon the work of early modernists in two key respects. First, they continued to mine the conventions of popular crime fiction, following its tradition of presenting the criminal as a formal as much as a social problem. Second, they embraced the early modernist form of the case study, with its insistence that the individual is productively understood as both a unique subject and a representative of larger patterns of human behavior. Employing a form with clear ties to early modernism and its debts to psychoanalysis, late modernists used the case study to present physical and psychological data about their fictional criminals, and thereby to demonstrate how criminality functions as a method of self-creation, while also emphasizing continuity between their work and that of their literary antecedents. As Freud maintained, the case study's value resides in its ability to align a patient's symptoms with specific disorders, demonstrating how the patient embodies a broader phenomenon. By grounding itself in the routine – Freud claims that it "depends for its coherence precisely upon the small details of real life" – the case study attends to minutiae of behavior, thought, and expression that, collectively, expose the general disorder.[10] Here arises the paradox of the case study as a diagnostic as well as a literary form, with Freud claiming to understand general patterns of subjectivity through individual instances. In his "Notes upon a Case of Obsessional

Neurosis" (1909), Freud attributes the Rat Man's fear that his sexual desires will inflict physical punishment upon his deceased father to a more general condition: "It was a complete obsessional neurosis, wanting in no essential element, at once the nucleus and the prototype of the later disorder – an elementary organism, as it were, the study of which could alone enable us to obtain a grasp of the complicated organization of his subsequent illness."[11] Late modernists turned to the case study to obtain a similar grasp, using the form to render the conventions of fictional narrative more useful in theorizing criminality as a broad category of subjectivity with which individuals might knowingly identify.

Just as the case study links late modernism to early modernism, it also links late modernism to crime fiction, as critics often frame the epistemo-logical imperatives of the latter genre alongside psychoanalysis's strategic use of narrative as a window into the unconscious. As Dennis Porter argues, "the psychoanalytic case history is a mystery story" because both represent "the recovery of a story," whether of neurosis or of crime.[12] Consequently, late modernism's interest in the case study as a tool for understanding the criminal's interiority solidifies connections between crime fiction and modernist fiction apparent since the late nineteenth century, and so provides another example of modernism's longstanding immersion in popular literary forms. Moreover, it also suggests the linked trajectories of modernism and crime fiction in the 1930s and after, as both were transformed by the efforts of authors eager to rethink them for new historical contexts. Though Dorothy Sayers published her first Lord Peter Wimsey novel in 1923, just six years before Dashiell Hammett debuted his first novel, *Red Harvest*, the emergence of the hard-boiled school blurred the boundaries between the detective and the criminal, shifting the genre's attention from the detective's reason (or unreason) to a more intensive examination of the criminal, with the explicit assumption that the line separating the two was no longer as firm as past writers had described. Hard-boiled authors figured the detective as a violent antihero, most often a private investigator whose violence makes him just as ethically ambiguous as the charismatic murderers, thieves, and gangsters he pursues. Of these authors, none attained a higher critical or popular reputation than Hammett, who combined the tenets of a popular genre with interrogations of form and subjectivity characteristic of modernism. This chapter begins by positioning Hammett's writing as itself a case study for understanding the evolution of the criminal in both modernism and genre fiction, and shows how Hammett's protean model of criminality inflects Graham Greene and Patricia Highsmith's late modernist deployment of the case study. In the process, it shows how the case study's prominence in late modernism signals a renewed concern with criminal typology, and the means by which individual criminals seek to embody the concept of criminality as a whole.

Dashiell Hammett's Career Criminals

For reasons both formal and thematic, Hammett's position in the modernist canon is firmer than that of any other crime novelist. His terse narration mirrors that of American modernists like Ernest Hemingway,[13] while his disregard for the epistemological certainty of earlier detective fiction echoes the modernist critique of ethical judgment.[14] Furthermore, despite the fact that other hard-boiled detectives existed before Hammett published his first stories in *Black Mask*, his reputation as an innovator within a historically restrictive genre ties him to modernism's experimental impulses. As John G. Cawelti observes, Hammett gave hard-boiled fiction "much of its distinctive style and atmosphere, developed its urban setting, invented many of its most effective plot patterns, and, above all, articulated the hard-boiled hero, creating that special mixture of toughness and sentimentality, of cynical understatement and eloquence that would remain the stamp of the hard-boiled detective, even in his cruder avatars."[15] Commonly viewed as an original within a sea of imitation, Hammett's aggressive reformulation of what many perceived as a derivative genre has led critics such as James Naremore to consider his work an example of popular modernism, responsive to evolving conceptions of generic form as well as the modernist assault on bourgeois cultural values. "The only difference between Hammett and the high modernists," Naremore argues, "was that he applied an emerging sensibility to popular adventure stories, attacking bourgeois culture from 'below' rather than from above."[16] Likewise, Jon Thompson characterizes Hammett's work as neither "a pale reflection of high modernism" nor a "second-tier" brand of genre fiction, but rather a modernist embrace of mass culture that signifies a dual commitment to formal experiment and convention.[17] Crucially, Hammett's decision to repurpose some of his genre's most important traditions – acting upon his desire to "make 'literature' of it," as he wrote to Blanche Knopf in 1928 – grants him a privileged position in both modernist and crime fiction criticism.[18] While opinions differ on what constitutes Hammett's modernism, few dispute its existence.

What this chapter aims to show is that Hammett also influenced the late modernism of the 1930s and after, particularly those authors interested in the potential of popular form to accommodate both generic and modernist conventions, and to reveal previously hidden aspects of criminality as a category of identity that individuals might inhabit in order to stabilize otherwise shaky senses of self. Following Hammett, late modernists such as Graham Greene and Patricia Highsmith employed the tropes of crime fiction in order to arrive at new ways of conceptualizing criminal identity, adapting for their own work the deep fascination with criminal subjectivity that Hammett displayed. Thus, while Hammett fits uneasily into the category of late modernism – the majority of his fiction appeared in the 1920s, and the years following his final novel, *The Thin Man* (1934), yielded little output except for a few scattered film stories and a brief run on the comic strip *Secret Agent X-9* – his shadow looms large over it.

So too do those of his quirky and oftentimes vicious fictional criminals, who range from inexperienced youths embroiled in crimes of passion to repeat offenders who know of no more lucrative or enjoyable enterprise than a life of crime. In every case, Hammett renders his criminals with a sharply defined psychology, and presents their individual motivations for crime in ways that refute notions of a general criminal type while at the same time evincing clear indebtedness to them, as people with few options style themselves as seasoned criminals in a world that responds to such an identity with a mixture of repulsion, awe, and attention. Through criminals who are equally capable of brutality and self-awareness, remorselessness and introspection, Hammett sets a precedent for interrogating the motives of fictional criminals in order to speculate on how criminality originates and develops, and demonstrates how one can utilize the conventions of the crime genre in order to give those characters a depth previously unknown.

Take, for instance, Hammett's first novel, *Red Harvest*, serialized in *Black Mask* from November 1927 through February 1928, in which the anonymous detective known only as the Continental Op bullies an anxious young man named Robert Albury, an assistant cashier at a local bank, into confessing to the murder of Donald Willsson, a prosperous muckraking journalist in the industrial city of Personville. While such an interrogation is a structural necessity in most crime fiction, as a killer must reveal his or her guilt in order to appease both a detective's appetite for justice and the reader's desire for narrative resolution, this particular confession is unique in lingering over the individual motivations for the murder rather than establishing closure. Admitting that his attraction to the avaricious Dinah Brand led him to murder Willsson, one of Brand's many lovers, Albury explains that his actions had less to do with unrequited love than with a deep-seated anger at the economic situation that blocked him from the object of his desires. Whereas Willsson could buy Brand's affections, Albury's job forced him to endure the indignity of cashing the very checks that pushed Brand out of his reach. Explaining his final interaction with Willsson, Albury laments that "[a]ll I could think about was that I had lost her because I had no more money, and he was taking five thousand dollars to her. It was the check. Can you understand that? . . . It was seeing the check – and knowing I'd lost her because my money was gone."[19]

The desperate youth who murders for money, to get it or to prevent its loss, is a common presence in crime fiction, and in fiction more generally. Indeed, economically motivated murder is a fairly predictable crime in literary history – as noted in the previous chapter, Stein found it the most believable of all possible motivations for violence – but it captivated American readers during the boom of the 1920s and the bust of the 1930s, two decades largely defined by economics. During that time, Hammett had ample opportunity to consider the role of money as a catalyst for one's actions. As a regular contributor to *Black Mask* he perfected the hard-boiled style that influenced generations of writers, yet he never earned a comfortable living from the work, and had to revise rejected stories to sell to other magazines.[20] He also harbored loftier aspirations, hoping to achieve a reputation traditionally reserved for more "serious" novelists while retaining the popular visibility he enjoyed with *Black Mask*. Effectively, Hammett sought to bridge the gap between modernist literature, with its focus on formal experiment, and the hard-boiled, with its unflinching depictions of urban decay, the banality of violence, and the harsh realities of the life of crime. As Mark McGurl puts it, Hammett's fiction "shows us both what modernism looks like to mass culture and what mass culture looks like to modernism, without canceling the relative autonomy of these two discourses."[21] Striving to make money while also making art, Hammett recognized his motivations for celebrity within an ideal professional identity that balanced seemingly opposite goals.

The tension between the mass-market visibility that came with pulp serialization and the prestige of collecting and reissuing his novels with Alfred A. Knopf, the most prominent American publisher for modernism, exerted an enormous influence over Hammett's career. Yet while Hammett's aspirations to critical and commercial success are well known, the ways in which his characters, particularly his criminals, wrestle with similar questions of profession, payment, and style have garnered comparatively little attention. Whereas critics tend to emphasize

Hammett's detective protagonists and their relation to the subversive sexuality of the femme fatale, or his novels' formal divergences from traditional murder mysteries, one can also consider Hammett's fiction from a different angle, by examining how the criminals that populate it consider themselves professionals in order to craft distinct identities within an otherwise indifferent society.[22] Regarding their grisly work as either a dubious enterprise beneath their talents or an opportune vehicle for self-creation, these criminals identify themselves professionally in much the same way that Hammett did. In fact, one of Hammett's most notable contributions to crime fiction lies in his depiction of crime as a marker of professional identity and status, coupled with his insistence that between the economic pinnacle of the roaring '20s and the opening throes of the Great Depression, the prospect of making money through violence attracted men and women from all walks of life, whether they were fictional characters or the authors who created them.

For Hammett's characters, the criminal persona represents an opportunity to solidify an otherwise confounded identity through a set of practices that signify fearlessness, aptitude, and distinction. Thus, crime provides a comfortable living as well as a stable professional and personal identity, becoming an invaluable method for constructing one's own subjectivity. To achieve this effect, Hammett employs the logic of the case study, rendering his characters with individual characteristics that also allude to a general criminal type. In *Red Harvest*, Albury's nervous tics and hyperactive talkativeness may distinguish him from other characters, but they also allow the Op to peg him as an inexperienced murderer. During the interrogation, the Op explains that he discerned Albury's guilt immediately after their first meeting: "You talked too much, son. You were too damned anxious to make your life an open book for me. That's a way you amateur criminals have. You've always got to do the frank and open business" (*RH*, 59). The fact that Albury is eager to reveal irrelevant personal details in order to mask his fear of being discovered as a murderer is precisely what makes him resemble so many other "amateur criminals," and thus easy to identify. The Op's language in this admonishment is telling, especially in its conflation of the pronoun "you," which refers to Albury and to all amateur criminals, interchangeably, as if the two are one and the same.

Whereas Albury represents the inexperienced, unsuccessful criminal whose attempts to hide his culpability peg him as an amateur, Hammett's other criminals are typically more hardened, and even derive pleasure from their status as dangerous professionals. Indeed, Hammett's career criminals make little effort to disguise their business from the detectives who pursue them. Rather than construct elaborate alibis to prove their innocence, they take evident pride in their work, publicly identifying themselves as professional criminals whose value emerges from that identification. It is unsurprising, then, that the police think of these criminals in terms of types, expecting that the self-proclaimed murderer, thief, or blackmailer will perpetually commit those crimes so intimately entwined with his identity. Hence, the concept of criminal rehabilitation is conspicuously absent from Hammett's writing, and detectives approach their work with the disillusionment of those who, like the Op, harbor no faith in the legal system's power to reform consistent offenders.

In depicting a world in which crime becomes a mode of identification, Hammett's fiction initially seems to present a radically simplified view of criminal psychology. Consider Albury, who, rejected by Dinah Brand because he could never summon enough money to retain her attention, blithely accepts her avarice. "She's money-mad," he admits, "but somehow you don't mind it. She's so thoroughly mercenary, so frankly greedy, that there's nothing disagreeable about it" (*RH*, 27). Because Brand emphasizes her greed Albury accepts it as an essential feature of her character, so prominent that it scarcely merits attention. Just as Brand's "money madness" defines her identity so thoroughly that one accepts it without passing judgment, Albury believes that his financial motivation for murder is so transparent that it marks him as a particular type of criminal, and becomes a shadow enveloping whatever remains of his life: "I can't now – quite understand – fully – why I did what I did. Do you know what I mean? That somehow makes the whole thing – and me – cheap" (*RH*, 62). While he claims not to understand his reasons for murdering Willsson, the language of his confession betrays him. Albury's humiliation does not arise from killing another person or from being caught, but from committing a crime inconsistent with what he believed himself to be. However, the state of being "cheap" alludes not only to Albury's resentment at carrying out an act he cannot fathom, but also to his empty wallet, a not-so-subtle reminder of the original murderous impulse. Though he hopes to live the incident down, when coupled with the poverty that drove him to murder in the first place it becomes the most distinguishing aspect of his identity. Even in his attempt to forget the killing Albury cannot avoid referencing his original intentions, trapped by the condition that defines him.

While Albury conforms to the identity he now believes he possesses, other characters in Hammett's work perceive their criminality as a malleable form that might be made to correspond to one's desires – or, in some cases, to aid in committing other, less expected types of crimes. These characters complicate the argument that Hammett's criminals remain locked in general categories of identity, and reveal their creator's fluctuation between ideas of the criminal as either a general or labile class of person. For instance, in "The Golden Horseshoe," published in *Black Mask* in 1924, a petty thief named Edward Bohannon explains to the Continental Op how he once stumbled upon a suicide in a Seattle hotel room and then assumed the identity of the dead man in order to procure money from the man's wife, who believed that her absent husband was in hiding, embarrassed by his drug addiction and poor prospects. The event, Bohannon argues, was pure accident. Seeking cover after robbing several of the hotel's rooms, he inadvertently took refuge in an empty room belonging to an architect named Norman Ashcraft, who returned to the room and shot himself while Bohannon hid in a closet. When confronted by police responding to the noise of the shot, Bohannon immediately claimed to be Ashcraft, anxious after shooting an anonymous burglar who had attempted to rob his room. Incredibly, the police believed Bohannon's story, and, as he tells the Op, "I stayed in Seattle for three days – as Norman Ashcraft. I had tumbled on to something rich and I wasn't going to throw it away."[23] The real Ashcraft's suicide provides Bohannon with a steady income as well as an identity he can adopt whenever it might prove lucrative. This new persona is "rich" in every sense of the term, earning money while offering fresh opportunities for crime that Edward Bohannon would not have been able to initiate.

What Bohannon finds most impressive about his new identity is the fact that others seem so easily fooled by it. The decision to take on the dead man's identity, he remarks, came easily, since "[t]here are thousands of us on the same order – blond, fairly tall, well set up."[24] Because so many men share this common physical type, Bohannon reasons that his impersonation should work seamlessly as long as he can replicate Ashcraft's more distinctive features, and so he rummages through Ashcraft's belongings to assist in his transformation: "after I went through the dead man's stuff I knew him inside and outside, backward and forward. He had nearly a bushel of papers, and a diary that had everything he had ever done or thought in it. I put in the first night studying those things – memorizing them – and practicing his signature."[25] In studying all that Ashcraft "had ever done or thought," Bohannon internalizes those elements of personality that are more unique than physical appearance yet can also be repeated successfully, memorizing Ashcraft's history in order to cast himself as a passable likeness. In so doing, Bohannon creates an identity that is uniquely his own – since only a few people seem to know what Ashcraft looked like – yet borrowed from an original source. Shifting between one identity and the other depending on which is more profitable at any given time, Bohannon picks and chooses between two different personae in a constant cycle of identification.

One could argue that Bohannon's adoption of Ashcraft's identity represents a simple case of a thief becoming a fraud, or of one species of criminal taking on the guise of another. After all, Bohannon is already a criminal before he presents himself as Ashcraft, and he remains a criminal after completing the transformation. Also, his impersonation of Ashcraft develops largely through an exchange of letters with Ashcraft's wife, and becoming another person through correspondence is obviously not the same thing as assimilating an entirely new identity. Still, the fact that Bohannon can change at all reflects Hammett's understanding of the fissures within supposedly stable categories of criminal identity, as does the story's implication that even the most individually specific traits can be repeated by other people. In recognizing that one can effectively adopt a foreign identity by studying the revelations of a diary, Bohannon and his newfound persona challenge conventional notions of criminality – and subjectivity more generally – as fixed, and undermine those fears of an inescapable criminal identity that haunt the doomed Albury.

Ironically, Hammett's detectives also share with his criminals an ambivalent sense of their professional identities. More violent than Hammett's other famous detective, Sam Spade, the Continental Op represents both the modern professional whose work permeates his life (hence his purely professional name) and the jaded lawman whose brutality equals that of the criminals he tracks. On occasion, the Op even enjoys violence, noting in *Red Harvest* the sense of calm he receives after pitting Personville's gangsters against one another: "Poisonville was beginning to boil out under the lid, and I felt so much like a native that even the memory of my very un-nice part in the boiling didn't keep me from getting twelve solid end-to-end hours of sleep" (*RH*, 115). As Sean McCann explains, while the Op aligns himself with the rule of law in *Red Harvest*, he is "as violent, cruel, and self-interested as anyone in Personville," and "all that distinguishes him from the criminals he betrays and kills is his purely formal adherence to laws that have been stripped of any ethical content."[26] Though the Op rarely questions the legality of his methods, he acknowledges their uneasy ethical footing. When Dinah Brand complains that the Op has "got the vaguest way of doing things I ever heard of," he argues that "[p]lans are all right sometimes ... [a]nd sometimes just stirring things up is all right – if you're tough enough to survive, and keep your eyes open so you'll see what you want when it comes to the top" (*RH*, 85). For him, the rule of law is not universally effective, as exceptions, which force detectives to skirt their legal obligations in order to find and punish their quarry, always arise. As he maintains, "[i]t's right enough for the Agency to have rules and regulations, but when you're out on a job you've got to do it the best way you can. And anybody that brings any ethics to Poisonville is going to get them all rusty" (*RH*, 117).

Though the Op's personal ethics buckle under the strain of Personville's corruption – the locals call the city "Poisonville" for its ability to infect anyone who enters it – they do so in service of his work as a private detective, and his compulsion to fulfill his professional obligations. Still, the Op's decision to fan the flames as Personville burns becomes unsettling as the novel progresses, conflicting with some essential element of his identity that the Op recognizes but cannot articulate. Complaining that he now finds humor in his ability to propose specific men as targets for the city's gangsters, he chastises himself for such callousness not because of any moral qualm with such a reaction, but because it seems out of character:

> I looked at Noonan [Personville's corrupt police chief] and knew he hadn't a chance in a thousand of living another day because of what I had done to him, and I laughed, and felt warm and happy inside. That's not me. I've got hard skin all over what's left of my soul, and after twenty years of messing around with crime I can look at any sort of a murder without seeing anything in it but my bread and butter, the day's work. But this getting a rear out of planning deaths is not natural to me. (*RH*, 157)

Throughout the novel, however, planning deaths seems entirely natural to the Op, and when his agency demands that he account for his actions, the Op busies himself by "trying to fix up my reports so they would not read as if I had broken as many Agency rules, state laws and human bones as I had" (*RH*, 215). By presenting the Op in this confounded manner – as an individual who perceives himself as both an ordinary private investigator and an agent provocateur – Hammett extends to his detective the protean subjectivity that characterizes his criminals. Using one's profession to establish a coherent identity may provide a measure of self-assurance, making one more recognizable to both crime fiction readers and the rule of law. However, as Hammett suggests, that comfort can easily collapse under the strain of circumstance, environment, and opportunity. Throughout his fiction, Hammett undertakes a complicated process of affirming general categories of identification, shattering them with characters that rebel against such constraints, and then reaffirming them in a manner that suggests their impermanence and fluidity. Thus, Hammett's work serves as a case study of how criminal identities are developed, cultivated, and reassembled, which in turn helps us understand why late modernists like Graham Greene found the tenets of crime fiction so productive in experimenting with representations of individuals who turned to such identities to construct unique senses of self.

Violent Entertainments

If one of late modernism's preoccupations is the tension between individual agency and social forces – Hammett's characters' obsession with money in an economic environment of dizzying gains and losses, or the Op's struggles with organized crime during a period when gang wars dominated newspaper headlines – then an early scene in Graham Greene's *Brighton Rock* (1938) explicitly dramatizes that condition. In the novel's opening pages, Ida Arnold, a vibrant woman characterized by her overt sexuality, unflagging optimism, and faith in the concept of justice, attempts to comfort a newfound acquaintance named Hale, who seems anxious in her embrace. Hoping that her reassurance will help him to relax, Ida repeats to Hale a variation on a common refrain: "It's a good world if you don't weaken."[27] Unbeknownst to Ida, however, Hale's anxiety stems not from his awkwardness as a lover, but from the knowledge that he is about to be murdered after exposing a local gang leader, and in this context Ida's words appear hopelessly shallow and ineffective. From its outset, Greene's novel undermines Ida's assertion of individual mastery over one's environment by juxtaposing that belief with a threatening urban landscape that, like Hammett's Personville, is scarred by poverty, gang warfare, and the static social condition of its youths, who, with no gainful source of employment and seemingly no future, turn to crime in order to obtain some sense of prominence and purpose.

Indeed, while the good world that Ida envisions is comically romanticized, the narrative world that she inhabits – late 1930s Brighton – is unsettling in that its badness is all too vivid. Unfailingly negative in its portrayal, Greene's novel depicts a popular tourist destination awash in violent and petty crime. The representation is not entirely unfair; a series of murders committed in Brighton between 1928 and 1934 earned the city the unfortunate nickname of "the Queen of Slaughtering Places,"[28] and its outward prosperity, exemplified by the numerous seaside shops, dance halls, and racetracks catering to a brisk tourist trade, masked high levels of poverty and unemployment.[29] The citizens of Brighton were understandably displeased with Greene's portrait of their community – local historian Clifford Musgrave maintained that the city's reputation as a lawless paradise for bookies, gangsters, and thieves was an exaggeration perpetuated in no small degree by Greene's novel[30] – yet *Brighton Rock* never yields in framing its setting as a battlefield, where rival gangs attack one another underneath the city's seaside piers while unsuspecting tourists remain oblivious to what occurs just beneath their feet. According to the narrator, Brighton's tourist crowds actually enable such violence, serving as "a thick forest in which a native could arrange his poisoned ambush" (*BR*, 9).

Just as Greene's depressed urban setting, permeated by the violence that emerges from economic despair, reflects some of late modernism's most prominent political and social critiques, it also affirms Thomas Davis's contention that "late modernism's encounter with everyday life is not primarily aesthetic or ethical," but "simultaneously aesthetic *and* political," as Greene's unruly Brighton, like the novel itself, is steeped in the formal conventions of crime fiction, particularly the hard-boiled aesthetics of authors such as Hammett.[31] From the novel's jarring, melodramatic opening line ("Hale knew, before he had been in Brighton three hours, that they meant to murder him"), to its detailed rendering of the colloquial speech of Brighton's gangsters, to its characterization of Ida as an ersatz detective bent on uncovering the circumstances of Hale's death, Greene establishes his narrative as, if not a full-fledged work of crime fiction, at least a fiction with clear footing in that genre (*BR*, 3). It also shares several of the formal characteristics of modernism: detailed accounts of the minutiae of everyday life, which equal in significance and narrative attention ruminations on the existence of God; gradual shifts in narrative voice, which move almost imperceptibly from the perspective of an omniscient narrator to those of the characters themselves; and abrupt cinematic cuts from one scene to the next, which provide a disorienting, decentered view of characters and events. Taken together, these elements signify a work that obscures the boundary between modernism and genre fiction much as the crime novels of Lewis and Stein did years earlier, and thus encapsulates the aesthetic aims of a late modernism determined to filter formal experiment and social critique through the lens of popular literature.

The epitome of this generic experiment is Pinkie Brown, a seventeen-year-old boy from the city's slums whose struggle to assume control of his gang following its leader's murder galvanizes the novel's plot. For Pinkie, the opportunity to command his own gang represents a chance at upward mobility, or a prospect of attaining a high status and material comfort in the most lucrative career option available to him. More fundamentally, it also reflects a belief in the powers of self-creation through established character types, as Pinkie hopes that casting himself as a professional criminal will lend his identity a firmness that it otherwise lacks. For him, criminality is not merely an attractive career choice, but a demonstration of agency that affirms the cultural purchase of labels in communicating those elements of one's character that one broadcasts in order to stabilize an otherwise unruly subjectivity. Fortunately for him, Pinkie has no shortage of criminal models upon which to draw; he aspires to the wealth and political power of Colleoni, a local gangster who runs his operation from the opulent Cosmopolitan Hotel, and finds physical security in the company of his gang's members, among whom he likens himself to "a physically weak but cunning schoolboy . . . who has attached to himself in an indiscriminating fidelity the strongest boy in the school" (*BR*, 61). Throughout *Brighton Rock*, crime functions not as an act of random violence or as a pathological character defect, but as a calculated social maneuver in which the weak individual can establish his identity through affiliation with the strong collective. In this way, the novel further ironizes Ida's statement regarding one's ability to make the world good through sheer willpower, in that Pinkie affirms the power of will in bending the world to one's desires, but only through a symbolic affiliation with a larger group. Thus, Pinkie's attitudes toward criminality – namely his eagerness to assert his social and individual value through violence – epitomize how late modernist authors such as Greene probe the connection between destruction and self-creation by studying the relationship between the individual and the subjective categories he adopts. Consequently, it is more productive to view Pinkie's criminality not as a reflection of the character's inherent sinfulness – an explanation favored by several of the novel's early critics – but rather as an assumed lifestyle that enables an identity far more desirable than anything else Brighton can offer.[32]

In his depiction of Pinkie's ability to forge an identity through crime, Greene utilizes the form of the case study to articulate the psychological impetus for such self-creation, and manipulates that form in a deliberately ironic vein. Indeed, Greene invites the reader to interpret his protagonist as a case study, for Pinkie's process of inventing himself as a career criminal is also an attempt to become a case study, or an exemplary instance of a larger whole. Pinkie's understanding of criminality, and of the behaviors expected of someone who occupies the position he covets, arises primarily through his knowledge of the stereotypes of criminal life, which he draws upon in order to style himself as the quintessential gangster. This approach to self-creation is all the more natural for Pinkie given that he seems to possess few individual characteristics in the first place. His approach to murder, for example, is entirely devoid of emotion: "The word murder conveyed no more to him than the word 'box,' 'collar,' 'giraffe.' . . . The imagination hadn't awoken. That was his strength. He couldn't see through other people's eyes, or feel with their nerves" (*BR*, 47). Here Pinkie's mind appears as an unfeeling blank, resembling in its lack of empathy what Mark Seltzer terms "the statistical person," or the "individual who, in the most radical form, experiences identity, his own and others, as a matter of numbers, kinds, types."[33] Pinkie is, at his core, a man without qualities, incapable of interpersonal connection except on the most general and dissociative of levels. The narrator reinforces that perception by referring to Pinkie only as "the Boy," highlighting the fact that this protagonist is both a typical Brighton teenager and a generic criminal type, lacking a unique identity apart from those taxonomies.

As noted earlier, several critics read Pinkie's blankness and lack of remorse for his crimes as evidence of a purely evil nature, much in keeping with the tenets of Greene's Catholicism.[34] At times, Pinkie affirms this assessment by speaking of himself in religious overtones that echo Lombroso's faith in born criminality. In a conversation with Rose, the girl he later marries in order to prevent her from testifying against him in Hale's murder case, he insists that his criminality has no basis in free will. "It's not what you do," Pinkie explains, "it's what you think . . . It's in the blood. Perhaps when they christened me, the holy water didn't take. I never howled the devil out" (*BR*, 136). The novel amplifies this perception of Pinkie as inherently evil by equating his appearance with a corresponding aura of villainy, alluding to the Lombrosian association of criminality with a degenerate physical type. Pinkie's eyes, for instance, evince "an effect of heartlessness like an old man's in which human feeling has died," and are "touched with the annihilating eternity from which he had come and to which he went" (*BR*, 6, 20). Additionally, Pinkie's face twitches and contorts when he grows nervous, and any attempt he makes at a smile comes out "stiffly," as he seems unable to "use those muscles with any naturalness" (*BR*, 26). Here, the criminal's pitiless visage and inability to control his own muscle movements reflect an utterly corrupted soul, or an innate criminality articulated through the body.

Though Pinkie's face might suggest that, for Greene and other late modernists, criminality remains the pathological inheritance of the unlucky child, his remarks to Rose on their shared Catholicism and its place in his peculiar system of morality possess a noticeably affected air, and undermine the essentialist notions of character that Pinkie's body otherwise conveys. Consistently, Pinkie delivers his thoughts on heaven, hell, and sin with the intention of strengthening his aura of violent expertise and thereby expanding the power he exerts over his listeners. His blasé statement regarding the possibility of heaven reveals this tendency to adopt the language of religion when it affirms his prominence as a career criminal:

> "These atheists, they don't know nothing. Of course there's Hell. Flames and damnation," he said with his eyes on the dark shifting water and the lightning and the lamps going out above the black struts of the Palace Pier, "torments."
>
> "And Heaven too," Rose said with anxiety, while the rain fell interminably on.
>
> "Oh, maybe," the Boy said, "maybe." (*BR*, 55)

The point of Pinkie's theological speculation is not to arrive at any consensus about the existence of heaven or hell, but instead to prove to Rose that his knowledge of the world trumps her own and earns him a position of power over her. He promotes a version of himself that invokes his self-created image as an irredeemable criminal doomed to exist in a heavenless world, and exposes his religious conviction as an ironic instrument of social climbing not unlike his belief in the power of the gang – a parallel that Greene exploits later in the novel when Pinkie ruminates on his impoverished childhood in a Brighton slum ironically called "Paradise Piece."

Indeed, practically all of Pinkie's mannerisms and gestures in *Brighton Rock* serve the purpose of distinguishing him as a certain kind of person – namely, an upwardly mobile, socially recognizable criminal type. Even Rose, dimly aware of Pinkie's involvement in gang activity yet hesitant to pry into his affairs, relishes the spotlight that Pinkie's criminal persona attracts. Scouring the crowds along the Brighton boardwalk, Rose tells Pinkie that "[i]t's wonderful being with you. Everyone knows you. I never thought I'd marry someone famous" (*BR*, 192). In spite of his marriage, Pinkie maintains that the life of crime represents a form of personal illumination through which he can pursue worldly experience and recognition unfettered by the bourgeois constraints of monogamy, parenthood, and conventional employment, effectively crafting an identity that carries some markers of economic respectability while also conveying a sense of menace and a rejection of social mores. He thus earns prestige for his abilities – organizing a mob, intimidating inferiors, killing rivals, and extorting money – while at the same time avoiding the traditional expectations of a middle-class professional. In fact, Pinkie prides himself on his simultaneous mimicry of class mobility and resistance to assimilation into bourgeois life: "his pride coiled like a watch spring round the thought that he wasn't deceived, that he wasn't going to give himself up to marriage and the birth of children, he was going to be where Colleoni now was and higher . . . He knew everything" (*BR*, 97).

One of Pinkie's greatest fears, though, is that the respect he earns through crime may not hold up to other measures of masculinity – especially sexual experience – and that the identity he labors to construct might crumble when faced with the materiality of the physical body. In spite of his assertions that he knows "everything" about organized crime, Pinkie knows almost nothing about sex, and admits that "he knew everything in theory, nothing in practice . . . He knew the moves, he'd never played the game" (*BR*, 124). To hide his inexperience, Pinkie insists on a system of personal restraint, abstaining from alcohol and spurning women in order to emphasize his professional dedication. Such abstention often veers toward disgust; even a glance at Rose elicits profound bitterness about the temptations of femininity:

> She got up and he saw the skin of her thigh for a moment above the artificial silk, and a prick of sexual desire disturbed him like a sickness. That was what happened to a man in the end: the stuffy room, the wakeful children, the Saturday night movements from the other bed. Was there no escape – anywhere – for anyone? It was worth murdering a world. (*BR*, 97)

For Pinkie, desire represents a pathological threat to subjective autonomy, a disorderly passion that threatens the edifice of detached professionalism. Yet if he can stifle his cravings to the point at which they cease to exist, he can fulfill the ideal self-image he has created – that is, he will remain an ideal criminal instead of becoming a conventional young man. At the same time, Pinkie acknowledges that his asceticism has limited social value, particularly within an all-male gang. "That was how they judged you," he complains, "not by whether you had the guts to kill a man, to run a mob, to conquer Colleoni" (*BR*, 95). By this logic, the cultivation of a criminal identity is also an attempt to steel oneself against the pressures of interpersonal entanglement. By presenting himself as an enterprising gang leader devoted entirely to his business, Pinkie shirks conventional social interaction – a bourgeois tradition that he fears might put an end to his uniqueness, which is itself derived through the dictates of another, broader category of subjectivity.

In addition to shoring up his sense of self, Pinkie's adoption of criminality as a new, more glamorous identity at once challenges and affirms the correspondence between subjectivity and place. When Pinkie persuades Rose to accompany him on a day trip to an area he refers to as "the country" – actually the outer limit of a Brighton slum – he reflects on his escape from an impoverished childhood. Worried that any commitment to Rose, legally necessary as it may be, will ensnare him in the family situation he left behind, Pinkie gazes upon

> the barred and battlemented Salvation Army gaff at the corner: his own home beyond in Paradise Piece: the houses which looked as if they had passed through an intensive bombardment, flapping gutters and glassless windows, an iron bedstead rusting in a front garden, the smashed and wasted ground in front where houses had been pulled down for model flats which had never gone up . . . He thought he had made his escape, and here his home was: back beside him, making claims. (*BR*, 95)

Despite his best efforts to remake himself as a model criminal, Pinkie cannot escape the fact that he has a past, and, moreover, a memory, both of which stubbornly remind him that he can never be a complete work of self-creation. In recalling his childhood home, Pinkie recognizes that Brighton, the city that makes his identity as a career criminal both possible and necessary, is also a place that will continually remind him of the nobody he used to be. This realization that he can never transcend his past brings him face to face with the paradox of the case study and its vacillation between the general and the specific. Although Pinkie strives to create a personal and professional identity based upon a generic sense of criminality, the unique history of his case will always set him apart. Likewise, Pinkie's hope of becoming a stereotypical gangster can never entirely fulfill his goal of becoming a distinct individual, as the act of modeling himself on a criminal type will only cause him to resemble everyone else who fits into that category. Greene alludes to this double bind in a 1926 letter in which he describes his practice of researching *Brighton Rock* by investigating London's slums, seeking out avenues with notably criminal reputations. Explaining the excitement of such work, Greene remarks that the "disreputable geography of London is a fascinating study ... It is funny how things run in streets. Half the blackmail or swindling cases live in Gerrard Street."[35] By referring to them as "cases," Greene characterizes Gerrard Street's criminal residents not as individuals, but as general types personified by the crimes they have committed. Even when highlighting certain crimes as significant – here, nonviolent crimes whose object is financial gain – Greene negates the specificity of those who commit them by describing those people in generalized legal terms.

Greene's metonymic conflation of the person with the crime – or, more accurately, of the person with the case – alludes to a persistent modernist concern with the relationship that the case study assumes between the individual and the aggregate. Just as Lauren Berlant describes the case study as a form that "hovers about the singular, the general, and the normative," *Brighton Rock* suggests that individual identity does the same.[36] That is, by offering Pinkie as a case study in criminality, Greene's novel troubles the separation between the character and the larger whole he represents, or at least aims to. Similarly, in his account of Freud's concerns over his case histories' resemblance to fictional characterizations, psychoanalyst Adam Phillips argues that Freud's tendency to worry over such disciplinary parameters begs the question of what case studies reveal about the tenuous relationship between eccentricity and conformity, and about the individual's desire to perceive him or herself in simultaneously general and specific terms:

> In psychiatric case histories the patient has to be a type, or is too much of a type; in short stories people are not too much like types, they are just the right amount. Free association as a method threatens to undo the patient as type; the patient's resistance to free association is a resistance to unfathomable singularity, to the delirium of idiosyncrasy. As a method it is Freud's antidote to the typecasting of everyday modern life.[37]

Greene takes the opposite approach, creating a protagonist who can never be "too much" like a type. The irony, though, in presenting an individual whose primary goal is to become a type, and thereby resist the "unfathomable singularity" of a distinctive subjectivity, is that Pinkie pursues his desire to become a typical criminal with the intention of reinventing himself as an absolutely singular individual. He works to exceed his ordinariness by becoming a stock character – in this case, the powerful and publicly feared gangster – which, by definition, is the epitome of the ordinary. Greene surely recognized the same paradox at work in his characterization of Gerrard Street's criminals as cases, a move that counters any view of criminality as aberrant by casting it as something utterly typical within particular circumstances. This focus on the banality of crime is what gives Greene's late modernism its sinister pall, and makes his depiction of the career criminal appear both menacing and mundane.

Such a perspective not only permeates *Brighton Rock*, but also Greene's earlier novel, *A Gun for Sale* (1936; published in America as *This Gun for Hire*). That text also focuses on the individual's position within larger criminal typologies, but exceeds the later novel's social imagination by engaging even more directly with the oppressive rigidity of class structures, which it links to both the specter of criminal anthropology within contemporary culture and the banal discourse of middle-class professionalism that applies equally to businessmen and killers. Published two years before *Brighton Rock*, *A Gun for Sale*'s interrogation of economic hierarchies and criminal subjectivity complicates the vision of professional crime depicted in Pinkie's grab for power, as it moves beyond the regional politics of a coastal resort to analyze the business of murder as signaling more pervasive and insidious social problems, exemplified in the figure of its tortured antihero, a professional assassin whose crimes have a direct influence on global affairs. In the process, the novel displays even more pointedly than *Brighton Rock* the potential of genre fiction to inform the aesthetic practices of late modernism, as well as the utility of the case study in representing the degrees of tension and symmetry between individual subjectivity and general criminal types.

A Gun for Sale makes its central claims about criminal identity through Raven, an assassin hired to murder an unnamed government minister and who, after the killing, is immediately double-crossed by his employers. Unlike Pinkie, who relishes the fact that his crimes bring him into the public eye, making him a major figure in a minor city, Raven expresses no desire that his murder of the Minister earn him recognition, even as that crime, initially suspected as the work of a foreign power and equivalent to a declaration of international war, radically affects European politics. More like Hammett's Continental Op in his indifference to violence, Raven goes about his job with the disinterestedness befitting a trained professional. He does not kill his targets out of rage or a desire for fame, but as the necessary outcome of a business transaction: "Murder didn't mean much to Raven. It was just a new job. You had to be careful. You had to use your brains. It was not a question of hatred" (*GFS*, 1). Whereas Pinkie craves notoriety, Raven attempts to blend in with the metropolitan crowd, partially in order to disguise the harelip that marks his physical difference from others, and partly because being known as a hired gun would effectively ruin his professional life. In order to go unnoticed, he adopts the appearance of a typical middle-class worker: "He carried an attaché case. He looked like any other youngish man going home after his work; his dark overcoat had a clerical air. He moved steadily up the street like hundreds of his kind" (*GFS*, 1).

Of course, passing as a white-collar worker whose bland uniform is priestly in its apparent innocence is not such a stretch for a criminal like Raven, who, after all, only commits crimes in exchange for payment. In this sense, his professionalism is even more characteristic of his identity than Pinkie's, in that Pinkie spends *Brighton Rock* in an increasingly desperate attempt to cement his professional position as a gang leader, never satisfied that he projects the air of criminal aptitude he desires, whereas Raven is so confident in his abilities that he projects an image that is both their embodiment and their exact opposite. Such ease with his own professional identity echoes what Lisa Fluet, in her study of the hit man in late modernist fiction, refers to as the process by which such figures "advance from poor or obscure origins to the relative stability of white-collar life via intelligence, talent, and some form of institutional legitimation."[38] It is important to note here that, for Fluet, the hit man's economic and professional stability is "relative," in that it compares well to other forms of white-collar work while still remaining fundamentally different in its procedures, outcomes, and public perception. Greene illustrates the same point when Raven meets with Mr. Cholmondeley, one of the men who contracts him to murder the Minster, at a local sweetshop. As he watches Cholmondeley devour a dish of ice cream, Raven picks at the distinctions between himself and his employer; Cholmondeley "was fat, he was vulgar, he was false, but he gave an impression of great power as he sat there with the cream dripping from his mouth. He was prosperity, he was one of those who possessed things, but Raven possessed nothing but the contents of his wallet, the clothes he stood up in, the hare-lip" (*GFS*, 9). Even with ice cream smudged across his face, Cholmondeley exemplifies professional success, though the narrator undermines that success by remarking that he "looked like a real-estate man, or perhaps a man more than usually successful in selling women's belts" (*GFS*, 8). While Raven registers Cholmondeley's prosperity through his ability to possess "things" – noting with envy his emerald ring, collared shirt, and eagerness to order rich and delicate foods – he classifies his companion not as an example of the enjoyment of prosperity, but as the embodiment of prosperity itself. Cholmondeley here becomes a stock character or case study – the gluttonous bankroller of lean and secretive killers, or the white-collar criminal who lives much farther up the corporate ladder, and whose social and economic prominence will likely absolve him of any legal troubles should his employees (i.e., Raven) be found out.

Just as Raven resembles Pinkie in his resentment of criminal hierarchies, begrudging the disparity between his lower status as a contract killer and Cholmondeley's conspicuous wealth, he reiterates Pinkie's rejection of emotionalism by perceiving murder as a banal, professional act. On this subject, Raven's mind works much like the mechanical apparatus ascribed to Sherlock Holmes, attentive to details and pertinent facts that help him achieve his goals more efficiently, but unwilling to conceive of those he encounters as anything more than a disembodied series of distinguishing characteristics. Here it is the criminal who behaves like a machine, his mind working "with mechanical accuracy like a ready-reckoner. You only had to supply it with the figures and it gave you the answer" (*GFS*, 14). More generally, Raven appears impervious to empathy, as he fails to imagine what another's thoughts might look like: "Raven could never realize other people; they didn't seem to him to live in the same way as he lived; and though he bore a grudge against Mr Cholmondeley, hated him enough to kill him, he couldn't imagine Mr Cholmondeley's own fears and motives" (*GFS*, 29). Like Pinkie, who cannot fathom a psychology beyond his own and for whom the word "murder" has no ethical connotations, Raven's mechanical mind can be prompted into rage, but cannot extend itself to a deeper consideration of another's subjectivity. Raven can feel pain, but he cannot imagine what it might be like for another.

Raven's emotional alienation comes under stress, however, when in an attempt to evade the police, who eventually suspect him of the Minister's murder, he kidnaps a young showgirl named Anne Crowder. When Anne hurls a cup of hot coffee in Raven's face in an effort to escape, the assassin instantly gains the ability to comprehend others' pain, and connects the experience both to his most recent victims and to his father, hanged in prison when Raven was six years old: "The pain drove him backwards with his hands to his eyes; he moaned like an animal; this was pain. This was what the old War Minister had felt, the woman secretary, his father when the trap sprang and the neck took the weight" (*GFS*, 38). In recognizing the existence of emotions in others, Raven acknowledges how his own feelings of hatred, bitterness, and disappointment contribute to his identity, and in turn to his aptitude for murder. After Anne escapes he spends a dreary night seeking refuge from a rainstorm, and wonders why Anne has not yet given him up to the authorities. Unaccustomed to such good fortune, Raven contrasts Anne's loyalty to the harrowing sequence of events that formed his character:

> He wasn't used to any taste that wasn't bitter on the tongue. He had been made by hatred; it had constructed him into this thin smoky murderous figure in the rain, hunted and ugly. His mother had borne him when his father was in gaol, and six years later when his father was hanged for another crime, she had cut her own throat with a kitchen knife; afterwards there had been the home. He had never felt the least tenderness for anyone; he was made in this image and he had his own odd pride in the result; he didn't want to be unmade. He had a sudden terrified conviction that he must be himself now as never before if he was to escape. It was not tenderness that made you quick on the draw. (*GFS*, 61)

In contrast to Pinkie's faith in a malleable identity subject to exertions of individual will, Raven evinces a belief in the formative nature of the past, and claims that only by "being himself" and drawing upon the source of his anger will he elude his trackers. Likewise, he also fears that he might somehow be "unmade," and so must remind himself to be himself in order to persevere.

"Being oneself," of course, is a curious expression, as it assumes that an individual might do otherwise. In a literal sense, being oneself is all one can ever do, and Raven's realization that his impoverished past will always haunt him suggests the unchanging character of subjectivity. Even more importantly, it alludes to those intractable systems of social and economic hierarchy whose rigidity prevents the poor from achieving prosperity without resorting to crime. In this sense, Raven resembles one of Mayhew's desperate London laborers, for whom crime serves as an illegitimate but potentially effective path out of poverty. In another sense, Raven's assertion that he must be himself follows the tradition of criminal anthropology, as it suggests a born criminal whose childhood trauma seems less important than the fact that it originates in the aftermath of a father's crimes. Too, it highlights Raven's uncanny evocation of nineteenth-century beliefs that distinguishing physical characteristics mark the criminal's body as innately prone to violence. Raven's harelip clearly invokes a Lombrosian perspective on hereditary deviance, and Raven recognizes it as a harbinger of what his life was to become: "If a man's born ugly, he doesn't stand a chance. It begins at school. It begins before that" (*GFS*, 40). Taking advantage of the shock his harelip elicits, Raven uses its status as an indicator of criminal character to disrupt the flow of conventional social situations, as when he accosts an unsuspecting shop girl:

A kind of subdued cruelty drove him into the shop. He let his hare-lip loose
on the girl when she came towards him with the same pleasure that he might
have felt in turning a machine-gun on a picture gallery. He said, "That dress
in the window. How much?"
    She said, "Five guineas." She wouldn't "sir" him. His lip was like a badge
of class. It revealed the poverty of parents who couldn't afford a clever
surgeon. (*GFS*, 10)

Ironically, Raven's attempt at inspiring horror only leads to embarrassment, as the girl reads his lip as a mark of poverty rather than criminality.
Still, Raven accepts this rejection, and shrugs off the hope that his lip might
communicate anything other than the material facts of his birth. Whereas
Pinkie immerses himself in the habits of a career criminal, pushing himself
to become the thing he has always wanted to be, Raven claims that he has
always been a criminal, has always been poor, and could never have become
anything else. Thus, Greene's characterization of Raven as a born criminal
hearkens back to a generic conceit mired in earlier criminological thought,
just as the later *Brighton Rock* reveals Greene's skepticism concerning the
arguments for hereditary deviance and its corporeal legibility.

    In representing criminal identity as a performative set of attitudes
conferring social status as well as a physical and economic pathology
from which one can never emerge, Greene's novels demonstrate the tension between the individual and the collective, suggesting that identity is
both fluid and fixed, labile yet wedded to social, economic, and biological
hierarchies. In the process, they shuttle between accounts of subjectivity
rooted in vastly different historical eras, illustrating a late modernist
imperative to filter the aesthetic aims of modernism through the lens of
popular culture – that is, the forms of characterization, plot, and structure
found in crime and detective fiction – while depicting social and economic
structures yoked simultaneously to nineteenth-century criminal anthropology and the British class system of the 1930s.

    Yet the question remains: if *Brighton Rock* and *A Gun for Sale* so readily
exemplify the historical and aesthetic liminality of late modernism, then
why is Greene overlooked in conversations about the period? Though his
professed antipathy to modernism is partly to blame – he infamously
compared Virginia Woolf's fiction to "a charming whimsical rather senti-
mental prose poem" – Greene's exclusion is due just as much to his
fondness for genre as to his critique of Woolf and others.[39] Indeed,
Greene was never entirely opposed to modernism, but preferred the
work of Henry James, Joseph Conrad, and Ford Madox Ford to later,
more experimental fictions because, as Andrzej Gąsiorek observes, the

innovations of the former were "arguably less destructive of the novel form than those of the post-war period," and remained "in touch with the social realm he himself wanted to explore."[40] As critics increasingly attend to modernism's investment in popular forms, however, Greene's genre work appears far more experimental than has previously been acknowledged. As Brian Lindsay Thomson argues, Greene's novels "played fast and loose with generic conventions in order to work out problems that intellectuals did not normally associate with the genres to which they assigned them . . . They neither required nor produced passive observers of stable genres . . . but rather active participants willing to take a hand in dismantling stereo-types and myths."[41] In other words, Greene was not a popular writer for the sake of profit alone, but interrogated the boundaries of genre in order to show how it might yield new insights into the practice of fiction more generally.

Nowhere is that interrogation more apparent than in Greene's "enter-tainments," a distinction he attached to multiple novels – including *A Gun for Sale* and *Brighton Rock*, in addition to *Orient Express* (1932), *The Confidential Agent* (1939), *The Ministry of Fear* (1943), *The Third Man* (1950), *Loser Takes All* (1956), and *Our Man in Havana* (1958) – and one that poses a unique set of categorical problems. While most of these novels share a taut, cinematic structure that fuses elements of the thriller and the detective story, Greene could never settle upon what, precisely, an entertainment entailed, or which of his fictions should fall under that designation. His used the term "entertainment" intermittently, and removed the label from later editions of his novels while affixing it to others years after their publication. One notable example of this habit is *Orient Express* (published in Great Britain as *Stamboul Train*), which was not categorized as an entertainment until 1936, when Greene decided that the novel fit comfortably into that genre. Such indecision is particularly apparent in *Brighton Rock*'s vexed publication history – Greene labeled the novel an entertainment for its first American edition, then removed the marker when the novel was published in Britain.[42]

Greene's critics have exhibited similar confusion. Murray Roston dis-misses the entertainments with the explanation that they "did not deal with the concerns confronting [Greene] as a serious novelist," and that, "although often exciting to read," they "were really pot-boilers intended to provide him with an income."[43] For his part, Greene did little to dissuade such criticisms. In a 1955 radio interview he separated the enter-tainments from his other novels by highlighting their emphasis on action rather than characterization, explaining that in writing an entertainment "one is primarily interested in having an exciting story as in a physical action, with just enough character to give interest to the action, because you can't be interested in the action of a mere dummy."[44] Years later, he claimed in his autobiography *Ways of Escape* (1980) that the decision to characterize certain novels as entertainments fulfilled his desire "to distinguish ... from more serious novels" those that participated in the suspense and thriller genres.[45] In both the interview and the autobiography, Greene shrugs off the entertainment as an exciting popular genre driven by the engine of plot, far removed from the "serious" novel with its emphases on character, philosophical speculation, and social problems.

Regarding the entertainments, however, it is important not to take the author at his word. Greene made no secret of his interest in the crime and detective genre, and none of his novels, entertaining or "serious," shirk the issue of psychology. In fact, some of Greene's most perceptive critics have defended the entertainments from charges of crass commercialism and formal simplicity on the grounds that they do, just as much as his other books, offer an incisive example of how generic conceits can help render interiority in unexpected ways. Roger Sharrock claims that in novels like *A Gun for Sale* and *England Made Me* (1935),

> the deceptions and betrayals of the mystery story, the isolation of the doomed or hunted hero, work at a deeper level than that of plot: the characters are separated not merely by the circumstances and withholding of information necessary to the thriller form but by incommunicable pasts and childhoods and by the incomprehensibility of a world without any recognizable total moral pattern.[46]

Similarly, Brian Diemert argues that "Greene's texts exist on and investigate the border of the frontier of genre," while Bernard Bergonzi contends that the entertainments "were ... not all that different from the books he regarded as novels, but ... drew more directly on the conventions of popular fiction and allowed Greene to indulge his liking for melodrama."[47] As these appraisals suggest, the entertainments allowed Greene to experiment with form in a way that exceeds the parameters of genre fiction while still relying upon them, and to illustrate how divisions between popular literature and the mid-century English novel might be far less pronounced than critics at the time suspected. Pioneering a genre that erases distinctions between late modernist and popular fiction by underlining their shared emphases on the problem of psychological representation, stock characters, and the upward mobility of violent self-creation, Greene initiated what he considered a necessary corrective to the classic

British mystery, which he felt was "lacking in realism" since it contained "too many suspects and the criminal never belonged to what used to be called the criminal class."[48]

Novels such as *Brighton Rock* and *A Gun for Sale*, then, do not reflect their author's desire for money or increased popularity, nor do they reveal an embarrassing indulgence in popular fiction. Like *Blood on the Dining-Room Floor* and *Mrs. Dukes' Million*, they show how literary convention can be mined for its creative potential, and how the formal principles of genre fiction might illuminate pressing aesthetic and historical concerns – illustrating, for instance, how a small-time gangster like Pinkie, by striving to reinvent himself as a stereotypical criminal, exemplifies a fragmentary and performative subjectivity, or how a clipped narrative voice can challenge early modernism's densely layered representation of individual impression while still emphasizing the primacy of interiority. Indeed, it is his keen attention to generic mandate that makes Greene such an influential figure for late modernism and its preoccupation with criminality as an unstable yet ubiquitous category of modern subjectivity. Thus, to classify Greene as a late modernist is not only to situate his work in relation to earlier modernist experiments with form, psychology, and crime, but also to view it as a complex response to the plight of the subject in an increasingly brutal, professionalized world. In so doing we can discern those points of contact between late modernism and popular fiction, as well as the more sinister aspects of late modernism that view the modern criminal and the modern professional as potentially two versions of the same thing.

Murderous Self-Fashioning

While Greene's entertainments represent a late modernist reappraisal of the key tropes of Hammett's hard-boiled fiction, furthering the modernist investment in popular culture by exploring criminal subjectivity through generic conventions, Patricia Highsmith's *The Talented Mr. Ripley* (1955) pushes that exploration to its extreme.[49] The first of five books to feature her eponymous protagonist, Highsmith's novel introduces Tom Ripley, a strangely likable sociopath with a uniquely self-serving approach to violence.[50] An earnest social climber who murders when it suits his interests, an aspiring art connoisseur whose undistinguished past bars him from the economic and social advantages enjoyed by lesser minds, and a cold, detached mimic whose talents in imitation mask the fact that he possesses few discernible traits of his own, Ripley is the late modernist criminal par excellence. Whereas Hammett and Greene envision the criminal as an opaque, unsteady subject caught between a set of innate characteristics and an adopted persona, Highsmith's protagonist appears entirely self-fashioned, delighted by the opportunities for advancement that a life of crime affords and unburdened by any sense of guilt over his actions (hence one of Highsmith's original titles for the novel, *Business is my Pleasure*).[51] In a chapter on late modernism's fascination with the relationships among violence, subjectivity, and genre, I end with Highsmith's novel as an example of how a character like Ripley participates in a long tradition of modernist engagement with criminality while forcing that tradition into startlingly original, if existentially uncomfortable, territory. Ripley, in this context, is what happens when the individual is unburdened of all subjective taxonomies, and then uses those taxonomies to embark upon a life of crime that yields a life of pleasure.

Just as late modernism simultaneously borrows from and critiques its predecessors, Highsmith's novel stands within and beyond the purview of its moment in literary history, expanding on prior notions of criminality while delivering an idiosyncratic perspective on the link between violence and self-creation. Though it bears little formal resemblance to other modernist fictions – save, perhaps, for Highsmith's eerily flat prose, which registers the banality of violence in sentences that Joan Schenkar describes as "plod[ding] along with the dull insistence of a headache" – its intense, even claustrophobic focus on the interior life of its criminal protagonist echoes those of earlier modernist authors at the same time that it signals a new approach to the subject.[52] Consequently, it is difficult to pinpoint the novel's relationship to the context from which it emerged, even as Leonard Cassuto dubs Highsmith "the quintessential fifties crime writer."[53] Cassuto's position is certainly persuasive in the case of *The Talented Mr. Ripley*, which, in its deliberate engagement with Cold War anxieties regarding sexual otherness, figures its protagonist as a prototypical outsider fighting for recognition within an oppressive cultural climate, and in the process exposes what Arthur Redding characterizes as "the dispiriting hollowness of postwar American life."[54]

At the same time, though, Highsmith's novel advances a trenchant critique of subjectivity rooted in earlier modernist paradigms, as it details the individual's ability to create himself through the destruction of another and then rejects conventional notions of justice, whether legal or literary, that surround the destructive act of violence, essentially suggesting that the traditional view of criminality as unequivocally evil or lamentable may no longer hold in a postwar, late modernist environment. The latter attribute has proven particularly germane for critics interested in the modernist revision of popular forms, who cite the Ripliad's moral ambiguity as evidence of Highsmith's sympathy for her protagonist, the reader's vicarious enjoyment of his consistently escaping punishment, and the series' resulting disruption of crime fiction's paradigms.[55] Stephen Kern, for example, maintains that Highsmith's modernism arises directly through her establishment of a "moral code" that Ripley scrupulously ignores: "[W]hat makes [*The Talented Mr. Ripley*] strikingly modern is that Highsmith almost makes her readers forget about that code. She does not condone murder but raises some modernist notions about the aptness of a moral framework for interpreting human existence."[56] In this way, Highsmith flouts the perception of crime fiction as a genre that insists upon narrative resolution, and her deliberate shirking of closure reflects earlier modernist invectives against such a tradition. By taking as her protagonist a murderer who succeeds spectacularly in evading the authorities, Highsmith departs from the crime novel's tendency to end with the death, arrest, or conviction of the criminal in favor of a more ambiguous and ethically unsettling conclusion. If, as D. A. Miller argues, the traditional detective novel emphasizes the triumph of law "not only by solving the crime, but also . . . by withdrawing from what had been, for an aberrant moment, its 'scene,'" then Highsmith's work refuses to depart the scene of Ripley's crimes by celebrating the fact that this narrative of unpunished violence precludes easy, ethically comfortable resolutions.[57]

While dismantling some of the crime genre's most recognizable formulae, the plot of *The Talented Mr. Ripley* also attends to the crises of representation, violence, and identity formation characteristic of other late modernist works. A twisted retelling of James's *The Ambassadors*, the novel begins with Ripley's search for Dickie Greenleaf, a wealthy American expatriate who refuses to inherit his family's business and instead settles on the Italian coast with a writer named Marge Sherwood. Fascinated by Dickie's leisurely lifestyle, financial resources, and outsized self-confidence, the demure Ripley attempts to befriend this moneyed aristocrat in hopes of establishing himself in a similar manner. His plan is all the more urgent due to the demoralizing poverty he experiences in Manhattan, a struggle that, prior to his European sojourn, he attempts to abandon through the pleasures of crime.[58] Like Pinkie in *Brighton Rock*, Ripley takes tentative steps toward economic advancement through acts of petty crime – in his case, forged letters from the IRS that attempt to trick recipients into sending him fictitious unpaid taxes. He also resembles Greene's young gangster in that he too blames an unfeeling social order for pushing him to crimes unworthy of his attributes: "What was he himself doing at twenty-five? Living from week to week. No bank account. Dodging cops now for the first time in his life. He had a talent for mathematics. Why in hell didn't they pay him for it, somewhere?" (*TMR*, 14). Here and elsewhere, Highsmith underscores the economic and social injustices that Ripley perceives as the root of his troubles. Upon losing a warehouse job for which he was physically unqualified, Ripley excoriates the prevailing system of mid-century American capitalism that he sees as ruining his prospects,

> deciding then that the world was full of Simon Legrees, and that you had to be an animal, as tough as the gorillas who worked with him at the ware-house, or starve. He remembered that right after that, he had stolen a loaf of bread from a delicatessen counter and had taken it home and devoured it, feeling that the world owed a loaf of bread to him, and more. (*TMR*, 42)

Ironically, Ripley arrived in New York with hopes of becoming an actor, and throughout the novel he perceives his features, movements, and thoughts at a remove, as when, studying himself in a mirror, he observes "every move he made as if it were somebody else's movements he were watching" (*TMR*, 17). Attending to his mannerisms in minute detail, Ripley examines himself in an eerily objective light, and disparages what he encounters as unremarkable. Even in the excitement of buying a new hat that he believes will allow him to resemble "a country gentleman, a thug, an Englishman, a Frenchman, or a plain American eccentric, depending on how he wore it," Ripley laments the ordinariness of his face: "He had always thought he had the world's dullest face, a thoroughly forgettable face with a look of docility that he could not understand, and a look also of vague fright that he had never been able to erase. A real conformist's face, he thought" (*TMR*, 37). Despite his efforts to assert his uniqueness, Ripley's face undermines his individuality by appearing both "forgettable" and "conformist," possessing a "docile" aspect that can either be dismissed entirely or suit itself to match the look of any average person. Ripley is at once like everyone else and able to become like everyone else, trapped between his lofty ambitions and the generality of his countenance.

The positive aspect of a "conformist's face," though, lies in its ability to resemble the visage of anyone else one might imagine, and so the liability of Ripley's face actually allows him to abandon his bland identity by inventing or assimilating new ones. Mark Seltzer describes Ripley's peculiar skill in emulation as a paradoxical indication of his self-reflexivity, which leads him to conceive of himself as both radically insubstantial and possessing an uncanny potential to transform. As Seltzer explains, Ripley's "singular talent might more simply be called, not impersonation, but *personation*. Ripley (like a range of other fictional and real-life serial killers) lives in the third-person singular."[59] Ripley's own account of his abilities emphasizes this talent for inhabiting roles besides his own, as he proudly proclaims that he "can forge a signature, fly a helicopter, handle dice, impersonate practically anybody, cook – and do a one-man show in a nightclub in case the regular entertainer's sick" (*TMR*, 58–59). Affirming his status as a "nonperson, a *man without content*," Ripley's talents coalesce around the goal of becoming someone else.[60] All reflect his eagerness to see himself as another person, preferably one whose life bears little resemblance to his own.

Ripley's ability not just to emulate but to *become* anyone else, and to perceive his identity as a pure surface that can be painted with any number of specific traits, establishes the case study as a framework for interpreting the web of associations, behaviors, and experiences that inform his ambiguous subjectivity. What makes Highsmith's novel so unique in its appropriation of the case study, however, is not simply its presentation of the protagonist as a case study – that is, the generalized "Mr. Ripley" of the title, simultaneously anonymous and specific – but the fact that Ripley perceives those around him as if they too were case studies, and tries to determine which characteristics, no matter how distinctive, he might absorb. He breaks down the gestures, possessions, and tastes of those he admires, creating a taxonomy of distinctions that, if assimilated successfully, promises to catapult him into the heretofore impermeable social and economic circles to which he aspires. In perceiving the world as an infinite series of case studies available to his critical eye, Ripley finds the pursuit toward which his talents might best be directed, and proves that everything one might consider unique is in fact completely repeatable.

Highsmith magnifies this tension between originality and authenticity in one of the novel's most disturbing scenes. Alone in Dickie's house, Ripley performs an elaborate imitation of his friend, dressing in Dickie's clothes and pretending to strangle Marge for undermining the bond that Ripley imagines between the two men:

> "Marge, you must understand that I don't *love* you," Tom said into the mirror in Dickie's voice, with Dickie's higher pitch on the emphasized words, with the little growl in his throat at the end of the phrase that

could be pleasant or unpleasant, intimate or cool, according to Dickie's mood. "Marge, stop it!" Tom turned suddenly and made a grab in the air as if he were seizing Marge's throat. He shook her, twisted her, while she sank lower and lower, until at last he left her, limp, on the floor. He was panting. He wiped his forehead the way Dickie did ... Even his parted lips looked like Dickie's lips when he was out of breath from swimming, drawn down a little from his lower teeth. (*TMR*, 77–78)

Ripley anatomizes his hatred of Marge as well as the minutia of Dickie's behavior in a performance that requires surprisingly minimal effort and seemingly no strain. After only a short time in Italy he has noticed such minor details as how Dickie enunciates certain words, and has catalogued those habits of speech into precise taxonomies corresponding to various emotions. Having made a case study out of his friend, Ripley imitates the details of Dickie's behavior so completely that he threatens to become an exact replica of the genuine article. He also realizes how thorough his physical imitation can be, surprised by "how much he looked like Dickie with the top part of his head covered. Really it was only his darker hair that was very different from Dickie. Otherwise, his nose – or at least its general form – his narrow jaw, his eyebrows if he held them right" (*TMR*, 78).

As he seizes upon the similarities between himself and his newfound obsession, Ripley becomes increasingly frustrated with Dickie's indifference to him, and with the widening gulf he perceives between his ambitions and the reality of his situation. In a moment of careful calculation and wounded pride, Ripley bludgeons Dickie to death in a boat, disposes of the body, and assumes Dickie's identity, eager to begin the new, financially stable life that had always been out of reach. His transformation is simple yet thorough, and the ease with which he achieves it exemplifies the novel's conception of criminality as a means to a larger subjective end. Murder, in fact, is not the novel's most serious crime, as Highsmith reframes physical violence as an instrumental action, or what Abigail Cheever characterizes as a "technology of self-transformation."[61] The desire to become a man of means and culture makes murder a necessity – a shocking act of violence that enables an even more shocking act of self-creation – and Ripley performs the task repeatedly, not as "frenetic *passages à l'acte*, or outbursts of violence in which he releases the energy accumulated by the frustrations of daily life," as Slavoj Žižek explains, but as welcome opportunities for reinvention.[62]

What makes Ripley's transformation so successful is not simply his uncanny ability to mimic Dickie's appearance, but rather his understanding that identity is primarily a psychological phenomenon, and that stealing it from another is largely a matter of forgetting one's own subjectivity and training oneself to think as someone else. Indeed, his physical resemblance to Dickie quickly becomes the least important component of his imitation, as, for him, it is vastly more important "to maintain the mood and temperament of the person one was impersonating, and to assume the facial expressions that went with them. The rest fell into place" (*TMR*, 127). His ability to act naturally in the guise of another, moving beyond performance to the conviction that he *is* Dickie Greenleaf, makes Ripley's impersonation entirely credible to those he encounters. Forced to invent stories of Dickie's whereabouts when Marge grows suspicious of his absence, Ripley persuades because he "imagined [his stories] intensely, so intensely that he came to believe them" (*TMR*, 239). Much like his impersonation, Ripley's fictional accounts of his time with Dickie are at once general and specific, combining details that seem generally consistent with Dickie's personality with those too unique to Dickie to be disputed. As a result, Ripley convinces potential skeptics with earnestness and improvisation, and convinces himself with the intensity of his lies. He furthers his convictions by practicing his imitation in solitude, performing specific behaviors in a manner commensurate with Dickie's general disposition. Because he has studied Dickie's case so well, Ripley can invent new behaviors that are nonetheless quintessentially Dickie's, secure in his ability to replicate a general impression of Dickie that will be universally believed.

This new identity also delivers a rare form of pleasure, similar to Pinkie's evident enjoyment of celebrity status in *Brighton Rock*, but different in that, for Ripley, delight in criminality comes from the rigors of imitation as they eradicate any trace of his old self. That is, the act of copying, rather than its result, is what Ripley deems the most satisfying aspect of the life he gains through murder. Living as Dickie Greenleaf

> gave his existence a peculiar, delicious atmosphere of purity, like that . . . which a fine actor probably feels when he plays an important role on a stage with the conviction that the role he is playing could not be played better by anyone else. He was himself and yet not himself. He felt blameless and free, despite the fact that he consciously controlled every move he made. But he no longer felt tired after several hours of it, as he had at first. He had no need to relax when he was alone. Now, from the moment when he got out of bed and went to brush his teeth, he was Dickie, brushing his teeth with his right elbow jutted out, Dickie rotating the eggshell on his spoon for the last bite. Dickie invariably putting back the first tie he pulled off the rack and

selecting a second. He had even produced a painting in Dickie's manner. (*TMR*, 132)

After such dedicated study, Ripley's performance is now more convincing than the original article, so unique that no one, not even Dickie himself, can replicate it. And yet, because Ripley believes that no subject is so original as to escape imitation, his attitude of singularity here is curious. By his own logic, he becomes unique only when he becomes someone else, and his claim that he is now both "himself and yet not himself" comes so matter-of-factly that it makes the transition from Ripley to Dickie appear even more seamless than when it first occurs. Such a paradoxical privileging of the duplicate clearly, if unintentionally, echoes Lewis's claims for mimicry in *Mrs. Dukes' Million*, as Highsmith questions the reverence for, and by extension the existence of, originality, dispelling through Ripley's transformation any notion that the copy, or the merely imitative, cannot be unique.

By embodying an identity both his own and someone else's, Ripley blurs the boundary between self and other so thoroughly that he destabilizes the concept of essential character altogether, effectively demonstrating how the act of imitation becomes even more central to his subjectivity than any quality that might be considered his own, original property. Fiona Peters argues that Ripley's "subjective universe remains a shell, a chameleon-like imitation of a human being," and that apparent paradox – the self defined by its own lack – is precisely what allows Ripley to create new, unprecedented forms of subjectivity founded on the presumption that an original identity is nothing more than an elaborate set of copies.[63] The tension becomes especially pronounced when he murders the boorish Freddie Miles, a friend of Dickie who discovers Ripley's impersonation. Preparing for his inevitable interview with the police, Ripley fabricates the details of the evening – he and Freddie drinking excessively before Freddie stumbled home alone – until he tricks his body into believing his mind's inventions. Surprised to find himself hung over without having ingested much alcohol, Ripley realizes the full extent of his mimicry: "He knew it was a matter of mental suggestion, and that he had a hangover because he had intended to pretend that he had been drinking a great deal with Freddie. And now, when there was no need of it, he was still pretending, uncontrollably" (*TMR*, 146). Here, Highsmith obscures the distinction between acting and being, as Ripley's life as Dickie Greenleaf moves from imitation to instinct, with the body disregarding its physical state and aligning itself with the events of Ripley's imagination. This conflict between mind and body also works the other way, as when Ripley glances into a mirror only to discover a visage that behaves independently of his carefully crafted thoughts: "He looked as if he were trying to convey the emotions of fear and shock by his posture and his expression, and because the way he looked was involuntary and real, he became suddenly twice as frightened" (*TMR*, 181). After such a rigid system of self-regulation, which demands that emotion function in a particular manner at a particular time, any thought that arises instinctively out of Ripley comes as a genuine surprise. Thus, Ripley's body behaves in a manner that is both entirely susceptible to suggestion and completely beyond control.

Ripley's identification with Dickie becomes so thorough, in fact, that when the risk of discovery forces him to abandon the ruse and assume his old role as Tom Ripley, he can only perform the part by approaching it as another personality to be learned and copied. Rather than resuming the life he had always led, Ripley must conceive of himself as his own case study, hamming up the features that once defined him in a dedicated attempt to become himself again: "He took a pleasure in it, overdoing almost the old Tom Ripley reticence with strangers, the inferiority in every duck of his head and wistful, sidelong glance" (*TMR*, 183). The pleasure again comes from the rigors of impersonation, but what is significant about this version of Tom Ripley is the fact that it comes about by a force of will, as Ripley's performance as Dickie had so thoroughly informed his own identity. Moreover, Ripley's return is only partial, as the persona that Ripley adopts represents yet another form of identity – a new version of Tom Ripley who applies Dickie Greenleaf's confidence and financial resources to Ripley's fixity of purpose and discriminating aesthetic tastes. This new identity is both self-created and borrowed, uniquely Ripley's own yet unabashedly stolen from another. As the narrator remarks, "[t]here was a sureness in his taste now that he had not felt in Rome . . . He felt surer of himself now in every way" (*TMR*, 203). This new identity constitutes itself primarily through material objects, which Highsmith depicts as markers of socio-economic status and physical indicators of an evolving persona. While he admires his collection of fine art, expensive clothing, and tasteful furniture, pausing to consider the beauty with which he has surrounded himself as an extension of his new self, Ripley takes comfort in the prospect of a life filled with exquisite possessions, all of which "reminded him that he existed, and made him enjoy his existence" (*TMR*, 236).[64]

Just as Ripley's fluctuation between multiple identities systematically repudiates the concept of a fixed, essential subjectivity, it also questions the idea that sexuality serves as a defining individual characteristic, or that it communicates anything unique about Ripley's criminality. In one sense, Ripley's queerness is the novel's open secret; his longing for a life with Dickie is decidedly homoerotic, and he characterizes his childhood as an unsuccessful attempt to dodge his Aunt Dottie's charge that he, like his father before him, is "a sissy from the ground up" (*TMR*, 96). According to George Haggerty, Ripley's "oddly amoral series of crimes are connected directly to his queer sensibility"; not only does Highsmith create in Ripley an ironic model of the homosexual that readers of the time would instantly recognize, she also links his criminality to a deeply ingrained stereotype of pathological sexuality.[65] As Haggerty contends, "[t]he risk that the homosexual poses [in the novel] is obvious; he is violent, hysterical, and prone to brooding passions. He is also deceitful, uncentered, and unsure of his feelings. In short, he is a sociopath, or even a psychopath, who hides a dark and debilitating power behind his shy or self-effacing demeanor."[66] In Haggerty's reading, Highsmith ironically exploits the conflation of queerness and pathological deviance in a purposeful challenge to a society that sought to marginalize the former as a criminal threat to an established order. In other words, by offering Ripley as an emblem of the period's most abusive conceptions of queer identity, Highsmith brashly characterizes her protagonist as a murderous queer subject who, in avoiding punishment, flouts the conventions of justice by moving freely within the society that shuns him.

As Michael Trask observes, however, those who categorize *The Talented Mr. Ripley* as a knowing inversion of Cold War mores, or an ironic rebuttal to equations of criminality and homosexuality, overlook the fact that Highsmith's narrative does not yield so easily to any interpretive structure founded upon stable notions of queer identity.[67] Indeed, just as Ripley's queerness appears as a given throughout the novel, so too does his palpable lack of physical desire, as he spends far more time disavowing any sexual urges than indulging them. Here too he resembles Greene's protagonist in *Brighton Rock*, though for Ripley, desire is not an impediment to professional renown, but instead only one component within a larger performance of identity. For instance, when Dickie chides Ripley for watching a group of scantily clad male acrobats building a human pyramid along the beach at Cannes, Ripley is both furious and nonchalant: "All right, Tom thought, the acrobats were fairies. Maybe Cannes was full of fairies. So what? ... Tom deliberately kept himself from even glancing at the acrobats again, though they were certainly more amusing to watch than the ocean" (*TMR*, 96). Here Highsmith lays bare the novel's sexual anxieties in the same moment that she alludes to their kinship with Ripley's talents in performance. To Dickie, the acrobatic spectacle is an undisguised queer display, but for Ripley it represents an aesthetic achievement – an act of mental and physical dexterity surpassing the sublimity of nature. Consequently, any eroticism that Ripley finds in the acrobatic display is bound up with its difficulty as an act of performance; he notes that the acrobats "must be professionals" because they sport identical g-strings, and while he feigns indifference in response to Dickie's disapproval, he secretly marvels at the "feet braced on bulging thighs, hands gripping forearms" as the acrobats complete their pyramid (*TMR*, 95–96). Like the precarious work of the acrobats, Ripley's disavowal of sexual desire is also a deliberate performance, or a balancing act undertaken before an audience, as is everything else he does. Through the erotically charged motions of the acrobats, Highsmith posits performance and sexuality as related forms of play, and suggests that sexuality might itself be a kind of high-stakes performance.

Against all the novel's contradictory attempts to define Ripley's sexuality – whether he is a pathological deviant who disrupts bourgeois convention or a repressed gay man living fearfully in the closet – Highsmith offers another, subtler possibility.[68] Detailing her suspicion of Ripley's sexual identity, Marge writes in a letter that Ripley "may not be queer. He's just a nothing, which is worse. He isn't normal enough to have *any* kind of sex life" (*TMR*, 118). Reversing the familiar equation of queerness with criminality, Marge complains that Ripley's apparent lack of sexuality is what makes him so unsettling, and potentially so dangerous. Similarly, Ripley often highlights his sexual ambiguity in a manner that emphasizes the labile, performative nature of identity as a whole. Reminiscing about his friends in New York, Ripley fixates upon a humiliating moment in which his flippant attitude toward sexuality failed to amuse a crowd of people he desperately wanted to impress:

> And he remembered, too, the humiliating moment when Vic Simmons had said, *Oh, for Christ sake, Tommie, shut up!* when he had said to a group of people, for perhaps the third or fourth time in Vic's presence, "I can't make up my mind whether I like men or women, so I'm thinking of giving them *both* up." Tom had used to pretend he was going to an analyst, because everybody else was going to an analyst, and he had used to spin wildly funny stories about his sessions with his analyst to amuse people at parties, and the line about giving up men and women both had always been good for a laugh, the way he delivered it, until Vic had told him for Christ sake to shut up, and after that Tom had never said it again and never mentioned his analyst again, either. As a matter of fact, there was a lot of truth in it, Tom

thought. As people went, he was one of the most innocent and clean-minded he had ever known. (*TMR*, 80)

Attempting to amuse this young, fashionable coterie, Ripley becomes disappointed when the joke of his sexual ambiguity fails to register with its audience. That failure, however, occurs not because his queerness is so obvious as to negate any other interpretations of his sexual identity, but because that identity is so patently a carefully crafted fiction. Ripley's friends recognize that his boasts of sexual indecision and hints at past affairs are inventions designed to ingratiate him to a smart social circle. Through the joke, Highsmith exposes Ripley's sexuality as another kind of performance much in keeping with his performance of Dickie or the performance of the acrobats, making it impossible to separate Ripley's actual desires (if such desires exist) from those he adopts in an effort to impress more sexually experienced peers with an intriguing, urbane persona. His attraction to Dickie may appear obvious, but it is not nearly as obvious as his attraction to the fictions he invents.

Through this conflation of identities – sexual, criminal, professional, individual – Highsmith gleefully upends traditional distinctions between the authentic and the inauthentic, and calls into question some of the most foundational categories for establishing the contours of subjectivity. For this reason, Mark Seltzer characterizes Ripley as entirely "without content or character," a man who "turns alter into ego albeit in the form of alter ego," and thus represents "the possibility of . . . interchangeability" between all subjects.[69] Similarly, Highsmith biographer Andrew Wilson argues that

> [w]hatever form Tom assumes . . . the fictional always seems more truthful than his "authentic" self, whatever that may be. Indeed, Ripley's sense of self . . . seems so dislocated and fragmented, he can hardly be said to have any essence whatsoever. It is clear that Ripley is just one of many personalities which jostle beneath the surface of the man.[70]

Wilson constructs his account of Ripley largely through Highsmith's notebooks – or "cahiers," as she called them – drawing attention to a 1949 entry as evidence of her position on the illusion of subjective authenticity. "Pretences when begun early enough become true character," Highsmith claims, and so "the curious truth in human nature, [is] that falsity becomes truth finally."[71] The novel that Highsmith eventually wrote, however, proposes an alternative position, suggesting that, when applied to subjectivity, terms such as "truth" and "falsity" simply lose their purchase. To proclaim that Ripley's identity is now false and was once true, or vice versa, is to miss the novel's larger contention that subjectivity is always a work in progress, an adaptive entity that responds to new situations independently of truth or falsity. This is not to claim, as Wilson does, that Ripley has no essence. Rather, it is to say that in the world of the novel, terms like "essence," "truth," and "falsity" fail to encapsulate the peculiar case of Tom Ripley, as they cannot capture the flow of influence and imitation that constitutes the amalgamation who gleefully escapes punishment at the end of the novel, and who never seemed so self-possessed when he was a young nobody struggling to make his way in New York.

While the fluidity of Ripley's identity may contradict Highsmith's early thinking about the role of truth and falsity in crime fiction – or, rather, "suspense fiction," the generic marker she employs in her manual for aspiring authors, *Plotting and Writing Suspense Fiction* (1966) – the elusive nature of the character makes him an ideal specimen of the uncanny, late modernist aesthetic that Highsmith perfected. When Highsmith maintains in her manual that works of suspense fiction can only achieve commercial and critical success when novelists understand that "characters should be given most serious consideration," and that they must continually "pay attention to what [their characters] are doing and why," she characterizes the act of authorship as a process of observation and invention strikingly akin to Ripley's obsessive methods of self-creation.[72] On its surface, this idea of the author as a witness to her characters' actions and motivations seems curious, as one wonders how an author can "pay attention" to characters who exist entirely within her imagination. Still, the fact that Highsmith's dictums appear in a crime writing handbook, and as such are aimed at a group of amateurs eager to follow the example of a professional author, epitomizes Ripley's conviction that one can create an entirely original identity by emulating another, and that inventing one's own, unique sense of self depends in large part on one's ability to find a suitable model.

In a sense, then, Ripley is not only a case study in late modernism's investment in criminal psychology, but also a case study of writing. Just as Ripley achieves self-authorship by scrutinizing external models, Highsmith's account of writing as a form of dictation, akin to transcribing overheard conversations, subtly attends to one of *The Talented Mr. Ripley*'s central questions – whether the identity theft upon which Ripley embarks, rather than constituting a crime, typifies instead a form of subjective play that improves upon an original source. As Highsmith attributed the novel's success to her ability to channel Ripley's voice, "thinking [herself] inside the skin of such a character" until her prose "became more self-assured than it logically should have been," so too does Ripley view his imitations as processes of discovery and improvement.[73] While his virtuosic performance as Dickie Greenleaf counters Highsmith's warning that "[t]here is no enthusiasm in copying," his transformation exemplifies her belief that literary creation renews one's sense of "individuality ... the joy of writing."[74] Such joy reflects the character's most provocative talents, as well as the benefits greeting those who heed Highsmith's advice – namely, the ability to take pleasure in the business of imitation, and an attentiveness to the possibilities for originality that emerge from obsessive observation. In this way, we can understand Highsmith's novel not just as an example of crime fiction attuned to the modernist fascination with criminal minds, bodies, and behaviors, but also as a late modernist refiguring of earlier cultural productions. In advancing her own, mutable conception of the criminal subject, Highsmith delivers a late modernist novel that charts a path toward future accounts of the criminal – as radically other, emotionally barren, remorseless, psycho- and sociopathic – just as it articulates the vagaries of a violent mind firmly rooted in earlier modernist conceptions of fictional criminality.

Notes

1. Graham Greene, *A Gun for Sale* (New York: Penguin, 2005), 1. Hereafter cited parenthetically, as *GFS*.
2. Patricia Highsmith, *The Talented Mr. Ripley* (New York: W. W. Norton, 2008), 182. Hereafter cited parenthetically, as *TMR*.
3. Will Norman, "The Big Empty: Chandler's Transatlantic Modernism," *Modernism/modernity* 20.4 (November 2013): 751.
4. On modernism's popular reception in the 1920s, see David M. Earle, *Re-Covering Modernism: Pulps, Paperbacks, and the Prejudice of Form* (London: Routledge, 2016), and Lise Jaillant, *Modernism, Middlebrow and the Literary Canon: The Modern Library Series, 1917–1955* (Abingdon: Routledge, 2016).
5. Thomas S. Davis, *The Extinct Scene: Late Modernism and Everyday Life* (New York: Columbia University Press, 2016), 11.
6. Tyrus Miller, *Late Modernism: Politics, Fiction, and the Arts Between the World Wars* (Berkeley: University of California Press, 1999), 13.
7. Jed Esty, *A Shrinking Island: Modernism and National Culture in England* (Princeton: Princeton University Press, 2003), 4.
8. Marina MacKay, *Modernism and World War II* (New York: Cambridge University Press, 2007), 15.
9. William Greenslade, *Degeneration, Culture and the Novel: 1880–1940* (Cambridge: Cambridge University Press, 1994), 254.

10. Sigmund Freud, *Three Case Histories*, ed. Philip Rieff (New York: Touchstone, 1996), 2.

11. Ibid., 9.

12. Dennis Porter, *The Pursuit of Crime: Art and Ideology in Detective Fiction* (New Haven: Yale University Press, 1981), 243.

13. On Hammett's relationship to American modernism, see John T. Irwin, *Unless the Threat of Death Is behind Them: Hard-Boiled Fiction and Film Noir* (Baltimore: Johns Hopkins University Press, 2006).

14. See Christopher Raczkowski, "From Modernity's Detection to Modernist Detectives: Narrative Vision in the Work of Allan Pinkerton and Dashiell Hammett," *Modern Fiction Studies* 49.4 (Winter 2003): 631.

15. John G. Cawelti, *Adventure, Mystery, and Romance: Formula Stories as Art and Popular Culture* (Chicago: University of Chicago Press, 1977), 163.

16. James Naremore, *More Than Night: Film Noir in Its Contexts*, expanded edition (Berkeley: University of California Press, 2008), 51.

17. Jon Thompson, *Fiction, Crime, and Empire: Clues to Modernity and Postmodernism* (Urbana: University of Illinois Press, 1993), 134.

18. Dashiell Hammett, *Selected Letters of Dashiell Hammett, 1921–1960*, ed. Richard Layman and Julie M. Rivett (Washington, DC: Counterpoint, 2001), 47.

19. Dashiell Hammett, *Red Harvest* (New York: Vintage, 1992), 60–61. Hereafter cited parenthetically, as *RH*.

20. See Julian Symons, *Dashiell Hammett* (San Diego: Harcourt Brace Jovanovich, 1985), 24.

21. Mark McGurl, *The Novel Art: Elevations of American Fiction after Henry James* (Princeton: Princeton University Press, 2001), 164.

22. On hard-boiled fiction's gender dynamics, see Christopher Breu, *Hard-Boiled Masculinities* (Minneapolis: University of Minnesota Press, 2005); Leonard Cassuto, *Hard-Boiled Sentimentality: The Secret History of American Crime Stories* (New York: Columbia University Press, 2009); and Greg Forter, *Murdering Masculinities: Fantasies of Gender and Violence in the American Crime Novel* (New York: New York University Press, 2000).

23. Dashiell Hammett, *The Continental Op*, ed. Steven Marcus (New York: Vintage, 1992), 89.

24. Ibid., 87.

25. Ibid., 88.

26. Sean McCann, *Gumshoe America: Hard-Boiled Crime Fiction and the Rise and Fall of New Deal Liberalism* (Durham: Duke University Press, 2000), 114.

27. Graham Greene, *Brighton Rock* (New York: Penguin, 2004), 17. Hereafter cited parenthetically, as *BR*.

28. Clifford Musgrave, *Life in Brighton: From the Earliest Times to the Present* (London: Faber and Faber, 1970), 388.

29. Suzanne Mackenzie, *Visible Histories: Women and Environments in a Post-War British City* (Montreal: McGill-Queen's University Press, 1989), 12.

30. Musgrave, *Life in Brighton*, 387.

31. Davis, *The Extinct Scene*, 6.

32. For an overview of the critical debate surrounding Pinkie's religiosity, see Cates Baldridge, *Graham Greene's Fictions: The Virtues of Extremity* (Columbia: University of Missouri Press, 2000), 129–140.

33. Mark Seltzer, *Serial Killers: Death and Life in America's Wound Culture* (New York: Routledge, 1998), 4.

34. Mark Bosco notes, however, that Greene's brand of Catholicism is extremely difficult to pin down, as Greene's views on his religion changed so frequently. Bosco, *Graham Greene's Catholic Imagination* (New York: Oxford University Press, 2005), 4.

35. Graham Greene, quoted in Norman Sherry, *The Life of Graham Greene: Volume I, 1904–1939* (New York: Penguin, 1989), 627–628.

36. Lauren Berlant, "On the Case," *Critical Inquiry* 33.4 (Summer 2007): 664.

37. Adam Phillips, *Side Effects* (New York: Harper Perennial, 2006), 51–52.

38. Lisa Fluet, "Hit-Man Modernism," *Bad Modernisms*, ed. Douglas Mao and Rebecca L. Walkowitz (Durham: Duke University Press, 2006), 271–272.

39. Graham Greene, *Collected Essays* (New York: Viking, 1969), 116.

40. Andrzej Gąsiorek, "Rendering Justice to the Visible World: History, Politics and National Identity in the Novels of Graham Greene," *British Fiction after Modernism: The Novel at Mid-Century*, ed. Marina MacKay and Lyndsey Stonebridge (Basingstoke: Palgrave Macmillan, 2007), 19–20.

41. Brian Lindsay Thomson, *Graham Greene and the Politics of Popular Fiction and Film* (Basingstoke: Palgrave Macmillan, 2009), 74. On Greene's work in the detective genre, see Elliott Malamet, *The World Remade: Graham Greene and the Art of Detection* (New York: Peter Lang, 1998).

42. Brian Diemert, *Graham Greene's Thrillers and the 1930s* (Montreal: McGill-Queen's University Press, 1996), 6.

43. Murray Roston, *Graham Greene's Narrative Strategies: A Study of the Major Novels* (Basingstoke: Palgrave Macmillan, 2006), 12–13.

44. Graham Greene, quoted in Peter Wolfe, *Graham Greene: The Entertainer* (Carbondale: Southern Illinois University Press, 1972), 5.

45. Graham Greene, *Ways of Escape* (New York: Simon and Schuster, 1980), 104.

46. Roger Sharrock, *Saints, Sinners, and Comedians: The Novels of Graham Greene* (Notre Dame: University of Notre Dame Press, 1984), 72.

47. Diemert, *Graham Greene's Thrillers and the 1930s*, 12; and Bernard Bergonzi, *A Study in Greene: Graham Greene and the Art of the Novel* (Oxford: Oxford University Press, 2006), 61.

48. Greene, *Ways of Escape*, 98.

49. Highsmith admired Greene's fiction, noting when she began her first novel, *Strangers on a Train*, in 1950, that she intended the book as "an 'entertainment' of the Greene school." Highsmith, quoted in Andrew Wilson, *Beautiful Shadow: A Life of Patricia Highsmith* (New York: Bloomsbury, 2003), 124.

50. The other novels in Highsmith's "Ripliad" are *Ripley under Ground* (1970), *Ripley's Game* (1974), *The Boy Who Followed Ripley* (1980), and *Ripley under Water* (1991).

51. Wilson, *Beautiful Shadow*, 191.

52. Joan Schenkar, *The Talented Miss Highsmith: The Secret Life and Serious Art of Patricia Highsmith* (New York: St. Martin's, 2009), 337.

53. Cassuto, *Hard-Boiled Sentimentality*, 135.

54. Arthur Redding, *Turncoats, Traitors, and Fellow Travelers: Culture and Politics of the Early Cold War* (Jackson: University Press of Mississippi, 2008), 107.

55. On Ripley's peculiar likability, see Tony Hilfer, *The Crime Novel: A Deviant Genre* (Austin: University of Texas Press, 1990), 129.

56. Stephen Kern, *A Cultural History of Causality: Science, Murder Novels, and Systems of Thought* (Princeton: Princeton Press, 2004), 321. Similarly, Marco Abel characterizes ethical judgment "as the defining problematic of [Highsmith's] entire oeuvre." Abel, *Violent Affect: Literature, Cinema, and Critique after Representation* (Lincoln: University of Nebraska Press, 2007), 90.

57. D. A. Miller, *The Novel and the Police* (Berkeley: University of California Press, 1988), 3.

58. On Highsmith's critique of upward mobility, see Josh Lukin, "Identity-Shopping and Postwar Self-Improvement in Patricia Highsmith's *Strangers on a Train*," *Journal of Modern Literature* 33.4 (Summer 2010): 21–40.

59. Mark Seltzer, *True Crime: Observations on Violence and Modernity* (New York: Routledge, 2007), 114.

60. Mark Seltzer, *The Official World* (Durham: Duke University Press, 2016), 105.

61. Abigail Cheever, *Real Phonies: Cultures of Authenticity in Post-World War II America* (Athens: University of Georgia Press, 2010), 124

62. Slavoj Žižek, "Not a desire to have him, but to be like him," *London Review of Books* 25.16 (August 21, 2003). www.lrb.co.uk/v25/n16/slavoj-zizek/not-a-desire-to-have-him-but-to-be-like-him. Accessed February 13, 2017.

63. Fiona Peters, *Anxiety and Evil in the Writings of Patricia Highsmith* (Surrey: Ashgate, 2011), 156.

64. On Ripley's fondness for material objects, see Peters, *Anxiety and Evil in the Writings of Patricia Highsmith*, 156–163; and Russell Harrison, *Patricia Highsmith* (New York: Twayne, 1997), 26–28.

65. George E. Haggerty, *Queer Gothic* (Urbana: University of Illinois Press, 2006), 162.

66. Ibid., 163.

67. See Michael Trask, "Patricia Highsmith's Method," *American Literary History* 22.3 (Fall 2010): 584–614.

68. On the closet's resistance to homogenizing models of authenticity, see Trask, "Patricia Highsmith's Method," 607–608.

69. Seltzer, *The Official World*, 32, 33.
70. Wilson, *Beautiful Shadow*, 295.
71. Patricia Highsmith, quoted in Wilson, *Beautiful Shadow*, 192.
72. Patricia Highsmith, *Plotting and Writing Suspense Fiction* (New York: St. Martin's Griffin, 2001), 137.
73. Ibid., 75.
74. Ibid., 141, 143.

Conclusion
The Criminal after Modernism

I'm not really interested in middle ways. The task, as I see it, is to be
genuinely radical. It means pushing experience right up against
language, and against the fact of its embedding within language,
and affirming the primacy of desire, and putting desire and the Law
on collision courses, again and again and again.

– Tom McCarthy[1]

It is tempting to end this study of modernist criminality with *The Talented
Mr. Ripley*, since to propose Highsmith's title character as the exemplary
self-fashioned criminal is also to label her novel an apotheosis of modernism's rejection of the criminal as defined by fixed, positivistic categories of
subjectivity. To do so would be disingenuous, however, for two related
reasons: first, because Highsmith returned to her favorite character in
1970's *Ripley under Ground*, and again in three subsequent novels,
and second, because modernism remains an unfinished project, its influence reverberating through twenty-first-century fiction. Indeed, the flour-
ishing of formal experimentation within the contemporary novel –
a deliberate reaction against the cultivated ironies of postmodernism that
several of its practitioners characterize as a belated example of modernist
aesthetics rather than a simple homage – has revived late modernism's
reconsideration of early modernist form from a new historical vantage
point. This modernist resurgence reflects what Aaron Jaffe, following
Ulrich Beck, calls "second modernism," or a modernism catalyzed by
"the unremitting need for continuously returning to the unfinished business of literary history and literary modernity."[2] It also resonates with the
concept of "metamodernism," a term that David James and Urmila
Seshagiri apply to twenty-first-century writing that, "[a]cross vastly divergent transnational literary registers . . . incorporates and adapts, reactivates
and complicates the aesthetic prerogatives of an earlier cultural moment."[3]
In each assessment, we can understand the return to modernist form as an

attempt to reckon with the past as it shapes the present, and to embrace literature's capacity to exceed its moment of production and influence future readers and literary histories in ways that are currently impossible to gauge.

Part of recognizing modernism's "unfinished business" in the contemporary novel, then, means confronting the possibility that modernism may be incapable of ending. If we define modernism as a mode of expression and critique rather than a discrete historical period – an aesthetic interrogation of cultural conditions applicable to various social and political realities – then such a modernism could easily continue in perpetuity, with authors chronologically far removed from modernism's initial salvoes painting themselves as forces for continuity. This is the irony that David James identifies when, in tracing modernism's formal and political influence on contemporary fiction, he notes the potential contradiction embedded in that process, as authors align themselves with a period commonly defined by rupture.[4] However, James also contends that these twenty-first-century writers differ from their early twentieth-century predecessors by utilizing the latter's formal techniques to address the subjective dilemmas posed by rapidly evolving social landscapes. These contemporary authors mine earlier formal innovations to underscore the changing conception of interiority as a fraught exchange between inner and outer, the personal and the political, in ways uniquely responsive to present conditions. In so doing, they

> reveal the potential for modernist fiction to be more than simply a laboratory for examining consciousness as a hermetic domain. Instead, they incorporate techniques for showing how mental experiences are shaped by material circumstances, how protagonists' psychological states adapt to and are mutually pervaded by the social realms they navigate – revealing their working definition of the modernist novel as a medium for connecting interiority and accountability, braiding the description of characters' innermost reflections into the fabric of worldly situations.[5]

Contemporary fiction sounds a good deal like early modernist fiction here. Yet James's appraisal of modernism as a medium, which later novelists can use to bridge experimental form and the material conditions of the twenty-first century as they impress themselves on an individual consciousness, more closely resembles the late modernist critiques of Greene and Highsmith in that it acknowledges modernism's temporal expiration while also proclaiming its continued relevance in forging new paths for fictional representation. If late modernism, as Thomas Davis puts it, "designates the moment when modernism no longer recognizes itself," then contemporary modernism marks a new, uncanny form of recognition, in which authors who never witnessed modernism's heyday regard the period's avant-garde aesthetics as uniquely suited to registering the complexities of the present.[6] Modernism, in this formulation, is not simply an unceasing project of aesthetic and cultural critique, but a powerfully responsive vehicle for framing current social conditions and individual experience through the rigors of experimental form.

Of all the writers linked to this contemporary strain of modernism, the most significant for a study of modernist criminality is British novelist Tom McCarthy, whose work explores the act of violence as a simultaneously disruptive and stabilizing force for twenty-first-century subjectivity. Having famously argued that "[t]he task for contemporary literature is to deal with the legacy of modernism," McCarthy routinely emphasizes his temporal distance from modernism while acknowledging its overwhelming influence on his work; "I'm not trying to be a modernist," he explains, "but to navigate the wreckage of that project."[7] Critics typically approach McCarthy's fiction as a blend of modernism's animating impulses – that is, a preoccupation with formal innovation, the fragmented minds of unreliable narrators, and burgeoning communication technologies – and the social, cultural, and psychic conditions produced through the twenty-first century's global networks of commerce and communication. What emerges is an avant-garde aesthetic that, as Justus Nieland contends, reveals McCarthy as a "forensic scientist of modernism" who understands that concept "not as a repertoire of forms ... but as a series of mediations between the noble subjectivity of the human and inhuman media."[8] McCarthy, in other words, does not treat modernism as an ossified set of formal paradigms, but as a more fluid aesthetic and philosophical phenomenon that allows writers to theorize the contemporary subject in ways that are unique to a specific historical moment while also indebted to earlier forms of representation and the technologies that engendered them. In practice, this means creating fictions that draw attention to their own formal construction, or a return to modernist self-consciousness about the subject's mediation through technologies of representation. Thus, for McCarthy, fiction does not serve as the expression of an individual consciousness (either the author or the character), but as "a labyrinthine entry into a realm of inauthenticity; or ... a surrender to a fact of being always inauthentic."[9] His novels employ experimental narrative forms in order to illuminate contemporary forms of selfhood that are curiously divorced from the self without claiming a privileged status as the authentic expression of a discrete subject.

As Mark Seltzer claims, McCarthy's novels reject "the confessional and
furtively self-assertive tone of the trauma novel" even as they acknowledge
trauma as a default condition of the contemporary world, and one that an
experimental aesthetic is ultimately best suited to represent.[10]

McCarthy's first novel, *Remainder* (2005), unearths modernism's
wreckage through its persistent questioning of experimental fiction's
potential to represent the everyday experience of global capitalism,
technological modernity, and subjective estrangement, all of which
have birthed new forms of violence that test the limits of criminal
identification according to legal or subjective taxonomies. The novel's
anonymous narrator, forced to relearn gross and fine motor skills after
a severe head injury, finds himself adrift in a body that seems painfully
inauthentic, incapable of performing actions without excessive self-
consciousness. Determining that the way to become authentic is, paradoxically, to perform gestures and interactions over and over, exploring
their nuances through patterns of repetition that he believes might lead
to more fluid modes of being, the narrator uses the fortune he acquires
as a settlement for his accident to recreate the events that stimulate him:
the mundane goings-on of a London apartment building, a mechanic's
garage in which a car mysteriously malfunctions, soaking its driver in
wiper fluid, and, most significantly, a murder. After he learns that
a man in his neighborhood has been fatally shot while attempting to
evade his killers on a bicycle, the narrator hires an elaborate cast to help
him re-enact the event, with him playing the part of the deceased. As he
ponders his obsession with the man's death, the narrator admits that,

> for me, this man had become a symbol of perfection. It may have been
> clumsy to fall from his bike, but in dying beside the bollards on the tarmac
> he'd done what I wanted to do: merged with the space around him, sunk
> and flowed into it until there was no distance between it and him – and
> merged, too, with his actions, merged to the extent of having no more
> consciousness of them. He'd stopped being separate, removed, imperfect.
> Cut out the detour. Then both mind and actions had resolved themselves
> into pure stasis.[11]

For the narrator, the man's violent end symbolizes an intriguing possibility: the subject who fuses with the material world around him until his
consciousness reaches a point of "pure stasis." The man becomes authentic
precisely when his interiority dissipates, no longer confined in a single,
distinct body. By re-enacting the event, the narrator practices a form of
abnegation somewhere between death and corporeal disintegration,
attempting to free himself from subjectivity by becoming part of a larger

material object – the tarmac – and thereby ridding himself of the self-consciousness that impedes his every thought and action.

In this re-enactment and in others, the narrator pursues experience that resembles a Joycean epiphany, even as he attempts to negate his subjectivity in the course of coming to a fuller realization of it. In this way, the re-enactment resembles what Paul Sheehan terms a "modernist event,"

> definable not so much by content as by duration. It is incarnated in those forms of instantaneity, or arrested intensity, that defy narrative continuity – impression, image, symbol, moment, epiphany. Indeed, the last and most famous of these moments of arrest is a pleasure-giving, aesthetic enhancing experience. The moment of epiphany thus represents a kind of counter-trauma, an inundation of consciousness that is enriching rather than wounding, the kind of stimulus or supraliminal excess that illuminates rather than scars. The epiphanic moment therefore moves beyond shock to realization and insight. If trauma bespeaks an absence of being, an emptying out or a displacement of self-cognizance, the modernist fixation on the arrested instant suggests a restorative, antipodal movement, freeing its violent aesthetic from the compulsions of antagonism and disharmony.[12]

McCarthy's narrator experiences precisely this "counter-trauma" in re-enacting the final moments of a gunshot victim; he performs and re-performs his part in order to feel the "enriching" liquidation of subjectivity within the violent event. Ironically, this enrichment occurs through the very "absence of being" that Sheehan offers as the traumatic negative to the positive, "restorative" functions of modernist epiphany. Reimagining epiphany as an ecstatic moment of self-knowledge in which consciousness is both "inundating" and "displaced," *Remainder* adapts the modes of epiphany available through the violent modernist event by suggesting that the contemporary subject is determined both positively and negatively, caught in the pleasurable process of realizing an impossibly evacuated identity.

McCarthy's theorization of subjectivity reaches its highest pitch in the novel's final re-enactment, in which the narrator stages an elaborate bank heist only to move his performers, without their knowledge, from the safe confines of a constructed stage to an actual bank, effectively transforming his performance of an armed robbery into an actual crime. The rationale for the change is, to the narrator, obvious: "to be real – to become fluent, natural, to cut out the detour that sweeps us around what's fundamental to events, preventing us from touching their core: the detour that makes us all second-hand and second-rate" (*R*, 264). Here criminality becomes the conduit to another form of being, similar to Ripley's attempt to fashion a new, improved version of himself but distinct in that it promises to allow the narrator to connect to the events he experiences rather than to himself. The narrator's goal is not to create an identity out of criminality – that is, to brand himself a thief – but rather, through the extremity of violence, to eliminate boundaries between individual, event, and environment, the subject and the world in which he participates. Becoming authentic, then, means performing the criminal act as a way of experiencing what C. Namwali Serpell describes as "a will to certainty – a desire to see patterns – bestirred by the experiential vibrations of uncertainty" that comes through the careful repetition of particular actions.[13] By practicing and ultimately committing a bank heist, McCarthy's narrator aims to link his actions to what is "fundamental to events," in which no separation exists between the actor and his deeds. Criminality, in this context, represents complete subjective transcendence rather than the fixity of character types. The modernist, criminal event becomes a letting go of one's individual characteristics, and an immersion in the larger material world that eliminates distinctions between person, place, and action.

As Zadie Smith observes in her review of *Remainder*, which famously proposes McCarthy as representing the future of the novel, "[o]ne of the greatest authenticity dreams of the avant-garde is this possibility of becoming criminal, of throwing one's lot in with Genet and John Fante, with the freaks and the lost and the rejected."[14] Throughout this book, I have endeavored to explain how the link between modernism's experimental aesthetics and criminality persists from the late nineteenth century well into the literature of the twentieth, moving from the psychological fictions of Poe and Doyle to the late modernist case studies of Greene and Highsmith. What McCarthy adds to this genealogy of criminality in the modernist novel is an affirmation of that subject's enduring presence in contemporary literature, as modernist aesthetics and criminal characters continue to test the boundaries of psychological representation and the limits of generic definition. While certainly not a work of crime fiction according to the conventional dictates of that genre, *Remainder* does become, in its closing chapters, an epistemological thriller that combines the rising action of Greene's late modernist entertainments with Highsmith's interrogation of interiority and the objects of the individual's violent desire. It is also a deliberate return to modernism's initial charge against Lombrosian positivism – namely, that the labeling of criminality as a type of identity denies both the multiplicity of motivations that inform the criminal act and the idea that those motivations might not be fully knowable through available means of representation. In both cases, one sees just how powerfully the violent criminal subject resonates within contemporary fiction, and how the work of earlier modernist authors allows us to understand how and why it does so.

Notes

1. Matthew Hart and Aaron Jaffe, with Jonathan Eburne, "An Interview with Tom McCarthy," *Contemporary Literature* 54.4 (Winter 2013): 680.
2. Aaron Jaffe, *The Way Things Go: An Essay on the Matter of Second Modernism* (Minneapolis: University of Minnesota Press, 2014), 19.
3. David James and Urmila Seshagiri, "Metamodernism: Narratives of Continuity and Revolution," *PMLA* 129.1 (January 2014): 93.
4. David James, *Modernist Futures: Innovation and Inheritance in the Contemporary Novel* (Cambridge: Cambridge University Press, 2012), 2.
5. Ibid., 9.
6. Thomas S. Davis, *The Extinct Scene: Late Modernism and Everyday Life* (New York: Columbia University Press, 2016), 11.
7. Tom McCarthy, quoted in James Purdon, "Tom McCarthy: 'To ignore the avant-garde is akin to ignoring Darwin," *The Observer* (31 July 2010). www .theguardian.com/books/2010/aug/01/tom-mccarthy-c-james-purdon. Accessed December 29, 2017.
8. Justus Nieland, "Dirty Media: Tom McCarthy and the Afterlife of Modernism," *Modern Fiction Studies* 58.3 (Fall 2012): 570.
9. Hart and Jaffe, "An Interview with Tom McCarthy": 669.
10. Mark Seltzer, *The Official World* (Durham: Duke University Press, 2016), 154.
11. Tom McCarthy, *Remainder* (New York: Vintage, 2007), 198. Hereafter cited parenthetically, as *R*.
12. Paul Sheehan, *Modernism and the Aesthetics of Violence* (Cambridge: Cambridge University Press, 2013), 172.
13. C. Namwali Serpell, *Seven Modes of Uncertainty* (Cambridge, MA: Harvard University Press, 2014), 247.
14. Zadie Smith, "Two Directions for the Novel," *Changing My Mind: Occasional Essays* (New York: Penguin, 2009), 94.

Bibliography

Abel, Marco. *Violent Affect: Literature, Cinema, and Critique after Representation.* Lincoln: University of Nebraska Press, 2007.

"A Crime Is a Crime." *Time* (June 14, 1948): 106.

Anderson, Amanda. *The Powers of Distance: Cosmopolitanism and the Cultivation of Detachment.* Princeton: Princeton University Press, 2001.

Antliff, Allan. *Anarchist Modernism: Art, Politics, and the First American Avant-Garde.* Chicago: University of Chicago Press, 2001.

Arata, Stephen. *Fictions of Loss in the Victorian Fin de Siècle.* Cambridge: Cambridge University Press, 1996.

Ardis, Ann L. *Modernism and Cultural Conflict, 1880–1922.* Cambridge: Cambridge University Press, 2002.

Ashton, Jennifer. *From Modernism to Postmodernism: American Poetry and Theory in the Twentieth Century.* Cambridge: Cambridge University Press, 2005.

Auden, W. H. "The Guilty Vicarage." *The Complete Works of W. H. Auden: Prose, Volume II, 1939–1948.* Ed. Edward Mendelson. Princeton: Princeton University Press, 2002. 261–270.

Avrich, Paul. *Anarchist Portraits.* Princeton: Princeton University Press, 1988.

The Haymarket Tragedy. Princeton: Princeton University Press, 1984.

Bakunin, Michael. *Statism and Anarchy.* Trans. and ed. Marshall S. Shatz. Cambridge: Cambridge University Press, 1994.

Baldridge, Cates. *Graham Greene's Fictions: The Virtues of Extremity.* Columbia: University of Missouri Press, 2000.

Baudelaire, Charles. "The Painter of Modern Life." *The Painter of Modern Life and Other Essays.* Trans. and ed. Jonathan Mayne. London: Phaidon, 1995. 1–41.

Bell, Kevin. *Ashes Taken for Fire: Aesthetic Modernism and the Critique of Identity.* Minneapolis: University of Minnesota Press, 2007.

Benjamin, Walter. *The Arcades Project.* Trans. Howard Eiland and Kevin McLaughlin. Cambridge, MA: Belknap, 2003.

Bergonzi, Bernard. *A Study in Greene: Graham Greene and the Art of the Novel.* Oxford: Oxford University Press, 2006.

Berlant, Lauren. "On the Case." *Critical Inquiry* 33.4 (Summer 2007): 663–672.

Berry, Ellen E. *Curved Thought and Textual Wandering: Gertrude Stein's Postmodernism.* Ann Arbor: University of Michigan Press, 1992.

"Modernism/Mass Culture/Postmodernism: The Case of Gertrude Stein." *Rereading the New: A Backward Glance at Modernism*. Ed. Kevin J. H. Dettmar. Ann Arbor: University of Michigan Press, 1993. 167–189.

Binyon, T. J. *"Murder Will Out": The Detective in Fiction*. Oxford: Oxford University Press, 1989.

Bosco, Mark. *Graham Greene's Catholic Imagination*. New York: Oxford University Press, 2005.

Bourdieu, Pierre. *The Field of Cultural Production: Essays on Art and Literature*. Ed. Randal Johnson. New York: Columbia University Press, 1993.

Breu, Christopher. *Hard-Boiled Masculinities*. Minneapolis: University of Minnesota Press, 2005.

Brown, Erica and Mary Grover, eds. *Middlebrow Literary Cultures: The Battle of the Brows, 1920–1960*. Basingstoke: Palgrave Macmillan, 2011.

Buck-Morss, Susan. "Aesthetics and Anaesthetics: Walter Benjamin's Artwork Essay Reconsidered." *October* 62 (Autumn 1992): 3–41.

Burstein, Jessica. *Cold Modernism: Literature, Fashion, Art*. University Park: Pennsylvania State University Press, 2012.

Butler, Christopher. *Early Modernism: Literature, Music, and Painting in Europe, 1900–1916*. Oxford: Oxford University Press, 1994.

Caillois, Roger. "The Detective Novel as Game." *The Poetics of Murder: Detective Fiction and Literary Theory*. Ed. Glenn W. Most and William W. Stowe. San Diego: Harcourt Brace Jovanovich, 1983. 1–12.

Caserio, Robert L. "G. K. Chesterton and the Terrorist God outside Modernism." *Outside Modernism: In Pursuit of the English Novel, 1900–30*. Ed. Lynne Hapgood and Nancy L. Paxton. New York: St. Martin's, 2000. 63–82.

Cassuto, Leonard. *Hard-Boiled Sentimentality: The Secret History of American Crime Stories*. New York: Columbia University Press, 2009.

Cawelti, John G. *Adventure, Mystery, and Romance: Formula Stories as Art and Popular Culture*. Chicago: University of Chicago Press, 1977.

Cecire, Natalia. "Ways of Not Reading Gertrude Stein." *ELH* 82.1 (Spring 2015): 281–312.

Chandler, Raymond. "The Simple Art of Murder." *Later Novels and Other Writings*. New York: Library of America, 1995. 977–992.

Cheever, Abigail. *Real Phonies: Cultures of Authenticity in Post-World War II America*. Athens: University of Georgia Press, 2010.

Chessman, Harriet Scott. *The Public Is Invited to Dance: Representation, the Body, and Dialogue in Gertrude Stein*. Stanford: Stanford University Press, 1989.

Chesterton, G. K. "The Anarchist." *Alarms and Discursions*. London: Methuen, 1924. 74–77.

The Collected Works of G. K. Chesterton. Volume 16. Ed. George J. Marlin et al. San Francisco: Ignatius Press, 1988.

The Man Who Was Thursday: A Nightmare. London: Penguin, 1986.

"Why I Am Not a Socialist." *The New Age* 2.10 (January 4, 1908): 189–190.

Chinitz, David E. *T. S. Eliot and the Cultural Divide*. Chicago: University of Chicago Press, 2003.

Claybaugh, Amanda. *The Novel of Purpose: Literature and Social Reform in the Anglo-American World*. Ithaca: Cornell University Press, 2007.

Clymer, Jeffory A. *America's Culture of Terrorism: Violence, Capitalism, and the Written Word*. Chapel Hill: University of North Carolina Press, 2003.

Cole, Sarah. *At the Violet Hour: Modernism and Violence in England and Ireland*. Oxford: Oxford University Press, 2012.

Cole, Simon A. *Suspect Identities: A History of Fingerprinting and Criminal Identification*. Cambridge, MA: Harvard University Press, 2002.

Conan Doyle, Sir Arthur. *The New Annotated Sherlock Holmes*. 3 volumes. Ed. Leslie S. Klinger. New York: W. W. Norton, 2005–2006.

The Sign of Four. London: Penguin, 2001.

Conlon, D. J., ed. *G. K. Chesterton: A Half Century of Views*. Oxford: Oxford University Press, 1987.

Conrad, Joseph. *The Secret Agent*. New York: Oxford University Press, 2004.

A Set of Six. Garden City: Doubleday, Page, and Co., 1925.

Under Western Eyes. London: Penguin, 2002.

Coren, Michael. *Gilbert: The Man Who Was G. K. Chesterton*. London: Jonathan Cape, 1989.

Cottom, Daniel. "Sherlock Holmes Meets Dracula." *ELH* 79.3 (Fall 2012): 537–567.

Coulson, Victoria. *Henry James, Women and Realism*. New York: Cambridge University Press, 2007.

Curtis, Jr., L. Perry. *Jack the Ripper and the London Press*. New Haven: Yale University Press, 2001.

Daly, Nicholas. *Modernism, Romance and the Fin de Siècle: Popular Fiction and British Culture, 1880–1914*. Cambridge: Cambridge University Press, 1999.

Davis, Thomas S. *The Extinct Scene: Late Modernism and Everyday Life*. New York: Columbia University Press, 2016.

Dean, Gabrielle. "Grid Games: Gertrude Stein's Diagrams and Detectives." *Modernism/modernity* 15.2 (April 2008): 317–341.

De Quincey, Thomas. "On Murder Considered as One of the Fine Arts." *On Murder*. Ed. Robert Morrison. New York: Oxford University Press, 2006. 8–34.

Dettmar, Kevin J. H. and Stephen Watt, eds. *Marketing Modernisms: Self-Promotion, Canonization, Rereading*. Ann Arbor: University of Michigan Press, 1996.

DeVine, Christine. *Class in Turn-of-the-Century Novels of Gissing, James, Hardy and Wells*. Aldershot: Ashgate, 2005.

DiBattista, Maria. "The Lowly Art of Murder: Modernism and the Case of the Free Woman." *High and Low Moderns: Literature and Culture, 1889–1939*. Ed. Maria DiBattista and Lucy McDiarmid. New York: Oxford University Press, 1996. 176–193.

Diemert, Brian. *Graham Greene's Thrillers and the 1930s*. Montreal: McGill-Queen's University Press, 1996.

Diepeveen, Leonard, ed. *Mock Modernism: An Anthology of Parodies, Travesties, Frauds, 1910–1935*. Toronto: University of Toronto Press, 2014.

Dydo, Ulla E. *Gertrude Stein: The Language That Rises, 1923–1934*. Evanston: Northwestern University Press, 2003.

Earle, David M. *Re-Covering Modernism: Pulps, Paperbacks, and the Prejudice of Form*. London: Routledge, 2016.

Eburne, Jonathan P. *Surrealism and the Art of Crime*. Ithaca: Cornell University Press, 2008.

Edwards, Paul. *Wyndham Lewis: Painter and Writer*. New Haven: Yale University Press, 2000.

Eksteins, Modris. *Rites of Spring: The Great War and the Birth of the Modern Age*. Boston: Houghton Mifflin, 2000.

Ellis, Havelock. *The Criminal*. London: Walter Scott, 1892.

Elmer, Jonathan. *Reading at the Social Limit: Affect, Mass Culture, and Edgar Allan Poe*. Stanford: Stanford University Press, 1995.

English, James F. "Anarchy in the Flesh: Conrad's 'Counterrevolutionary' Modernism and the *Witz* of the Political Unconscious." *Modern Fiction Studies* 38.3 (Autumn 1992): 615–630.

Esteve, Mary. *The Aesthetics and Politics of the Crowd in American Literature*. Cambridge: Cambridge University Press, 2003.

Esty, Jed. *A Shrinking Island: Modernism and National Culture in England*. Princeton: Princeton University Press, 2003.

Eysteinsson, Astradur. *The Concept of Modernism*. Ithaca: Cornell University Press, 1992.

Faulkner, William. *Sanctuary: The Corrected Text*. New York: Vintage, 1993.

Ferguson, Rex. *Criminal Law and the Modernist Novel: Experience on Trial*. Cambridge: Cambridge University Press, 2013.

Fluet, Lisa. "Hit-Man Modernism." *Bad Modernisms*. Ed. Douglas Mao and Rebecca L. Walkowitz. Durham: Duke University Press, 2006. 269–297.

Forter, Greg. *Murdering Masculinities: Fantasies of Gender and Violence in the American Crime Novel*. New York: New York University Press, 2000.

Foucault, Michel. *Discipline and Punish: The Birth of the Prison*. Trans. Alan Sheridan. New York: Vintage, 1995.

Freedman, Ariela. "Dorothy Sayers and the Case of the Shell-Shocked Detective." *Partial Answers* 8.2 (June 2010): 365–387.

Freemantle, Anne. "Review of Gertrude Stein, Blood on the Dining-Room Floor." *New York Times* (August 1, 1948): BR13.

Freud, Sigmund. *Three Case Histories*. Ed. Philip Rieff. New York: Touchstone, 1996.

Gąsiorek, Andrzej. "Rendering Justice to the Visible World: History, Politics and National Identity in the Novels of Graham Greene." *British Fiction after Modernism: The Novel at Mid-Century*. Ed. Marina MacKay and Lyndsey Stonebridge. Basingstoke: Palgrave Macmillan, 2007. 17–32.

"War, 'Primitivism,' and the Future of 'the West': Reflections on D. H. Lawrence and Wyndham Lewis." *Modernism and Colonialism:*

British and Irish Literature, 1899–1939. Ed. Richard Begam and Michael Valdez Moses. Durham: Duke University Press, 2007. 91–110.

Gibson, Mary. *Born to Crime: Cesare Lombroso and the Origins of Biological Criminology.* Westport: Praeger, 2002.

Gillis, Stacy. "Consoling Fictions: Mourning, World War One, and Dorothy L. Sayers." *Modernism and Mourning.* Ed. Patricia Rae. Lewisburg: Bucknell University Press, 2007. 185–197.

Gilman, Sander L. *Difference and Pathology: Stereotypes of Sexuality, Race, and Madness.* Ithaca: Cornell University Press, 1985.

Goble, Mark. *Beautiful Circuits: Modernism and the Mediated Life.* New York: Columbia University Press, 2010.

GoGwilt, Christopher. *The Fiction of Geopolitics: Afterimages of Culture, from Wilkie Collins to Alfred Hitchcock.* Stanford: Stanford University Press, 2000.

Goldman, Jonathan. *Modernism Is the Literature of Celebrity.* Austin: University of Texas Press, 2011.

Gould, Stephen Jay. *The Mismeasure of Man.* Revised edition. New York: W. W. Norton, 1996.

Greene, Graham. *Brighton Rock.* New York: Penguin, 2004.

Collected Essays. New York: Viking, 1969.

A Gun for Sale. New York: Penguin, 2005.

Ways of Escape. New York: Simon and Schuster, 1980.

Greenslade, William P. *Degeneration, Culture and the Novel, 1880–1940.* Cambridge: Cambridge University Press, 1994.

Habermann, Ina. *Myth, Memory and the Middlebrow: Priestley, du Maurier and the Symbolic Form of Englishness.* Basingstoke: Palgrave Macmillan, 2010.

Haggerty, George E. *Queer Gothic.* Urbana: University of Illinois Press, 2006.

Hammett, Dashiell. *The Continental Op.* Ed. Steven Marcus. New York: Vintage, 1992.

Red Harvest. New York: Vintage, 1992.

Selected Letters of Dashiell Hammett, 1921–1960. Ed. Richard Layman and Julie M. Rivett. Washington, DC: Counterpoint, 2001.

Hammill, Faye. *Sophistication: A Literary and Cultural History.* Liverpool: Liverpool University Press, 2010.

Hansen, Miriam Bratu. "Benjamin and Cinema: Not a One-Way Street." *Critical Inquiry* 25.2 (Winter 1999): 306–343.

Harker, Jaime. *America the Middlebrow: Women's Novels, Progressivism, and Middlebrow Authorship between the Wars.* Amherst: University of Massachusetts Press, 2007.

Harrison, Russell. *Patricia Highsmith.* New York: Twayne, 1997.

Hart, Matthew and Aaron Jaffe, with Jonathan Eburne. "An Interview with Tom McCarthy." *Contemporary Literature* 54.4 (Winter 2013): 656–682.

Hartley, Lucy. *Physiognomy and the Meaning of Expression in Nineteenth-Century Culture.* Cambridge: Cambridge University Press, 2001.

Hepburn, Allan. *Intrigue: Espionage and Culture.* New Haven: Yale University Press, 2005.

Herman, David. "1880–1945: Re-minding Modernism." *The Emergence of Mind: Representations of Consciousness in Narrative Discourse in English.* Ed. David Herman. Lincoln: University of Nebraska Press, 2011. 243–272.

Highsmith, Patricia. *Plotting and Writing Suspense Fiction.* New York: St. Martin's Griffin, 2001.

The Talented Mr. Ripley. New York: W. W. Norton, 2008.

Hilfer, Tony. *The Crime Novel: A Deviant Genre.* Austin: University of Texas Press, 1990.

Holquist, Michael. "Whodunit and Other Questions: Metaphysical Detective Stories in Postwar Fiction." *The Poetics of Murder: Detective Fiction and Literary Theory.* Ed. Glenn W. Most and William W. Stowe. San Diego: Harcourt Brace Jovanovich, 1983. 149–174.

Horn, David G. *The Criminal Body: Lombroso and the Anatomy of Deviance.* New York: Routledge, 2003.

Horsley, Lee. *Twentieth-Century Crime Fiction.* Oxford: Oxford University Press, 2005.

Houen, Alex. *Terrorism and Modern Literature, from Joseph Conrad to Ciaran Carson.* New York: Oxford University Press, 2002.

Humble, Nicola. *The Feminine Middlebrow Novel, 1920s to 1950s: Class, Domesticity, and Bohemianism.* Oxford: Oxford University Press, 2001.

Hutcheon, Linda. *A Theory of Parody: The Teachings of Twentieth-Century Art Forms.* Urbana: University of Illinois Press, 2000.

Huxley, Aldous. *Point Counter Point.* Normal: Dalkey Archive, 2001.

Huyssen, Andreas. *After the Great Divide: Modernism, Mass Culture, Postmodernism.* Bloomington: Indiana University Press, 1986.

Irwin, John T. *Unless the Threat of Death Is behind Them: Hard-Boiled Fiction and Film Noir.* Baltimore: Johns Hopkins University Press, 2006.

Jaffe, Aaron. *Modernism and the Culture of Celebrity.* Cambridge: Cambridge University Press, 2005.

The Way Things Go: An Essay on the Matter of Second Modernism. Minneapolis: University of Minnesota Press, 2014.

Jaillant, Lise. *Modernism, Middlebrow and the Literary Canon: The Modern Library Series, 1917–1955.* Abingdon: Routledge, 2016.

James, David. *Modernist Futures: Innovation and Inheritance in the Contemporary Novel.* Cambridge: Cambridge University Press, 2012.

James, David and Urmila Seshagiri. "Metamodernism: Narratives of Continuity and Revolution." *PMLA* 129.1 (January 2014): 87–100.

James, Henry. *Letters.* Volume II, 1875–1883. Ed. Leon Edel. Cambridge, MA: Harvard University Press, 1975.

The Princess Casamassima. London: Penguin, 1987.

Jameson, Fredric. *Fables of Aggression: Wyndham Lewis, the Modernist as Fascist.* Berkeley: University of California Press, 1979.

"On Raymond Chandler." *The Poetics of Murder: Detective Fiction and Literary Theory.* Ed. Glenn W. Most and William W. Stowe. San Diego: Harcourt Brace Jovanovich, 1983. 122–148.

Jensen, Richard Bach. *The Battle against Anarchist Terrorism: An International History, 1878–1934.* Cambridge: Cambridge University Press, 2014.

Joyce, Simon. *Capital Offenses: Geographies of Class and Crime in Victorian London.* Charlottesville: University of Virginia Press, 2003.

Kadlec, David. *Mosaic Modernism: Anarchism, Pragmatism, Culture.* Baltimore: Johns Hopkins University Press, 2000.

Kavanagh, Thomas M. *Dice, Cards, Wheels: A Different History of French Culture.* Philadelphia: University of Pennsylvania Press, 2005.

Kenner, Hugh. *Paradox in Chesterton.* New York: Sheed and Ward, 1947.

—— *Wyndham Lewis.* Norfolk: New Directions, 1954.

Kern, Stephen. *A Cultural History of Causality: Science, Murder Novels, and Systems of Thought.* Princeton: Princeton University Press, 2004.

Klein, Scott W. *The Fictions of James Joyce and Wyndham Lewis: Monsters of Nature and Design.* Cambridge: Cambridge University Press, 1994.

—— "Modern Times against Western Man: Wyndham Lewis, Charlie Chaplin and Cinema." *Wyndham Lewis and the Cultures of Modernity.* Ed. Andrzej Gąsiorek, Alice Reeve-Tucker, and Nathan Waddell. Surrey: Ashgate, 2011. 127–143.

Knight, Stephen. *Crime Fiction since 1800: Detection, Death, Diversity.* Second edition. Basingstoke: Palgrave Macmillan, 2010.

—— *Form and Ideology in Crime Fiction.* London: Macmillan, 1980.

Kopley, Richard. *Edgar Allan Poe and the Dupin Mysteries.* New York: Palgrave Macmillan, 2008.

Lacan, Jacques. "Seminar on 'The Purloined Letter.'" *The Poetics of Murder: Detective Fiction and Literary Theory.* Ed. Glenn W. Most and William W. Stowe. San Diego: Harcourt Brace Jovanovich, 1983. 21–54.

Landon, Brooks. "'Not Solve It But Be In It': Gertrude Stein's Detective Stories and the Mystery of Creativity." *American Literature* 53.3 (November 1981): 487–498.

Latham, Sean. *"Am I a Snob?": Modernism and the Novel.* Ithaca: Cornell University Press, 2003.

—— *The Art of Scandal: Modernism, Libel Law, and the Roman à Clef.* Oxford: Oxford University Press, 2009.

Le Bon, Gustave. *The Crowd: A Study of the Popular Mind.* Mineola: Dover, 2002.

Leick, Karen. *Gertrude Stein and the Making of an American Celebrity.* New York: Routledge, 2009.

Levenson, Michael H. *Modernism.* New Haven: Yale University Press, 2011.

—— *Modernism and the Fate of Individuality: Character and Novelistic Form from Conrad to Woolf.* Cambridge: Cambridge University Press, 1991.

Levine, Caroline. *Forms: Whole, Rhythm, Hierarchy, Network.* Princeton: Princeton University Press, 2015.

Lewis, Pericles. *Religious Experience and the Modernist Novel.* Cambridge: Cambridge University Press, 2010.

Lewis, Wyndham. "Berlin Revisited." *Modernism/modernity* 4.2 (April 1997): 175–180.

*Creatures of Habit and Creatures of Change: Essays on Art, Literature and Society,
1914–1956*. Ed. Paul Edwards. Santa Rosa: Black Sparrow Press, 1989.

The Letters of Wyndham Lewis. Ed. W. K. Rose. London: Methuen, 1963.

Mrs. Dukes' Million. Toronto: Coach House Press, 1977.

Lewis, Wyndham, ed. *BLAST 1*. Santa Rosa: Black Sparrow Press, 2002.

Liebow, Ely M. *Dr. Joe Bell: Model for Sherlock Holmes*. Madison: Popular Press, 2007.

Lombroso, Cesare. *Criminal Man*. Ed. and trans. Mary Gibson and Nicole Hahn Rafter. Durham: Duke University Press, 2006.

Lukin, Josh. "Identity-Shopping and Postwar Self-Improvement in Patricia Highsmith's *Strangers on a Train*." *Journal of Modern Literature* 33.4 (Summer 2010): 21–40.

Macdonald, Kate, ed. *The Masculine Middlebrow, 1880–1950: What Mr. Miniver Read*. Basingstoke: Palgrave Macmillan, 2011.

MacKay, Marina. *Modernism and World War II*. New York: Cambridge University Press, 2007.

MacKay, Marina and Lyndsey Stonebridge, eds. *British Fiction after Modernism: The Novel at Mid-Century*. Basingstoke: Palgrave Macmillan, 2007.

Mackenzie, Suzanne. *Visible Histories: Women and Environments in a Post-War British City*. Montreal: McGill-Queen's University Press, 1989.

Mahaffey, Vicki. *Modernist Literature: Challenging Fictions*. Malden: Blackwell, 2007.

Malamet, Elliott. *The World Remade: Graham Greene and the Art of Detection*. New York: Peter Lang, 1998.

Mao, Douglas. *Solid Objects: Modernism and the Test of Production*. Princeton: Princeton University Press, 1998.

Mao, Douglas, and Rebecca L. Walkowitz, "The New Modernist Studies." *PMLA* 123.3 (May 2008): 737–748.

Mayhew, Henry. *London Labour and the London Poor. Volume IV*. New York: Dover, 1968.

McCann, Sean. *Gumshoe America: Hard-Boiled Crime Fiction and the Rise and Fall of New Deal Liberalism*. Durham: Duke University Press, 2000.

McCarthy, Tom. *Remainder*. New York: Vintage, 2007.

McCrea, Barry. *In the Company of Strangers: Family and Narrative in Dickens, Conan Doyle, Joyce, and Proust*. New York: Columbia University Press, 2011.

McGregor, Robert Kuhn, and Ethan Lewis. *Conundrums for the Long Week-End: England, Dorothy L. Sayers, and Lord Peter Wimsey*. Kent: Kent State University Press, 2000.

McGurl, Mark. *The Novel Art: Elevations of American Fiction after Henry James*. Princeton: Princeton University Press, 2001.

McHale, Brian. *Postmodernist Fiction*. London: Routledge, 1987.

Melchiori, Barbara Arnett. *Terrorism in the Late Victorian Novel*. London: Croom Helm, 1985.

Mellow, James R. *Charmed Circle: Gertrude Stein and Company*. New York: Owl Books, 2003.

Menand, Louis. *The Metaphysical Club: A Story of Ideas in America*. New York: Farrar, Straus and Giroux, 2001.

Meyers, Jeffrey, ed. *Wyndham Lewis: A Revaluation*. London: Athlone, 1980.

Micale, Mark S., ed. *The Mind of Modernism: Medicine, Psychology, and the Cultural Arts in Europe and America, 1880–1940*. Stanford: Stanford University Press, 2003.

Miller, D. A. *The Novel and the Police*. Berkeley: University of California Press, 1988.

Miller, Elizabeth Carolyn. *Framed: The New Woman Criminal in British Culture at the Fin de Siècle*. Ann Arbor: University of Michigan Press, 2008.

Miller, Tyrus. *Late Modernism: Politics, Fiction, and the Arts Between the World Wars*. Berkeley: University of California Press, 1999.

Mix, Deborah M. *A Vocabulary of Thinking: Gertrude Stein and Contemporary North American Women's Innovative Writing*. Iowa City: University of Iowa Press, 2007.

Monk, Leland. *Standard Deviations: Chance and the Modern British Novel*. Stanford: Stanford University Press, 1993.

Moretti, Franco. *Signs Taken for Wonders: Essays in the Sociology of Literary Forms*. London: Verso, 1988.

Morrisson, Mark S. *The Public Face of Modernism: Little Magazines, Audiences, and Reception, 1905–1920*. Madison: University of Wisconsin Press, 2001.

Moses, Omri. *Out of Character: Modernism, Vitalism, Psychic Life*. Stanford: Stanford University Press, 2014.

Musgrave, Clifford. *Life in Brighton: From the Earliest Times to the Present*. London: Faber and Faber, 1970.

Nabers, Deak. "Spies Like Us: John Buchan and the Great War Spy Craze." *Journal of Colonialism and Colonial History* 2.1 (Spring 2001): 28 paras.

Naremore, James. *More than Night: Film Noir in Its Contexts*. Expanded edition. Berkeley: University of California Press, 2008.

Nieland, Justus. "Dirty Media: Tom McCarthy and the Afterlife of Modernism." *Modern Fiction Studies* 58.3 (Fall 2012): 569–599.

Nordau, Max. *Degeneration*. Lincoln: University of Nebraska Press, 1993.

Norman, Will. "The Big Empty: Chandler's Transatlantic Modernism." *Modernism/modernity* 20.4 (November 2013): 747–770.

North, Michael. *Machine-Age Comedy*. Oxford: Oxford University Press, 2009.

Reading 1922: A Return to the Scene of the Modern. Oxford: Oxford University Press, 1999.

O'Brien, Geoffrey. *Hardboiled America: Lurid Paperbacks and the Masters of Noir*. Expanded edition. New York: De Capo Press, 1997.

Ó Donghaile, Deaglán. *Blasted Literature: Victorian Political Fiction and the Shock of Modernism*. Edinburgh: Edinburgh University Press, 2011.

Olson, Liesl. "'An invincible force meets an immovable object': Gertrude Stein Comes to Chicago." *Modernism/modernity* 17.2 (April 2010): 331–361.

O'Keeffe, Paul. *Some Sort of Genius: A Life of Wyndham Lewis*. London: Jonathan Cape, 2000.

Otis, Laura. *Membranes: Metaphors of Invasion in Nineteenth-Century Literature, Science, and Politics*. Baltimore: Johns Hopkins University Press, 1999.

Parkes, Adam. *A Sense of Shock: The Impact of Impressionism on Modern British and Irish Writing*. Oxford: Oxford University Press, 2011.

Pease, Allison. *Modernism, Mass Culture, and the Aesthetics of Obscenity*. Cambridge: Cambridge University Press, 2000.

Peppis, Paul. *Literature, Politics, and the English Avant-Garde: Nation and Empire, 1901–1918*. Cambridge: Cambridge University Press, 2000.

"Querying and Queering Golden Age Detection: Gladys Mitchell's *Speedy Death* and Popular Modernism." *Journal of Modern Literature* 40.3 (Spring 2017): 120–134.

Perrin, Tom. *The Aesthetics of Middlebrow Fiction: Popular US Novels, Modernism, and Form, 1945–75*. New York: Palgrave Macmillan, 2015.

Peters, Fiona. *Anxiety and Evil in the Writings of Patricia Highsmith*. Surrey: Ashgate, 2011.

Phillips, Adam. *Side Effects*. New York: Harper Perennial, 2006.

Phillips, W. M. *Nightmares of Anarchy: Language and Cultural Change, 1870–1914*. Lewisburg: Bucknell University Press, 2003.

Pick, Daniel. *Faces of Degeneration: A European Disorder, c.1848–c.1918*. Cambridge: Cambridge University Press, 1989.

Pippin, Robert B. *Modernism as a Philosophical Problem: On the Dissatisfactions of European High Culture*. Second edition. Malden: Blackwell, 1999.

Pittard, Christopher. *Purity and Contamination in Late Victorian Detective Fiction*. Burlington: Ashgate, 2011.

Plain, Gill. *Women's Fiction of the Second World War: Gender, Power and Resistance*. New York: St. Martin's, 1996.

Plotz, John. *The Crowd: British Literature and Public Politics*. Berkeley: University of California Press, 2000.

Poe, Edgar Allan. *Selected Tales*. Ed. David Van Leer. Oxford: Oxford University Press, 1998.

Porter, Dennis. *The Pursuit of Crime: Art and Ideology in Detective Fiction*. New Haven: Yale University Press, 1981.

Porter, Roy. *London: A Social History*. Cambridge, MA: Harvard University Press, 2001.

Porter, Theodore M. *The Rise of Statistical Thinking, 1820–1900*. Princeton: Princeton University Press, 1986.

Posnock, Ross. *The Trial of Curiosity: Henry James, William James, and the Challenge of Modernity*. New York: Oxford University Press, 1991.

Pound, Ezra. *The Letters of Ezra Pound, 1907–1941*. Ed. D. D. Paige. New York: Harcourt, Brace, 1950.

Purdon, James. "Tom McCarthy: 'To ignore the avant-garde is akin to ignoring Darwin.'" *The Observer* (July 31, 2010). www.theguardian.com/books/2010/aug/01/tom-mccarthy-c-james-purdon.

Quéma, Anne. *The Agon of Modernism: Wyndham Lewis's Allegories, Aesthetics, and Politics*. Lewisburg: Bucknell University Press, 1999.

Rabaté, Jean-Michel. *Given: 1° Art 2° Crime: Modernity, Murder and Mass Culture.* Brighton: Sussex Academic Press, 2007.

Raczkowski, Christopher T. "From Modernity's Detection to Modernist Detectives: Narrative Vision in the Work of Allan Pinkerton and Dashiell Hammett." *Modern Fiction Studies* 49.4 (Winter 2003): 629–659.

Radway, Janice A. *A Feeling for Books: The Book-of-the-Month-Club, Literary Taste, and Middle-Class Desire.* Chapel Hill: University of North Carolina Press, 1997.

Rafter, Nicole. *The Criminal Brain: Understanding Biological Theories of Crime.* New York: New York University Press, 2008.

Rafter, Nicole Hahn. *Creating Born Criminals.* Urbana: University of Illinois Press, 1997.

Rainey, Lawrence. *Institutions of Modernism: Literary Elites and Public Culture.* New Haven: Yale University Press, 1999.

Redding, Arthur. *Raids on Human Consciousness: Writing, Anarchism, and Violence.* Columbia: University of South Carolina Press, 1998.

———. *Turncoats, Traitors, and Fellow Travelers: Culture and Politics of the Early Cold War.* Jackson: University Press of Mississippi, 2008.

Reizbaum, Marilyn. "Yiddish Modernisms: Red Emma Goldman." *Modern Fiction Studies* 51.2 (Summer 2005): 456–481.

Reynolds, Barbara. *Dorothy L. Sayers: Her Life and Soul.* New York: St. Martin's, 1997.

Rodensky, Lisa. *The Crime in Mind: Criminal Responsibility and the Victorian Novel.* Oxford: Oxford University Press, 2003.

Ross, Stephen. *Conrad and Empire.* Columbia: University of Missouri Press, 2004.

Roston, Murray. *Graham Greene's Narrative Strategies: A Study of the Major Novels.* Basingstoke: Palgrave Macmillan, 2006.

Rothfield, Lawrence. *Vital Signs: Medical Realism in Nineteenth-Century Fiction.* Princeton: Princeton University Press, 1992.

Rowbotham, Judith, and Kim Stevenson, eds. *Criminal Conversations: Victorian Crimes, Social Panic, and Moral Outrage.* Columbus: Ohio State University Press, 2005.

Rubin, Joan Shelley. *The Making of Middlebrow Culture.* Chapel Hill: University of North Carolina Press, 1992.

Rzepka, Charles J. *Detective Fiction.* Malden: Polity, 2005.

———. "Introduction: What Is Crime Fiction?" *A Companion to Crime Fiction.* Ed. Charles J. Rzepka and Lee Horsley. Malden: Wiley-Blackwell, 2010. 1–9.

Sayers, Dorothy L. *Clouds of Witness.* New York: HarperCollins, 1995.

———. "Introduction." *The Omnibus of Crime.* Ed. Dorothy L. Sayers. New York: Harcourt, Brace, 1929. 9–47.

———. *Unnatural Death.* New York: HarperCollins, 1995.

———. *The Unpleasantness at the Bellona Club.* New York: HarperTorch, 2006.

———. *Whose Body?* New York: HarperCollins, 1995.

Scaggs, John. *Crime Fiction.* London: Routledge, 2005.

Scanlan, Margaret. "Terrorism and the Realistic Novel: Henry James and *The Princess Casamassima.*" *Texas Studies in Literature and Language* 34.3 (Fall 1992): 380–402.

Schenkar, Joan. *The Talented Miss Highsmith: The Secret Life and Serious Art of Patricia Highsmith.* New York: St. Martin's, 2009.

Schnapp, Jeffrey T., and Matthew Tiews, eds. *Crowds.* Stanford: Stanford University Press, 2006.

Schoenbach, Lisi. *Pragmatic Modernism.* Oxford: Oxford University Press, 2012.

Seitler, Dana. *Atavistic Tendencies: The Culture of Science in American Modernity.* Minneapolis: University of Minnesota Press, 2008.

Sekula, Allan. "The Body and the Archive." *October* 39 (Winter 1986): 3–64.

Seltzer, Mark. *Henry James and the Art of Power.* Ithaca: Cornell University Press, 1984.

    The Official World. Durham: Duke University Press, 2016.

    Serial Killers: Death and Life in America's Wound Culture. New York: Routledge, 1998.

    True Crime: Observations on Violence and Modernity. New York: Routledge, 2007.

Serpell, C. Namwali. *Seven Modes of Uncertainty.* Cambridge, MA: Harvard University Press, 2014.

Sharrock, Roger. *Saints, Sinners and Comedians: The Novels of Graham Greene.* Notre Dame: University of Notre Dame Press, 1984.

Sheehan, Paul. *Modernism and the Aesthetics of Violence.* Cambridge: Cambridge University Press, 2013.

Sherry, Norman. *Conrad's Western World.* Cambridge: Cambridge University Press, 1971.

    The Life of Graham Greene: Volume I, 1904–1939. New York: Penguin, 1989.

Sherry, Vincent. *Ezra Pound, Wyndham Lewis, and Radical Modernism.* Oxford: Oxford University Press, 1993.

Shpayer-Makov, Haia. "Anarchism in British Public Opinion 1880–1914." *Victorian Studies* 31.4 (Summer 1988): 487–516.

Siraganian, Lisa. *Modernism's Other Work: The Art Object's Political Life.* Oxford: Oxford University Press, 2012.

Smajić, Srdjan. *Ghost-Seers, Detectives, and Spiritualists: Theories of Vision in Victorian Literature and Science.* Cambridge: Cambridge University Press, 2010.

Smith, Zadie. "Two Directions for the Novel." *Changing My Mind: Occasional Essays.* New York: Penguin, 2009. 72–96.

Sonn, Richard D. *Anarchism.* New York: Twayne, 1992.

Stein, Gertrude. *Blood on the Dining-Room Floor.* Mineola: Dover, 2008.

    Everybody's Autobiography. Cambridge, MA: Exact Change, 1993.

How Writing Is Written: Volume II of the Previously Uncollected Writings of Gertrude Stein. Ed. Robert Bartlett Haas. Los Angeles: Black Sparrow Press, 1974.

Narration: Four Lectures. Chicago: University of Chicago Press, 2010.

Selections. Ed. Joan Retallack. Berkeley: University of California Press, 2008.

Sullivan, Melissa and Sophie Blanch. "Introduction: The Middlebrow – Within or Without Modernism." *Modernist Cultures* 6.1 (May 2011): 1–17.

Symons, Julian. *Dashiell Hammett.* San Diego: Harcourt Brace Jovanovich, 1985.

"A Master of Disguise." *Times Literary Supplement* 30 (30 June 1978): 726–727.

Szalay, Michael. *New Deal Modernism: American Literature and the Invention of the Welfare State.* Durham: Duke University Press, 2000.

Tarde, Gabriel. *Penal Philosophy.* Trans. Rapelje Howell. Boston: Little, Brown, and Co., 1912.

Taylor, Charles. *Sources of the Self: The Making of the Modern Identity.* Cambridge, MA: Harvard University Press, 1989.

Taylor, David. *Crime, Policing and Punishment in England, 1750–1914.* New York: St. Martin's, 1998.

Thomas, Matthew. *Anarchist Ideas and Counter-Cultures in Britain, 1880–1914: Revolutions in Everyday Life.* Aldershot: Ashgate, 2005.

Thomas, Ronald R. *Detective Fiction and the Rise of Forensic Science.* Cambridge: Cambridge University Press, 1999.

Thompson, Jon. *Fiction, Crime, and Empire: Clues to Modernity and Postmodernism.* Urbana: University of Illinois Press, 1993.

Thomson, Brian Lindsay. *Graham Greene and the Politics of Popular Fiction and Film.* Basingstoke: Palgrave Macmillan, 2009.

Trask, Michael. "Patricia Highsmith's Method." *American Literary History* 22.3 (Fall 2010): 584–614.

Tratner, Michael. *Modernism and Mass Politics: Joyce, Woolf, Eliot, Yeats.* Stanford: Stanford University Press, 1995.

Trilling, Lionel. "The Princess Casamassima." *The Moral Obligation to Be Intelligent: Selected Essays.* Ed. Leon Wieseltier. New York: Farrar, Straus, Giroux, 2000. 149–177.

Walkowitz, Judith R. *City of Dreadful Delight: Narratives of Sexual Danger in Late-Victorian London.* Chicago: University of Chicago Press, 1992.

Walkowitz, Rebecca L. *Cosmopolitan Style: Modernism beyond the Nation.* New York: Columbia University Press, 2007.

Walton, Samantha. *Guilty but Insane: Mind and Law in Golden Age Detective Fiction.* Oxford: Oxford University Press, 2015.

Watt, Ian. *Essays on Conrad.* Cambridge: Cambridge University Press, 2000.

Weir, David. *Anarchy and Culture: The Aesthetic Politics of Modernism.* Amherst: University of Massachusetts Press, 1997.

Whelehan, Niall. *The Dynamiters: Irish Nationalism and Political Violence in the Wider World, 1867–1900.* Cambridge: Cambridge University Press, 2012.

Wiener, Martin J. *Reconstructing the Criminal: Culture, Law, and Policy in England, 1830–1914.* Cambridge: Cambridge University Press, 1990.

Wilde, Oscar. "Pen, Pencil, and Poison." *The Complete Works of Oscar Wilde.* Volume 4. Ed. Josephine M. Guy. Oxford: Oxford University Press, 2007. 104–122.

Wilson, Andrew. *Beautiful Shadow: A Life of Patricia Highsmith.* New York: Bloomsbury, 2003.

Wilson, Edmund. "Who Cares Who Killed Roger Ackroyd?" *Classics and Commercials: A Literary Chronicle of the Forties.* New York: Farrar, Straus and Giroux, 1950. 257–265.

Wisnicki, Adrian S. *Conspiracy, Revolution, and Terrorism from Victorian Fiction to the Modern Novel.* New York: Routledge, 2008.

Wolfe, Peter. *Graham Greene: The Entertainer.* Carbondale: Southern Illinois University Press, 1972.

Wollaeger, Mark A. *Joseph Conrad and the Fictions of Skepticism.* Stanford: Stanford University Press, 1990.

Woodcock, George. *Anarchism: A History of Libertarian Ideas and Movements.* Peterborough: Broadview, 2004.

Woolf, Virginia. "Mr. Bennett and Mrs. Brown." *Collected Essays.* Volume 1. London: Hogarth Press, 1966.

Worthington, Heather. "Identifying Anarchy in G. K. Chesterton's *The Man Who Was Thursday.*" *To Hell with Culture: Anarchism and Twentieth-Century British Literature.* Ed. H. Gustav Klaus and Stephen Knight. Cardiff: University of Wales Press, 2005. 21–34.

Žižek, Slavoj. *Looking Awry: An Introduction to Jacques Lacan through Popular Culture.* Cambridge, MA: MIT Press, 1992.

Žižek, Slavoj. "Not a Desire to Have Him, but to Be Like Him." *London Review of Books* 25.16 (August 21, 2003). www.lrb.co.uk/v25/n16/slavoj-zizek/not-a-desire-to-have-him-but-to-be-like-him.

Index